# 5

Rochester College Lectures on Preaching
Volume 5

# *Preaching the Eighth Century Prophets*

David Fleer and Dave Bland, editors

*Preaching the Eighth Century Prophets*

# A·C·U
# PRESS

ACU Box 29138
Abilene, TX 79699
www.acu.edu/acupress

Cover Design and Typesetting by Sarah Bales

Printed in the United States of America

ISBN 0-89112-139-0

Library of Congress Control Number: 2004104014


1,2,3,4,5

# Table of Contents

# Acknowledgements

We express our gratitude to Spencer Furby, Chris Altrock, Jon Partlow, Josh Pattrick, and Royce Dickinson, Jr. for their careful reading of the chapters and manuscript at various stages of development. Thanks to Thom Lemmons, our editor, for his constant support and encouragement for these volumes on preaching.

# Dedication

For eight years, my colleagues in the Religion Department have been extended family, supportive friends, and academic partners in Rochester's Sermon Seminar and the volumes it has inspired. I dedicate this volume to Craig Bowman, Ron Cox, Rex Hamilton, Greg Stevenson, and Mel Storm, whose professional and spiritual encouragement daily sustain me.

*–David Fleer*

My wife, Nancy, and I dedicate this volume to the church at White Station. For the past eleven years, you have modeled for us the prophets' call to practice steadfast love and walk humbly with God. You have shared with us your lives and showed us what the vision statement of this church means: "Walk with God and care for people." We are deeply grateful to you for allowing our family to be a part of your family.

*– Dave Bland*

# Biographical Sketches

## Dave Bland

For more than two decades, Dave Bland has devoted his life to preaching tenures with the Eastside Church of Christ in Portland, Oregon and currently with the White Station congregation in Memphis. Dave complements his life's activity in preaching with a background in rhetoric (Ph.D., University of Washington) and an interest in wisdom literature. In addition to preaching, Dave serves as full-time Professor of Homiletics at Harding University Graduate School of Religion in Memphis and co-editor of this preaching series.

## David Fleer

David Fleer's devotion to preaching first found expression through a long-tenured pulpit ministry with the Vancouver Church of Christ in the state of Washington. His Ph.D. in Speech Communication at the University of Washington moved him into teaching, where he is currently Professor of Religion and Communication at Rochester College. Co-editor of the current series on preaching, David's work is characterized as a thoughtful and passionate attempt to walk afresh in the world of Scripture, that readers and listeners may experience the reality of the Gospel of God.

## *John Fortner*

John Fortner is at home both in the classroom and in the pulpit. Over the course of more than three decades, John has served churches in five states in either a teaching or preaching capacity. In his seventeen years of university teaching, first at Lubbock Christian University and now at Harding University, John reflects a passion for the God of the biblical text and for exploring theological and hermeneutical approaches that bridge the "then" and "now."

## *Rick Marrs*

Rick Marrs has taught at Pepperdine University since 1987, where he specializes in Old Testament studies. He especially has an interest in the use of the Old Testament in preaching. Besides his teaching responsibilities, he currently serves as the Associate Dean for Seaver College at Pepperdine and as an elder for the Conejo Valley Church of Christ in Thousand Oaks, California.

## *Robert Reid*

Bob served as Senior Minister for two congregations as well as a long-term interim minister for several congregations during graduate work. He holds the Ph.D. degree in rhetoric from the University of Washington, an M.Div. degree from Fuller Theological Seminary, and is currently Director of the Master of Arts in Communication program at the University of Dubuque. Author of several books and essays concerning homiletics, he is ordained to the American Baptist ministry and currently functions as a teaching elder for a congregation in Dubuque, Iowa.

## Timothy Sensing

Tim received his Ph.D. in Curriculum and Instruction of Rhetoric, focusing on the pedagogy of preaching, from the University of North Carolina (Greensboro) in 1998, where he concluded that preachers learn to preach primarily in the church more so than in a classroom. His research about the training of African-American preachers in Churches of Christ confirmed this pedagogy of preaching. Tim puts his theories to practice teaching homiletics at the Graduate School of Theology at Abilene Christian University, where he serves as the Director of Supervised Practice of Ministry, overseeing its ministerial internship program.

## William H. Willimon

William H. Willimon has been Dean of the Chapel and Professor of Christian Ministry at Duke University in Durham, North Carolina since 1984. He preaches each Sunday in the Duke Chapel at the center of Duke's campus and directs the program of campus ministry there. He also serves as a professor at the Duke Divinity School and is the author of fifty books (over a million copies of his books have been sold). His *Worship As Pastoral Care* was selected as one of the ten most useful books for pastors in 1979 by the Academy of Parish Clergy. In 1996 an international survey conducted by Baylor University named him one of the Twelve Most Effective Preachers in the English-speaking world.

# Foreword

## Donald E. Gowan

Reading the excellent essays and sermons in this book reminded me of an article by Sibley Towner, written during an earlier tumultuous period in American history, in which he reflected on the popular use of the term "prophet": "On Calling People 'Prophets' in 1970."[1] He reminded his readers that contemporaries—as different as Pope John XXIII, Martin Luther King, Bob Dylan, and Billy Graham—were being called "prophets"; Towner then set about to describe Old Testament prophecy, claiming the word should be used in our age only of people who fit that description. A key sentence, which accounts for his claim and which leads me to offer a few comments on preaching from the prophetic books, appears early in the article: "As Christians and Jews, we are concerned whenever an appeal is made to this tradition (whether from inside the religious communities or outside of them) in the attempt to lend authority to the utterance of some contemporary speaker."[2] *Authority* is an issue whenever the term "prophetic" appears. One of the questions that underlies every discussion of "prophetic preaching" is thus "What kind of authority does the preacher dare to claim?"

I checked a recently-published denominational hymnal and found that it does not include the hymn that was often

---

[1] Sibley W. Towner, "On Calling People 'Prophets' in 1970," *Interpretation* 24 (1970), 492-509.

[2] Towner, 494.

used in the past at ordination services, "God of the Prophets, Bless the Prophets' Sons." The reason is obvious, for "sons and daughters" doesn't fit the text very well, and perhaps it is just as well to abandon it for another reason as well; after all, "Prophet" and "prophetic" are tricky terms. One description of the pastor's role, which I read long ago, acknowledged that sometimes it may be necessary to be prophetic—clearly meaning in that context *to do something that will get one into trouble.* There are some whose personalities seem to impel them toward "prophetic" activity of that kind, and the label itself is attractive to them. But, as Towner reminds us, there are true prophets and false prophets.

"Prophetic preaching" is a popular term, and it is used in responsible ways in this book. However, for a few paragraphs, I will go against the grain in order to suggest that it may not be wise to set out intentionally to become that kind of preacher. To do so may involve making claims for oneself and one's own words that cannot be justified, because "prophetic," in the Old Testament sense of the word, involves a claim to divine authority, having special access to the truth. And, notice that there are no self-appointed prophets in the Old Testament— except those who are condemned as false prophets!

We may and we must preach from the prophetic books, however, and that is a different matter. Authority in no way resides in us, but remains with the word of Scripture. The preacher must be a faithful interpreter of that authoritative word. Although the contemporary message our congregations need will seldom and perhaps never be identical to the messages of Amos and Isaiah, their unparalleled insights into who God is, and who we are, need to be heard and understood in every generation. I especially appreciate the sermons contained in the volume you're now holding; they are excellent examples of the responsible use of texts from the prophetic books.

For much of history, the books of prophecy were used in a highly selective way—as sources of texts predicting the coming of Christ and as descriptions of the last days. Thus, Isaiah has always been a favorite book in the church, but until recently Amos was seldom used, since his message contained few texts of that kind. In our own time, their concern for the oppressed and calls for justice have attracted greater interest, and Amos has been found to be a relevant book after all. The former approach corresponds to ways the New Testament writers used the prophets, but the emphasis on justice reflects very well the teachings and activity of Jesus himself. "Prophecy" continues to be used today to refer to messages about the end time, but "prophetic" is likely to be a term of approval used of those who are active in the fight against injustice.

The canonical prophets were neither evangelists, preachers of repentance, nor reformers, with a program that might establish justice among their people. As to the latter, they did preach the law, but only to explain why judgment was about to fall. Note the context of passages such as Isaiah 1:16-17 and Micah 6:8. As to the former, the historical books do speak of prophets sent to call for repentance; yet, promises that repenting now can avert the impending announced judgment are almost entirely missing from the prophetic books.[3] The prophets spoke at a time when God was about to do an utterly new thing. Unless one of us has really been authorized by God to offer such a message for our time (and we had better be very sure of it), our central message is more that of the apostles than of the prophets—declaring the utterly new thing that God *has done* in Jesus Christ. Thus, our call is to evangelize and reform.

This by no means makes the prophetic books irrelevant, evidence only for ancient history, however; they speak with unparalleled power of what has gone wrong in human life and of God's insistence on bringing his will to fulfillment on earth in spite of what we do. The word of judgment, for which the prophetic books are mostly known, had to be proclaimed, but it would have accomplished little or nothing had there not been gospel in these books as well. And the promises God offered through the prophets are messages founded entirely on grace. I see in these books some remarkable foreshadowings of the theology of Paul. Long before Paul's time, the prophets had

---

[3] See A. Vanlier Hunter's convincing demonstration in his *Seek the Lord! A Study of the Meaning and Function of the Exhortations in Amos, Hosea, Isaiah, Micah, and Zephaniah* (Baltimore: St. Mary's Seminary and University, 1982). Isaiah 1:18-20 is one of the rare passages indicating that obedience might avert the judgment that is proclaimed everywhere else.

learned that people cannot save themselves: "The heart is devious above all else; it is perverse—Who can understand it?" (Jer 17:9; cf. 13:23). Humanity under fully deserved divine judgment is the major theme of the early prophetic messages, the same theme found in Romans 1-3. From Amos through Ezekiel, they speak of the death of Israel ("The end has come upon my people Israel," Amos 8:2; "These bones are the whole house of Israel," Ezek 37:11)—as if there were no possible future for them as a people of God. So much for human potential! But it is clear that they believe in a God who cannot be defeated by anything, even the worst human failings. They said there is no basis for a future in *us*, but in God there is. Hosea dares to speak of what judgment costs God and insists that it is God's nature for grace to prevail over judgment: "How can I give you up, Ephraim? How can I hand you over, O Israel?" (Hos 11:8). Then Ezekiel speaks of God raising Israel from the dead, and of God's intention to transform people so they can obey (giving them a new heart and a new spirit; 36:26). Death and resurrection thus already appear in the Old Testament as the most potent possible ways of telling us how bad it is, and how insistent God is in his intention to make it right. When the Son of God appeared among us, we saw again how bad it is—he died. But God said if I have to raise the dead to accomplish my purpose I will do it. The famous restoration passages in the book of Isaiah (as elsewhere in the prophets) contain no "ifs"; they speak solely of works of divine grace (cf. Isa 2:3-4 [Mic 4:1-4]; Isa 4:2-6; 9:6-7; 11:1-16).

The prophetic concept of the death and resurrection of God's people in history thus took on two new forms in the New Testament: first, the physical death and resurrection of the man Jesus, then death and resurrection as a way to speak of the transformation of our persons that becomes possible when we believe in him: "The saying is sure: If we have died with him, we will also live with him" (2 Tim 2:11; cf. Rom 6:5; 2 Cor 4: 10-12; Phil 3:10-11).

Bringing the dead back to life is not the only aspect of God's redeeming power that surpasses our powers of reason. God's triumph over human failure also appears in the Old Testament's use of justice language to speak of salvation, and especially in the way *tsedaqah* (justice, righteousness) prefigures Paul's language about the justice/righteousness of God, which saves the unworthy (Rom 3:21-26). God's "justice," in both testaments, is not identical to our conception of it—getting what we deserve. For example,[4] Daniel seems appropriate to offer a few words concerning a striking passage in one of the eighth century prophets, Micah 7:9:

> I must bear the indignation of the LORD,
> because I have sinned against him,
> until he takes my side
> and executes judgment for me.
> He brings me out to the light;
> I shall see his vindication.

It contains a cluster of legal terms, which most often would be used of God's judgment of sinners. But the prophet knows God's justice also involves intervening on behalf of the helpless, without regard to what they deserve, and he dares to present himself to God as one who is helpless because of his sin.[5] So Micah wrote, "I must bear the indignation of the LORD, because I have sinned against him, until he takes my side." "Takes my side" is the NRSV translation of *riv*, which is usually God's lawsuit against sinful Israel (note RSV: "pleads my cause"), but now the prophet expects God to be on his side, although he is a sinner. He continues with "and executes judgment for me," *mishpat*—another striking use of justice-language—to speak, not of condemnation, but of God's saving action. Then he concludes, "He will bring me out to the light; I shall see his vindication," namely his *tsedaqah*, the kind of justice that redeems a sinner.

---

[4] I dealt with this issue recently in my commentary on Daniel 9:15-19, "Daniel," *Abingdon Old Testament Commentaries* (Nashville: Abingdon Press, 2001): 138-140.

[5] As John Goldingay said with reference to the Daniel passage, "Those who suffer as a consequence of sin are still seen as those who suffer and need to be restored. John Goldingay, "Daniel," *Word Biblical Commentary* (Dallas: Word Books, 1989): 243.

How this could be remains a mystery to us, but it is the divine mystery that made possible the death of a just man on the cross, to bear the sins of the unjust.

There is more to the prophetic books than judgment of sin and promise for a glorious restoration at some future time. The eighth century prophets were theologians who understood the human predicament in all of its ramifications; but what is more important are their insights, matched by few other humans, into the true character and purpose of God.

# Introduction

## The World Imagined by the Eighth Century Prophets: Moving Toward a New Preaching Paradigm

### David Fleer and Dave Bland

Since the 1960s, church historians have been describing Protestant Christianity's evolution into *two parties*: Evangelical and Mainline, Conservative and Liberal. Based on doctrinal positions and experiences, United Methodists apparently have more in common with Disciples than they do with Free Methodists, and the Christian Church seems to align with Free Methodists better than with Disciples. Once familiar denominational identities and allegiances have faded and two parties have emerged, evidenced by our journals (*Christianity Today* on the right and *Christian Century* on the left), seminaries, and even the way we read the Bible.

However, in the last few years, the *two-party* description has become too confining. While no one is moving back and reclaiming old denominational loyalties, nonetheless we are witnessing an original migration to a reforming *center*—where large numbers from each party are finding they share substantive Christian views. Some Evangelical and Mainline Christians are discovering that they hold in common absolute devotion to this essential issue: the transcendent realm is more real than the material world and therefore the Bible should claim central position in our living and preaching. We are witnessing what we have longed for: a community that desires a new paradigm for reading and preaching from the world imagined in Scripture.

This reforming center in Protestant Christianity, however, reflects something far more significant than common doctrinal affinities. At the core of our current shift is a rupture from our modernist moorings. We have strong reason to claim that up until the recent past we all were theological modernists. That is, the modern world consumed both Christian parties, liberals and conservatives. Evangelical and Mainline Protestants were two sides of the same modern coin. Modernity had limited interest in Christianity but demanded that Scripture satisfy its criteria. Liberals caved in to the pressure by requiring that biblical stories be verified by extra-biblical sources. Thus, miracles were challenged and replaced with natural explanations. Conservatives likewise capitulated with debates over historical and scientific detail, defending the earth's young age and Mosaic authorship. Both parties thus ignored biblical emphases, shackling the Bible with external standards,[1] consuming reading and preaching energies in the process.

These modern distractions allowed a series of crises to arise in our pulpits. While we were busy fighting battles conceived and governed by modernism, we misplaced the church's language, and our identity began to erode. We allowed ourselves to be defined by our opponents. These exigencies were exacerbated when the church addressed political issues by employing the language of sociology, defined personal piety with the images of psychology, and relinquished authority to the world of business.[2] And so today we overhear Christians speak of the church's work in terms of "fiscal responsibility," threatening "budget trimming" of various programs if we experience a "financial shortfall." Our revealing metaphors, "you can take that to the bank," or "we've got to capitalize on opportunities," or the ever-present "bottom line," determine what we can and cannot "afford," as if we might be able to track God's movement by the rise and fall of the stock market.

We are now at a juncture where we fluently speak the dialect of other disciplines but have misplaced our biblical images and

---

[1] For a more thorough discussion of this theme, see William H. Willimon, Martin B. Copenhaven, and Anthony B. Robinson, *Good News in Exile: Three Pastors Offer a Hopeful Vision for the Church* (Grand Rapids: Eerdmans, 1999) and William H. Willimon, *Shaped by the Bible* (Nashville: Abingdon, 1990).

[2] *Good News*, 93.

vocabulary. We are apt, in Stephen Carter's indictment, to choose first a political position and then turn to Scripture for verification. We are more clearly Republicans or Democrats than we are Christians. We weren't surprised, therefore, when a friend in Iowa called with news that his city's churches, from Lutheran to Roman Catholic, were awash with the "flag controversy." Some wanted the American flag to stand in the sanctuary, while others were opposed. Passions ran high, he reported. One church came to the following compromise. At the moment the concluding "amen" was uttered, ushers quickly positioned the American flag in the foyer so that, to quote our friend, "parishioners might be reminded of their allegiances to America as they left the church." Our friend asked, "What do you think?" What do we think? We think that the time has come for Christians to set aside worldly allegiances and ask how we might live and preach the world imagined in Scripture.

What would happen if we did *not* approach the Bible as a location for modern debate or as "occasions to illustrate prior theological notions?"[3] What would happen if we learned to see the Bible as imagining a reality capable of recasting our human agendas to fit God's greater purpose? What would happen if we turned to Scripture for insights beyond us, for a word that didn't serve our preconceived interests? What if the church became the imaginative projection of the biblical text? What if we allowed the Bible to form us as a covenant community, a people encountered by the living Lord who meets us in Scripture and thereby changes us? What if we allowed ourselves to live in this new paradigm that grants the Bible a reality-defining power over the church and thus creates "an alternative story of the world?"[4]

The Christian landscape is radically changing. The fundamentals of denominationalism have been re-sculptured

The latter phrase is borrowed from Stanley Hauerwas. "Rheinhold Neibuhr." *Concise Encyclopedia of Homiletics*, William H. Willimon and Richard Lischer, eds. (Louisville: Westminster John Knox Press, 1995), 348.

See Willimon, *Shaped by the Bible*, 21, 42, 61.

into two parties, from which is now emerging a new center.
"We stand at the collision of two cultures, on a battleground
of two great faiths: the secular 'faith' of modernity, and the
theocentric faith of the Bible." Longing to move beyond
modern constructions of desire and need, we are unwilling
to exploit the Bible with the limitations of contemporary
culture. We wish instead to "interpret our reality to match the
demands of the Bible"[5] by seriously weighing Willimon's
restorationist-like claim, "A congregation is Christian to the
degree that it is confronted by and attempts to form its life in
response to the Word of God."[6] And so this volume turns its
attention to the world revealed by the eighth century prophets.
This is a call for a new paradigm for reading Scripture and a new
paradigm for preaching the world revealed in Scripture.

The eighth century prophets—Amos, Hosea, Isaiah, and
Micah—imagined the world as God intended it, ruled in the
righteousness and justice originally illuminated in the Torah.
Isaiah holds up a vision of Yahweh creating a world in which
his messiah will rule in a spirit of wisdom and knowledge of the
Lord. Humans who are filled with this knowledge will treat one
another with respect and dignity, which in turn will influence
the natural world. The wolf then will live in peace with the lamb
and the lion with the calf (Isa 11:1-9). This is the world God
is bringing about, the world in which the prophets call people
to participate.

Israel, however, chose to create her own realm to serve
special interests and promote particular causes by amassing land
and material goods, oppressing the poor, abusing creation, and
worshipping the god Baal who promised health and wealth. God
charged the prophets to call Israel out of this ghetto and into an
experience where justice and righteousness reigned. Thus the
prophets were not foretellers of the future and neither were they
innovators of a new religion; rather, they called the people of
God back to God's Torah. The world imagined by the prophets
is rooted in God's Word.

---

[5] *Shaped by the Bible*, 63.

[6] *Shaped by the Bible*, 11.

Since the Bible wishes to convert us to such a vision biblical preachers "do not just massage the world as we find it. We create a new world."[7] This is why William Willimon calls preachers to re-learn the grammar of biblical faith, claiming that "Biblical language has shown, time and again, that it has power…to evoke that of which it speaks. The Bible is able to create…the people it desires."[8] Remarkable changes can happen when a preacher moves into the world imagined in Scripture. We invited Willimon to contribute to this volume because, in these times of crisis, his words are daringly out of sync with what we wish to hear. We have chosen a writer who embodies the very kind of prophet he defines. Like the prophets, Willimon makes little distinction between the religious, economic, social, and personal. He stokes our imaginations as he speaks from within and for the community. His orienting essay ends with a sermon from a Gospel text, in which Jesus works "in much the same guise as the prophets of the eighth century."

For insights beyond us and words that do not serve our preconceived interests, Rick Marrs focuses on oracles of doom in the books of Amos, Hosea, and Micah. He identifies the reason for the impending judgment, which is related to Israel's abuse of her covenant with God. Israel felt that the covenant was for her benefit. Thus she was a privileged people, which led to Israel's mistreatment of others. The prophets, beginning with Amos, come on the scene delivering blistering social criticism against the people. The prophets stand over against the popular prophets of the day who preached what the people *wanted* to hear. Amos, Hosea, and Micah spoke to what the people *needed* to hear.

Another premier Old Testament scholar, John Fortner, addresses oracles of hope. In particular, Fortner reflects on the two oracles located at the conclusion of Amos. Fortner demonstrates how these oracles of hope express the flip side of the doom oracles in the covenant relationship. Through visions of what the world could be through God's grace, the prophets call

---

[7] William H. Willimon, *Peculiar Speech: Preaching to the Baptized* (Grand Rapids: Eerdmans, 1992), 86.

[8] *Peculiar Speech*, 22.

the people to participate in that new world instead of the realm ruled by wealth, power, and self-interests. Fortner's challenging essay creates a deeper appreciation for the prophetic vision and its power to reshape our world.

Craig Bowman carefully explores a variety of perspectives on what it means to live in the world of Hosea and Gomer as illuminated in Hosea 1–3. After looking at how other communities interpreted and lived in this text, Bowman considers the possibility of Hosea 1–3 orienting the reader to the entire Book of the Twelve. These three chapters accomplish this direction by introducing the theological theme of Yahweh's return to his people and the people's return to Yahweh. To live in the imaginative projection of this particular text means that one participates in the experience of restoration. Thus, Bowman discloses how he unexpectedly found himself in the world of Hosea and Gomer. His personal story serves as a powerful testimony to the radical obedience necessary to remain faithful in a season of unfaithfulness. In practicing faithfulness, we participate in God's vision for a new world.

In his chapter on "Reimagining the Future," Timothy Sensing is concerned with how Scripture interprets and reapplies the eighth century prophets and how these texts then interpret us. He examines in particular how Zechariah reinterprets the eighth century prophets for his sixth century audience. Sensing demonstrates that the eighth century prophets continue to speak to a new context two centuries later not by explaining but by re-envisioning the earlier prophets. Zechariah calls on his people to participate in the new world envisioned in Scripture.

Engaging both theory and praxis, Robert Reid lives in two worlds: the church and the academy. It is to our benefit that he straddles both worlds so well because his intelligent and helpful essay encourages us to think about our voice in Sunday's pulpit. Calling for an authentic pulpit, Reid analyzes four distinct voices with example sermons from Amos. Providing helpful perspectives for preachers who desire to enhance the hearing of God's word, Reid answers the very question he asks of his homiletic students, "What did you want to have happen as a result of people hearing your sermon?" The chapter claims that unless the preacher knows the sermon's rhetorical intention, the congregation will judge his or her voice inauthentic.

As in our previous volumes, we conclude with nine sermons by four preachers. These sermons are intended to flesh out theological themes and demonstrate homiletical principles developed in the book's essays. The six sermons by Dave Bland include two each from Amos, Hosea, and Isaiah. The three remaining sermons by Mark Frost, Royce Dickinson, and David Fleer all come from key texts in eighth century prophetic material.

As we launch this fifth volume, our desire is to renew our incentive to preach the eighth century prophets, to enlighten the power of God's Word to change lives, and in this process invite the church to be shaped by the world of Scripture and to participate in the radical new world that God is creating.

# I | Essays on Preaching The Eighth Century Prophets

# 1

# Pastors Who Are Preachers Who Are Prophets

## William H. Willimon

Some time ago, a man, a layperson in a large church in the Midwest, said to me, at the conclusion of my lecture on preaching, "The trouble with you preachers is that you just don't speak my language. You don't say anything that relates to my world."

He meant it as damning criticism, I'm sure. I replied, in love, "Where in the world would you get the notion that I, or any of my pastoral sisters and brothers, would want to speak in your language or to your world? I don't want to speak to your world. I want to rock your world! I want to give you a new language that you wouldn't know without my preaching. I want to destroy your world and offer you another. I'm a prophet, for God's sake!"

The prophets, both major and minor, have a word for us contemporary preachers. It is a word that, like so many prophetic words, is both judgment and grace. Among the insights of contemporary scholars into the testimony of the prophets that have relevance for preachers are these:

- The essays in this volume speak to various aspects of the prophetic vocation with particular reference to the eighth century prophets: Amos, Isaiah, Hosea, and Micah. They enable us to see who prophets were and what they did and said. However, if you want to skip these learned essays and go instead with an initial thumbnail definition of a prophet, here it is: *a prophet, in the biblical tradition, is someone with uncommon access to matters of God's will and purpose that usually remain hidden to other people.*[1]

• Prophets crop up from time to time in Yahweh's history with Israel, often *during times of national crisis*, such as the eighth century. Yet their words are daringly out of synch with what the community may long to hear in its crisis. During some of Israel's worst moments, languishing in exile, without hope for a future, the prophets dared to utter some of their most extravagant, pushy, sweeping claims for the power of God.

• Prophets seem to appear from out of nowhere, with inadequate precedents and neither portfolio nor preparation: Amos the farmer from the South, Isaiah and Jeremiah the young and the inept. Prophets seem to preach outside the realm of conventional discourse. Luther noted, "They have a queer way of talking, these prophets." Their speech seems to specialize in imaginative *disruption* in order to provoke social *transformation*, all in service of Yahweh who creates new worlds through the Word (Gen 1; John 1).

• The earliest prophets appear to have been recipients of ecstatic episodes (1 Sam 10:9-13; 19:20-24). This ecstatic, charismatic source of prophecy continues to characterize the speech of prophets. The word "ecstasy" means literally (in the Greek) "to stand outside." Prophets are those who get pulled outside of conventional power arrangements in order to speak in behalf of God. Such divinely initiated revelation was embodied in the stories of call that became

---

[1] This is Walter Brueggemann's definition, found in his *Reverberations of Faith: A Theological Handbook of Old Testament Themes* (Louisville: Westminster John Knox Press, 2002), 159-162. I am heavily dependent on Brueggemann's article, "Prophets," for the organizing thought behind this chapter. Indeed, I am indebted to him for my own continuing fascination with the prophets and an understanding of prophecy as the basis for the pastoral ministry.

a virtual requirement for a prophet (Jer 1:4-10; Isa 6:1-8). A prophet is born in the mind of God, in God's determination to have a hearing, in good times and bad, among those with whom God has made covenant. Thus a prophet's authorization rests upon *the miracle of divine vocation.* Every word uttered by the prophet is a continuing exercise of divine vocation. The prophet's call keeps on happening in prophetic speech. That vocation enables the prophet to utter the characteristic "Thus saith the LORD" (KJV). The prophet's call means that the prophet's words arise neither from royal patronage nor popular appeal. This divine authorization accounts for why, when all is said and done, biblical prophecy tends to be a strange and essentially inexplicable phenomenon because it rests not upon social or historical dynamics but upon the dynamics of a covenanting, calling God who will not let his people free from his Word.

Though there is much variety in their speaking, prophetic pronouncements tend to be shaped by *three typical prophetic moves*:

- *Judgment that indicts Israel for disobedience to God's covenant and punishment that fits the crime. Grief.*[2]
- *Call to repentance and return to covenantal obedience. Change.*
- *Promise of the gift of new life and open future that comes from a gracious and merciful God. Hope.*[3]

*No area of life is excluded from the purview of the prophet.* The prophet seems to make little distinction between the

---

[2] Jeremiah comes to mind as the great prophet of grief and tears: "O that my head were waters, and my eyes a fountain of tears that I might weep day and night for the slain daughter of my people!" (Jer 8:23).

[3] Jeremiah is also a great prophet of hope. He is called not only to "pluck up and tear down, to destroy and overthrow" (Jer 1:10), but also to plan and to build. Chapters 29-33 contain great oracles of hope enunciated by Jeremiah.

"religious" and the economic, political, social, and personal. God notices everything and intends for it all to be brought within the sphere of divine summons. Nothing and no one is above the judgment of free and sovereign Yahweh, and no one is below his care.

Prophets tend to read history morally, asserting that issues of justice and righteousness are at stake in the community's deeds. The community's false faith in money, power, and armaments is characterized as a moral matter, as a failure to worship the true and living God, as idolatry. The prophets tend to be disinterested in concerns about utility, practicality, and expediency, placing everything under the sovereign judgments of a righteous God.

A prophet works primarily through words. The prophet is a poet, not the carping social critic of some contemporary characterizations. Through words, imaginative metaphors, and symbolic gestures, a prophet invites the covenant community to a reconstruction of reality, sub specie aeternitatis ("in light of eternity").[4]

This the prophet does through heavily metaphorical and symbolic speech and actions. Only the later prophets resort to prose. Striking metaphors are used to assault conventional understandings of reality and to offer a richly metaphorical and highly imaginative alternative to royal arrangements.[5] Paul says that the gift of prophecy is part of the ministries of learning and encouragement (1 Cor 14:31). Peter Gomes calls the Bible "a book of the imagination."[6] Prophets are those whose peculiar ministry it is to stoke, to fund, to fuel the covenant community's imagination through their words.[7]

---

[4] For instance, Jeremiah calls God an abandoned bridegroom (2:2), a fountain (2:13), a betrayed father (3:19), a lion, a wolf, a leopard (5:6), an engineer (5:22), a potter (18:1), and a host of striking poetic images too numerous to mention.

[5] The image of prophet as poet is worked most beautifully by Walter Brueggemann in his Finally Comes the Poet: Daring Speech for Proclamation (Philadelphia: Augsburg Fortress, 1989).

[6] Peter J. Gomes, The Good Book (New York: Bard, 1998).

[7] Paul Ricoeur first showed us that people are transformed, not by ethical urging, but by transformed imaginations. The Philosophy of Paul Ricoeur, ed. C. E. Reagan and D. Steward (Boston: Beacon Press, 1979).

The subject of prophetic speech is a holy God whose judgments are terrifying and who will not be constrained by human expectation. Though the covenant community is characterized by recurring failures to live up to its covenantal obligations, though the community faces repeated dead ends in its national life, the God for whom the prophets dare to speak is not limited by the community's infidelity or lack of imagination. Time and again the community that *claims* to want to hear a word from the Lord shows its ambivalence and downright rejection of that word by its persecution of prophets (Matt 5:12). Yet as King Jehoiakim learned in his dealings with Jeremiah (Jer 36:32), the words and acts of the prophet have a resilient power that adheres to speech that is divinely authorized and instigated.

It is most important that pastors who are called to speak like prophets get over some historic misconceptions of the prophetic vocation:

- Some Evangelical Christians still think of the prophets as "predictors," fortune-tellers of the future, prognosticators. Israel rejected attempts to fix and know the future (Deut 18:9-14), and so did Jesus (Mark 13:32). When prophets speak of the future, it is from their intimate knowledge of, and past experience with, the workings of a faithful God.[8] Prophets often speak in order to dislodge and transform, to offer a future that, without repentance, would be tragic.

- Some Mainline Christians think of prophets as social activists, those who engage in "prophetic ministry" and moral exhortation. Biblical prophets in fact have little to say about the specific problems of their day and offer little specific prescription. While they are concerned about issues of justice, it is always justice

---

[8] Donald Gowan makes the observation that the way in which God dealt with his people in the past was the basis for projecting a hope for the future. It also served as a check on the imagination, which might be tempted to introduce wishful thinking into the scenario. See Donald Gowan, *Eschatology in the OT* (Philadelphia: Fortress, 1986): 25-26. The volume was reprinted by T & T Clark in 2000.

defined as the working out of the righteous demands of God, not some sort of political or economic system. In all that a prophet says, it is clear that Yahweh is the decisive factor, the real speaker, the final judge, the only hope. Perhaps that is why, when Paul speaks of prophecy as a gift, it is a gift associated with faith (Rom 12:6).

- When many of us think of "prophetic preaching," we think of someone who is in opposition to the institutional church. True, much prophetic pronouncement does seem antagonistic to the community of faith. Amos, Isaiah, and Jeremiah have some stinging words for Israel's worship practices, particularly when they are divorced from the ethical demands of the covenant community. When Martin Luther King, Jr. wrote his "Letter from Birmingham City Jail," expressing his disappointment with the moderation and lukewarm support of city clergy, he was within the tradition of those prophets who afflicted those who were "at ease in Zion."[9]

However, it is important to realize the ways in which prophets spoke, not simply in opposition to the community but *from within* and *for* the community. The image of prophet as antagonistic critic of the faith community is based more upon the work of Max Weber, Adolf von Harnack, and Ernst Troeltsch than the prophetic testimony of the Bible.[10] Harnack contrasted the supposedly earlier "charismatic" prophet to the faith community with the later "institutional office" of the priests who defended and tended the institution. This is the enduring misinterpretation that is the basis for our contemporary popular contrast of prophetic with pastoral ministry. A pastor shows

---

[9] See J. M. Washington, ed., in *Testament of Hope: The Essential Writings of Martin Luther King Jr.* (San Francisco : Harper & Row, 1986)289-302.

[10] Stephen Long, "Prophetic Preaching," in William H. Willimon and Richard Lischer, eds., *A Concise Encyclopedia of Preaching,* (Louisville: Westminster John Knox Press, 1995), 385-389.

charity; a prophet preaches justice. A prophet cares for the truth; a pastor worries about the congregation.

From this misunderstanding flows the notion that as a preacher I am being most "prophetic" when I speak without regard to the rules, conventions, traditions, and institutional demands of the church. This understanding of the prophetic role was particularly popular among nineteenth century Protestant scholars who contrasted the freedom-loving Paul with his "legalistic," institutionally-bound "Judaizer" critics. In this view, prophetic Paul defended the free gospel against those who would constrict it by the law. Protestants found this view helpful in their polemic against the institutional strictures of the rules, rites, and offices of Roman Catholicism. The contrast lives on in much of the work of the "Jesus Seminar." Jesus is the wandering cynic philosopher and mystic, the anti-institutional critic who was eventually crucified because of his prophetic critique of the establishment.[11]

Biblical prophets, those in the eighth century and others, often speak about the future, but they do so as those who stand upon Israel's experience of the Sovereign God who meets us in the past. It is an oversimplification and an anachronistic misunderstanding to characterize the prophets as preachers who, in contrast to the priests, force their hearers to choose between the unencumbered freedom of the "prophetic" and the "legalism" of the priestly. A preacher, in this view, can serve either the free, prophetic word *or* the institutionalized traditions of the church. This sets the prophet against the faith community, justice against charity, and the future against the past in a way that is very different from what we have learned about biblical prophets.

True, when prophets dare to speak the truth, they have often provoked hostile response from many within the community. But the hostility is based, not so much on a contrast between allegiance to the past and faith in the future, but rather on an

---

[11] For example, Marcus Borg and N.T. Wright in chapter two of *The Meaning of Jesus: Two Visions* (San Francisco: HarperSanFrancisco, 1998), and Thomas Cahill, chapter two, "The Last of the Prophets," in *Desire of the Everlasting Hills: the World Before and After Jesus* (New York: Doubleday, 1999).

argument within the faith community about the significance of Israel's past with Yahweh for the present and future. The opposition is often so fierce and sometimes violent because the prophet instigates a debate within the covenant community about the very basis of its identity as covenant community.

Stephen Long says that one of the greatest impediments to truly prophetic preaching is our enduring blending of the prophetic with the heroic.[12] Romanticism sees the hero as an isolated, self-sufficient individual who is faithful to the degree that he or she is able to detach from the faith community in order to oppose the conventions of the community. If the community eventually overcomes its stubborn resistance to the truth that the hero speaks, then the hero is vindicated as a truthful visionary and can depart, confident that the hero's lone opposition to the community has transformed the community.

In contrast to the romantic hero, the biblical prophet speaks from within the community in service to the God who created the community and who continues to hold it accountable to its originating covenant.[13] A favorite prophetic word is thus "return." The prophet calls the community to a return to fidelity. Prophets, seen from this perspective, are more traditionalists than innovators. As Long says, "Prophetic preaching seeks to discover what *is*, not to create that which is *not*."[14] In the Hebrew Scriptures, prophetic preaching restates the abiding demands of being in covenant with Yahweh. In the New Testament, prophetic preaching continues to assert Christ as the all sufficient, normative, and sovereign Lord and Savior. All must be subservient to and judged by this lordship. The prophet

---

[12] Long, 388.

[13] "…the shaping of Israel took place from inside its own experience and confession of faith and not through external appropriation from somewhere else…. If the church is to be faithful it must be formed and ordered from the inside of its experience and confession and not by borrowing from sources external to its own life." Walter Brueggemann, *The Prophetic Imagination* (Philadelphia: Fortress, 1978), 15. Micah, for example, is willing to suffer with the community (1:8-9; 7:1-7) and repeatedly refers to Judah as "my people" (some 8 or 9 times). Micah sees the necessity of identifying with the community as he speaks.

[14] Long, 388.

is not so much about action, though need for action is often implied in what the prophet preaches. The prophet is mainly about *identity*. Who are we as those who have been bought, delivered, commandeered in covenant with Yahweh? Prophets preach "This is who we are; therefore, this is how we ought to order our life together. This is what God in Christ has done. Therefore, how then should we live?" Prophets continue to see that which the rest of us have lost sight of. Prophets continue to submit to the sovereign demands of a God who creates a new people, an alternative community through the Word.

As preachers, we are not only the beneficiaries of but we are also judged by the biblical prophetic tradition. Nobody is being "pastoral" who is not also being "prophetic." A major vocation of preachers is to speak the truth about God so that a community of prophets (church) can speak and live the truth before the world. Among the prophetic implications for us preachers I see these:

1. Prophetic preaching is vividly tethered to a sovereign, active, loquacious, opinionated, totalitarian God. Thus, prophetic preaching renders a God who is quite a contrast to contemporary North American Christianity that tends toward a deistic, stoic sort of God who cares deeply about us but never actually acts or speaks.[15]

2. The purpose of prophetic preaching is the production of a community of prophets called the Body of Christ. The preacher is not the surrogate prophet for the congregation but rather the one who gives the people the words, the images, and the demonstration of dependency upon God that equips them for the prophetic ministry that is theirs by virtue of their baptism.[16] Too much of our

---

[15] Walter Brueggemann notes that "Jeremiah has a robust view of God.... This God is a vital, free conversation partner to whom Jeremiah can speak candidly and who surely is free to say anything back to Jeremiah." *Hopeful Imagination: Prophetic Voices in Exile* (Philadelphia: Fortress, 1986), 14.

[16] See my discussion of the way in which a prophetic community is the goal of prophetic preaching in my section, "Would That All the Lord's People Were Prophets," *Pastor: The Theology and Practice of Ordained Ministry* (Nashville: Abingdon, 2002), 252-265.

preaching is an individualizing, more specifically a
pop-psychologizing, of good news that is meant to be
inherently communal. Prophetic preaching is always
an experiment in faith—can the Trinity still produce a
people who are gathered on the basis of nothing more
than the Word?

3. Prophetic preaching tends toward the metaphorical
and highly charged symbolic discourse that wants
to fire and to fuel the imagination of the church.
As Walter Brueggemann puts it, "The task of
prophetic ministry is to nurture, nourish, and make
a consciousness and perception alternative to the
consciousness and perception of the dominant culture
around us."[17] The prophet criticizes the present order
in order to energize the faithful through a promise of a
new future. To paraphrase the poet Auden, one doesn't
have to be a poet in order to be a preacher, but if one
hopes to be a prophetic preacher, it is a necessity to be
a poet. Most of Mainline Protestantism today is in dire
need of some pushy, bold, extravagant speech.

4. All biblical preaching is an experience in vocation.
Our words become God's word as God calls our word
into his service. Prophetic preaching arises from within
and is demonstrably dependent upon the originating
vocation of Israel and Church. The prophetic preacher
will want to demonstrate, whenever possible, that we
preach what we have been told to preach. Use of the
lectionary as a source of biblical texts for preaching
is helpful; making visible to the congregation that
the word we preach is not self-derived, not what we
ourselves might have wanted to preach, but that which
we under compulsion must preach, is a requisite for
preaching that would be considered prophetic.

5. Prophetic preaching is unashamedly "miraculous." It
rests upon divine summons and is a gift, grace, an act

[17] Brueggemann, *The Prophetic Imagination*, 13.

of God, not an achievement of the preacher. The entire prophetic dynamic is set in motion by God after the human inquiry, "Is there any word from the LORD?" (Jer 37:17). The only reason a prophet speaks is because God speaks. The only authorization, validation, or consolation a preacher has is divine. Every prophetic sermon is a redoing of Genesis 1, a demonstration within the congregation of a God who loves to raise the dead and to make something out of nothing. The resurrection gives not only something to preach but the means to preach. All preaching that presumes to be the Word of God rests upon the prophetic vision of an interventionist, intrusive, invasive God.

6. Tom Long has called contemporary preaching's "turn to the listener" the most momentous event in twentieth-century homiletics. Much of current homiletic literature therefore tends to be mostly rhetoric, strategies for gaining a hearing, speculation upon the limits and capabilities of contemporary congregations. Prophetic preaching cares about none of this. Prophetic preaching worries more about listening to and speaking for God and less about listener approval, visible results, church growth, seeker sensitivity, user friendliness, and other ways that we pay more attention to what the congregation is able to hear than to what the Trinity is able to say.

7. Because nothing is beyond the purview of Yahweh, prophetic preaching is not about religion, or faith, or doing justice. Prophetic preaching is about *everything*—the feet of the poor, empty stomachs, the fate of children are all fair game for prophetic sermons. Everything is to be placed under the judgments of a righteous God. The apparent ease with which churches in America combine the flag and the cross, tie yellow ribbons on the front doors of their sanctuaries, and pray exclusively for our troops (despite Jesus' prophetic injunction to pray for our enemies) suggests that popular sentimentality and patriotic fervor mean

more to us clergy than the righteousness of a God who laughs at kings, even democratically elected kings (Ps 2).

8. The prophets preach against a backdrop of faith in Yahweh's ability ultimately to make a new heaven and a new earth, to transform, convert, and rebirth. Though our situation is grim, the prophet's fundamental faith in Yahweh's ability to get the family he deserves enables him or her to be not only brutally honest but also extravagantly hopeful. Any preacher who believes that things are unchangeably fixed, unalterably frozen by sociological, psychological, genetic, or economic determinisms, is not being true to the God of the prophets who creates, plucks up, plants, brings fresh a new heaven and a new earth. Prophets can sound so very pessimistic about human prospects for renewal because they are so unabashedly optimistic about God's ability to transform.

Though our chief concern is with the great prophets of the eighth century, one reason for our concern is our faith that the dynamics and the message of those prophets continues, by the grace of God, in the preaching of the church. I was surprised, midway through my preparation of this essay, to have the Gospel of John present Jesus as a prophet in much the same guise as the prophets of the eighth century. In preaching this text, again only by the grace of God, I got to stand in line with those prophets who preceded me, thus experiencing the continuing relevance of the prophetic way of God.

## *Spring House Cleaning - John 2:13-22*

### *Third Sunday in Lent*

I saw something the other day that I hope never to see again. Even now, it's hard for me to describe it, so painful, so upsetting was it. The day began as most any other. I got here about eight thirty or nine that morning, parked my car, walked up the way from the parking lot to the Chapel. I love walking that way—on every other morning but this one. The sun was shining, even though it was February. The morning sun on the polychrome stone of the Chapel, rising up before one in neogothic splendor, is a sight to behold.

But the sight I saw that morning was something else again. I could hear commotion as I got within range, clatter and clamor, things crashing.

"No, you can't do that! Stop! Who do you think you are?" I was hearing the voices of our Janitor, along with that of the Attendant.

I approached the door and was shocked, yes, even horrified, to see a couple of hymnals come flying out the door. The new hymnals that we had bought only a few years ago, the twenty-dollars apiece hymnals with the gold letters stamped on them for two dollars extra! Those precious books were being thrown out the door by some raving lunatic.

Then came the big Bible—the leather bound, genuine Moroccan, gold embossed lectern Bible that was given as a memorial. The two hundred dollar Bible! That one. Flying out the door, flopping half opened on the flagstones in front of the Chapel.

What kind of nut would throw around the Word of God? Had the police been called?

Then came the furniture: a couple of pews, sailing out the door, ripped out of the floor where we had them carefully bolted down. The Attendant's desk—the one where he guards the entrance to the Chapel. Splintering into a hundred pieces on the sidewalk. How are we supposed to ensure the safety and preservation of the Chapel building without that desk?! The computer, which keeps the Chapel calendar, that holds all the records of those would-be brides and grooms who have met our requirements for getting married in the Chapel. How are we supposed to police this place without that computer?

The sacred computer burst into a pile of rubble when it hit the ground.

The altar! No, not our altar! We have to hire four football

players to move that thing whenever we need it placed somewhere else. How on earth did that lunatic lift it? There it sailed out the door. The beautiful paraments and hangings (hand embroidered, European hand embroidered, silk European hand embroidered), now crumpled in the yard.

I ducked just in time or the silver communion chalice would have cold conked me, sailing out the door. Then the sterling silver paten, the engraved one. Then the huge hand carved oak baptismal font, out the door! Where are those police when you need them? Probably writing parking tickets and here our place of worship is being ravished.

Then I saw fly the Methodist *Book of Discipline*, a large bishop came flying out by the seat of his pants, landing hard on the front steps in a very undignified heap, then the Dean of the Divinity School, then one by one all of the members of the Committee of Ministerial Credentials, the Study Commission on Homosexuality and the Church, the Chairperson of the Altar Guild, the large vase in which we put the flowers on special Sundays. All out the door.

The Attendant came running out, his clothes half torn off, cuts and bruises on his face, screaming, "Jesus is in there, and he's cleaning house!"

"Jesus?" I asked. "My Jesus, Jesus meek and mild? The compassionate Jesus? Our best friend and most loyal patron? Jesus?"

"Yep," said the attendant, "I saw him myself. Burst in this morning while we were praying. Boy, is he mad!"

At that moment, the entire Judicial Council of the United Methodist Church sailed between us and hit the ground with a thud, almost exactly on the ground where the Clergy Pension Fund lay.

Jesus is cleaning house. To my knowledge, this is the first time Jesus has been in the Temple since he was a kid. He was brought here, as I recall, as a babe in arms to be dedicated to God. Then he was here again when he was about twelve. Things didn't go that well on his last visit. He got into a big argument (the nerve of the kid!) with the biblical scholars, embarrassing them with his extensive knowledge of biblical exegesis.

That was about his last time in the Temple until today. It's spring, Passover time, time when Jews celebrate their deliverance from Egyptian slavery. It's a religious ritual that commemorates that time when once we had to bow down to the Pharaoh. Now we're free; thus the Passover.

Jesus comes in the temple, encounters the vendors selling cattle, sheep, and doves, and goes ballistic. Why? All of this is religious! The livestock are for the necessary, biblically prescribed temple sacrifice. You can't make a sacrifice to God, can't get your sins forgiven, can't get right with God without a sacrifice. The rich folk are buying oxen to sacrifice. The upper middle class buy sheep, and the poorer folk purchase doves. Take your sacrifice to the priest up at the altar and get tight with God.

"What if you don't have even enough money to buy a dove?" you ask. Well, too bad. It takes money to run any organization, even a religious one. Without the Friends of Duke Chapel, none of this would possible. Please give generously when the offering plate is passed, etc.

Look, people need a little help when they worship. Sure, you can meet God walking in the woods or sitting quietly at home, but here in this beautiful building, with the organ, and the hymnals, the choir and the clergy, well, it's just better this way. Easier. We need the oxen, doves, hymnals, bread, and wine to help us do business with God—and to help God do business with us.

You ask if we need this nice a building, this large a choir, this costly a clergy in order to worship God? Well, you pay for what you get. We do quality Christian worship here, and quality costs. "Give of your best to the Master," "take my silver and my gold, not a mite would I withhold"; it's in the hymnal.

And Jesus? Jesus makes a whip, kicks over the tables, destroys the bird cages, stampedes the cows, dumps out the cash drawers of the money changers, and throws the rest of them out the door.

"Stop making my Father's house into Southport Mall!" he screamed to them as he popped that whip on their backsides.

It was about then that his disciples remembered where it is written, "Passion for God's house has consumed me."

In just a few years, the beloved temple would be in ruin, thanks to the Romans. And if you couldn't get right with God by buying a dove or a sheep, how could you get to God? If the sheep and the rites and rituals, the prayer books and the praise choruses and the bread and the wine are not the way that we get to God (and God gets to us), then how are we supposed to do that? Where is the Temple now?

Jesus told them, "Your Temple is not such a big deal. Destroy this Temple. In three days, I will build it back."

Get it? *Who* is the Temple now?

There's now a new way to God. The altar of God has come down to us. The high altar has become a dinner table. The sacred, mysterious sacrificial act has become everyday bread and wine. The Word of God has become flesh and dwelt among us.

All our beloved aids to worship, our church, our books, our ideas, our songs, our graven images and our sacred spaces, as helpful as they often are, pale in comparison with the new "temple," the one that was not built with human hands, not dependent upon human contributions. Sadly, these beloved means of worship, those ways we have to climb up to God, sometimes, in our hands, become "gods." Idols. We invest too much of ourselves in them, expect too much from them, allow them to expect too little of us. Our freedom to worship becomes enslavement to false gods. Jesus sets us free. We pass over to worship in Spirit and in truth.

Just as sad, our beautiful places of worship that we have so lavishly, lovingly furnished become a barrier between us and the poor, a barrier to the poor who are beloved by God but don't know how to return that love in such an extravagant, beautifully adorned Temple.

If even the very House of God can become an idol, a substitute for, a way of evading God, what next might we make our idol?

The good news is that Jesus is just consumed with passion for God's house. Jesus loves us, but loves the righteousness, truth, and holiness of God even more. He not only quotes the prophets, he *is* one. If you thought prophecy died with Isaiah, think again. He will purify God's house, transform our little play church into his very Body. Jesus is a prophet, a wild, obedient, obsessed lover of the righteousness of God. He will, whip in hand, drive out the idolatry in us. He will cleanse us until we shine like the sun. He will take our church, our fumbling attempts to praise, and transform it and us into a purified acclamation of the true God.

So this Sunday, amid the rubble of our "religion," we pray:

*Lord Jesus, drive out our self-contrived demons, whip our worship into shape, clean us up, dust us off, until we are able to worship you—in word and in deed, in spirit and truth, on Sunday and on Monday—as we ought. Amen.*

# 2

# The Proclamation of Doom in the Eighth Century Prophets:

Want vs. Need

Rick Marrs

To cite an overused famous opening, "It was the best of times, it was the worst of times." Such ably captures the world of the eighth century prophets. During the eighth century B.C., Israel (and Judah) experienced an economic explosion and geographical expansion unknown since the glory days of David and Solomon. The abundant documentation from this period evidences a vibrant and dynamic society, a society flush with national pride and a seemingly glowing future, a future that could only return Israel to a place of honor and recognition in the larger Near Eastern political arena.

However, by the middle of the eighth century, Israel's glorious days under Jeroboam II were rapidly drawing to a close. Exploiting Assyrian weakness, Jeroboam II and his Judean counterpart, Uzziah, had constructed impressive kingdoms in North Israel and South Judah. During the reign of Jeroboam II, the mercantile sector prospered, key Israelite cities were enlarged and re-fortified, and boundaries were expanded and secured. Not surprisingly, a sense of self-confidence pervaded the land. Religious activity bolstered this confidence in external trappings. At the temples, sacrifices were offered, God's praises were sung, prayers were made, and the salvific acts of God were recounted. God's people seemed secure; external obedience to God's will manifested itself regularly in cultic activities.

A horizon currently bright with economic prosperity, military expansion, and societal confidence would soon be shadowed with Assyrian troops. Tiglath-Pileser III rose to power in Assyria and quickly implemented crucial changes into the governmental structure and international policies that boded ill for satellite countries. However, until Tiglath-Pileser III actually marched against Syria-Palestine, destroying Damascus and annexing Galilee from North Israel, most Israelites remained blissfully ignorant of their impending troubles.

The complexity of the remainder of the eighth century in many ways rivals the complexity of today's world. In 722/21 B.C., Samaria fell, leaving no doubt that the glorious days of Jeroboam II (and Uzziah) were long past. This catastrophe resulted in a large influx of northern refugees into southern Judah (specifically Jerusalem).[1] Such an influx certainly had tremendous social and economic consequences upon both the urban and rural sectors of Judah. Resources were taxed; income was affected.[2]

In 713, Philistia revolted against Sargon of Assyria. According to Sargon's annals, Hezekiah of Judah joined Ashdod in this move for freedom. Later, in 705-701, Hezekiah, encouraged by the death of Sargon far from home and prodded by Merodach-Baladan of Babylon and Piankhi of Egypt, ceased paying tribute to Assyria. As a result, the Judean countryside was ravaged; Jerusalem narrowly escaped annihilation.

In the midst of this tumultuous period of unprecedented hope, boundless optimism, and eventual turmoil, Yahweh sent his messengers the prophets, preachers armed with oracles from the Lord, but oracles of doom! He called Amos and Micah from Judah and Hosea from Israel. Though different in geographical and social origins and rhetorical style, these three prophets shared a common homiletic stance—they each brought a profound theological vision to bear upon their proclamation.

---

[1] Archaeological data suggest that the population of Jerusalem more than doubled during this period.

[2] Many scholars have suggested that during this time there arose an extra incentive to own land, and reduced wages resulted. Interestingly, a number of stamped jar handles have been discovered in the Shephelah (Micah's home territory). These handles are stamped *lmlk* ("to/for the king"). Although some questions remain, it has been suggested that these artifacts evidence increased royal involvement in the life of rural Judah. Specifically, agrarian Judah may have been substantially financing the policies of the capital.

They each integrated fully their theological worldview with the social milieu in which they were placed. Amos, a shepherd from rural Judea, went north and tackled cherished ideologies of salvation history. Hosea, a true northern prophet, personalized the covenant theology through relational images to demonstrate the insanity of melding Canaanite religious thought and practices with the worship of Yahweh. Micah, a rural southerner commissioned to proclaim God's word in urban Jerusalem, powerfully challenged the reigning ideology of the powerful elite. These three prophets brought their theological vision to bear powerfully upon the various social issues of their day and their audience. Each courageously stepped forth to proclaim the divine message of doom in the midst of a society unwilling and unable to accept such a word.

## Doom in Amos: the Reversal of Salvation History

Amos, called from the flocks to proclaim God's word, journeyed north to the great Israelite cities and sanctuaries to prophesy. To a society saturated with self-confidence and celebrating success, Amos delivered blistering social criticisms. Where the wealthy saw unlimited growth and prosperity, Amos saw social injustice; where the powerful saw a flourishing cult and fulfillment of God's decrees, Amos saw the hollow trappings of religiosity with no ethical impact on the daily lives of its worshipers. Amos lamented a community devoid of righteousness, a society lacking a true moral compass. Although an "outsider" lacking recognized credentials, Amos faithfully decried the creation of a community differentiating people by socio-economic status.[3]

---

[3] Recent sociological analyses of this period in Israelite history have emphasized the apparent movement within the society from an agrarian based economy to a mercantile based society. This movement, coupled with a move away from a covenant ideology of egalitarianism to a monarchical ideology of hierarchy, spelled disaster for numerous inhabitants of the land. Perhaps Amos, as sheepbreeder and merchant moving between the two sectors, stepped forth as God's prophet to denounce the abuses resulting from such changes. For further discussion of this period of Israelite history for the message of the prophets, see R. Coote, *Amos among the Prophets* (Philadelphia: Fortress Press, 1981); J. Hayes, *Amos. The Eighth-Century Prophet* (Nashville: Abingdon, 1988).

Amos, infused with a theology rooted in the majestic sovereignty of God and fully cognizant of the ethical implications of living in right relationship with this majestic creator, is called to communicate that message to a people lacking such a vision. Following the superscription, Amos declares:

*The Lord roars from Zion, and utters his voice from Jerusalem; the pastures of the shepherds wither, and the top of Carmel dries up.* (1:2)

Two images appear in this verse, each of them somewhat surprising. That Amos would picture God as a roaring lion suggests a powerful God ever ready to spring forth from his lair and ferociously defend his people; that Amos would present God as a roaring lion poised to pounce upon his own people surely must have startled his listeners. Yahweh's capacity to fight meant security for most Israelites; Amos graphically unleashes an image of God stalking his own people (see also 3:8; 5:19). In a different direction, the roar of the divine voice often appears in contexts heralding the advent of a rainstorm. Since God sustained the created order, rain (and its attendant peals of thunder) signaled divine presence and activity (see Ps 29). Hearing the roar of the Lord's voice should result in beneficent rain falling upon the pastures and Carmel range. However, in most unexpected fashion, drought ensues! From this first prophetic utterance, Israel must have realized that for this prophet, things were not as they appeared; the trappings of success, in which Israel placed so much confidence, were a potentially deadly chimera.

A gripping display of motif reversal unfolds in the oracles against the foreign nations (Amos 1-2).[4] The audience must have delighted as Amos recounted with rhetorical flourish and methodical precision the atrocious war crimes of such neighbors as Damascus, Gaza, Tyre, Edom, Ammon, and Moab. These acts of inhumanity, ranging from brutally killing innocent victims to enslaving the powerless, could only receive

---

[4] For a discussion of these oracles from a covenant perspective, see M. Barre, "The Meaning of *l' 'sybnw* in Amos 1:3–2:6," *JBL* 105 (1986), 611-31.

responses of righteous indignation from his listeners. Surely such acts decisively demonstrated Israel's moral superiority over her neighbors. However, as Amos brings this section to a close, he saves for last the nation exhibiting the rankest demonstrations of inhumanity. To the shock (and perhaps horror) of his audience, that nation was none other than Israel! God's own chosen people outpaced the foreign nations in acts of inhumanity.

Amos's conclusion, while perhaps startling to his audience, reflects clearly his theology; his argument masterfully demonstrates his grasp of the power of rhetoric. Before detailing God's intended reversal of Israel's saving history, Amos first articulates Israel's absolute reversal of the divine intent for her:

> *Thus says the Lord: For three transgressions of Israel, and for four, I will not revoke the punishment; because they sell the righteous for silver, and the needy for a pair of sandals—they who trample the head of the poor into the dust of the earth, and push the afflicted out of the way; father and son go in to the same girl, so that my holy name is profaned; they lay themselves down beside every altar on garments taken in pledge; and in the house of their God they drink wine bought with fines they imposed.* (2:6-8)[5]

In comparison to the foreign nations, Israel's crime is doubly heinous. Whereas the crimes committed by Israel's neighbors were against "outsiders," Israel enacts criminal activity against her *own* citizens! Further, none other than Yahweh's own covenant partner, recipient of the full array of divine grace and deliverance, commits these vicious atrocities.[6]

---

[5] See also 5:12; 8:4-6.

[6] The heinous nature of these criminal acts is particularly poignant. The proceeds confiscated from the poor by the rich are subsequently used in cultic activities! For a survey of interpretation of these verses, see H. Barstad, *The Religious Polemics of Amos: Studies in the Preaching of Am 2, 7B-8; 4, 1-13; 5, 1-27; 6, 4-7; 8, 14* (SVT 34; Leiden: Brill, 1984), 11-36.

> *Yet I destroyed the Amorite before them, whose height was like the height of cedars, and who was as strong as oaks; I destroyed his fruit above, and his roots beneath. Also I brought you up out of the land of Egypt, and led you forty years in the wilderness, to possess the land of the Amorite. And I raised up some of your children to be prophets and some of your youths to be nazirites. Is it not indeed so, O people of Israel? says the Lord. But you made the nazirites drink wine, and commanded the prophets, saying "You shall not prophesy."* (2:9-11)[7]

Israel's complete failure to grasp the ethical implications of living in covenant relationship with Yahweh can only result in a reversal of her salvation history and a collapse of one of her most trusted securities—the military.

> *Flight shall perish from the swift, and the strong shall not retain their strength, nor shall the mighty save their lives; those who handle the bow shall not stand, and those who are swift of foot shall not save themselves, nor shall those who ride horses save their lives; and those who are stout of heart among the mighty shall flee away naked in that day, says the Lord.* (2:14-16)[8]

Israel's consistent reversal of God's intent for her brings a divine response fully committed to reversing her presumption upon the divine blessings.

Amos continues his effective use of reversal language in the collection of social justice oracles (Amos 3-6). Beginning with a striking series of rhetorical questions (3:3-8), the prophet returns to his portrayal of the lion Yahweh stalking his prey Israel: "The lion has roared; who will not fear? The Lord God

---

[7] Ironically, the effort to silence the prophets was not entirely successful, since Amos remains dramatically "unsilenced" (see also 3:8; 7:10-17).

[8] Although Israel verbally affirmed her trust in God, her activities belied her claim. In reality, Israel trusted in military power (so here and 6:8, 13), savvy political leaders and foreign alliances (6:1-2, 4-6), wealth (3:15), and correct religious practice (5:21-23).

has spoken; who can but prophesy?" (3:8). Contrary to the false
security pervading the land, Amos envisions the imminent
danger approaching Israel; he can only proclaim impending
doom. "Fearless" Israel lives out of touch with covenant reality
(3:2). Her refusal to live out the covenant obligations results in
a most striking scene:

> Proclaim to the strongholds in Ashdod, and to the
> strongholds in the land of Egypt, and say, "Assemble
> yourselves on Mount Samaria, and see what great
> tumults are within it, and what oppressions are in
> its midst." They do not know how to do right, says
> the Lord, those who store up violence and robbery
> in their strongholds. Therefore thus says the Lord
> God: An adversary shall surround the land, and strip
> you of your defense; and your strongholds shall be
> plundered. (3:9-11)

Incredibly, Yahweh invites these foreigners to take
front row seats, not so they can see God's will righteously
implemented and demonstrated by his covenant people,
nor so they can themselves receive God's chastening critique
of their own behavior, but so they can witness the moral
mayhem and chaos of a society devoid of God's just and
righteous presence![9]

The prophetic assault upon Israel's cherished securities
continues in Amos 4 with a devastating reversal of her salvific
traditions. Amos opens with a stinging critique of Israel's cult
(4:4-5), sarcastically calling Israel to multiply those cultic
activities in which she takes so much pride and security.[10] He

---

[9] For a similar motif, see Isa 1:21-26 where Isaiah tragically depicts
Jerusalem as a city devoid of justice and righteousness. For a striking contrast,
see Ps 2, where the nations come to scoff at God's people and find themselves
the recipients of divine scorn; here they are invited by the Lord to engage in
that very task!

[10] The language is noteworthy. Amos utilizes the customary psalmic
language of invitation to worship: "O, come, let us sing to the Lord; let us
make a joyful noise to the rock of our salvation! Let us come into his presence
with thanksgiving; let us make a joyful noise to him with songs of praise!....O,
come, let us worship and bow down, let us kneel before the Lord, our Maker!"
(Ps 95:1-2, 6). Yahweh's true reaction to Israel's worship appears in 5:21-23.

immediately follows with a rehearsal of Yahweh's persistent inbreakings into Israelite history, not for weal, but for woe. With rigor and dispatch, he recounts the multiple divine attempts to reverse the direction of Israel's activities. Yahweh has authored famine, drought, crippling crop failures, and insect infestation to awaken Israel to the serious nature of her situation. Not only has Israel remained oblivious to this divine intervention, she has also failed to see the similarities of her situation to ominous historical forebears:

> *I sent among you a pestilence after the manner of Egypt;[11] I killed your young men with the sword; I carried away your horses; and I made the stench of your camp go up into your nostrils; yet you did not return to me, says the Lord. I overthrew some of you, as when God overthrew Sodom and Gomorrah, and you were like a brand snatched from the fire; yet you did not return to me, says the Lord.* (4:10-11)[12]

Amos eloquently attacks rampant social injustices and flagrant cultic abuses in chapters 5-6. Through the use of wordplay, he exposes the moral bankruptcy of Israel's extensive cultic activities. They have failed completely to effect proper social behavior. Where Israel sees power and prestige,

---

[11] The reference to the "pestilence of Egypt" may simply connote the frequent maladies encountered in Egyptian agricultural life, or it may hauntingly echo the plagues Egypt experienced at the Exodus. The latter would surely clash with the popular theology of the day. To suggest that the wealthy and powerful in Israel might find themselves recipients of Yahweh's former treatment of Egypt would surely meet with strong opposition (see also 5:16-17).

[12] Later the book of Amos envisions the ultimate famine. Having failed to produce repentance through physical famine and deprivation, Yahweh absents himself from Israel: "The time is surely coming, says the Lord God, when I will send a famine on the land; not a famine of bread, or a thirst for water, but of hearing the words of the Lord. They shall wander from sea to sea, and from north to east; they shall run to and fro, seeking the word of the Lord, but they shall not find it" (8:11-12). This final tragic divine action counters Yahweh's true desired action toward his people. (Note especially Amos 9:11-15, where Yahweh longs to shower his people with abundance and blessing.)

Amos sees death and decay (5:1-2). Amos calls the people to
"worship," but it is a worship that manifests itself in the street!

> *Seek the Lord and live, but do not seek Bethel, and
> do not enter into Gilgal or cross over to Beersheba....
> Seek the Lord and live, or he will break out against
> the house of Joseph like fire, and it will devour Bethel,
> with no one to quench it. Ah, you that turn justice to
> wormwood, and bring righteousness to the ground![13]
> Seek good and not evil, that you may live; and so the
> Lord, the God of hosts, will be with you, just as you
> have said. Hate evil and love good, and establish
> justice in the gate; it may be that the Lord, the God
> of hosts, will be gracious to the remnant of Joseph.*
> (5:4-5a, 6-7, 14-15)

Using the traditional language of gathering for worship
("seek"), Amos turns the focus away from one place (the
sanctuary) to another place (the city square). Seeking the Lord
becomes nothing less than activating justice and righteousness
in every daily activity and social interaction. The stakes are
high.[14] Because Israel has completely reversed God's intention
for her, Yahweh will reverse her intentions.

> *Therefore because you trample on the poor and take
> from them levies of grain, you have built houses of
> hewn stone, but you shall not live in them; you have
> planted pleasant vineyards, but you shall not drink
> their wine.* (5:11)[15]

---

[13] Elsewhere Amos utilizes an apt analogy to express the ludicrous nature
of subverting justice and righteousness: "Do horses run on rocks? Does one
plow the sea with oxen? But you have turned justice into poison and the fruit of
righteousness into wormwood" (6:12).

[14] Yahweh promises Israel the same punishment as that of the foreign nations
(chs. 1-2)–devastating fire (5:6; cf. 7:4).

[15] The language strikingly reverses that of Deut 6:10-12; 8:11-13, where
Moses admonishes the future inhabitants of the land not to forget that their
houses and vineyards are sheer gifts from their gracious God.

Amos climaxes his reversal in his stinging critique of the "day of the Lord" tradition.

> *Alas for you who desire the day of the Lord! Why do you want the day of the Lord? It is darkness, not light; as if someone fled from a lion, and was met by a bear; or went into the house and rested a hand against the wall, and was bitten by a snake. Is not the day of the Lord darkness, not light, and gloom with no brightness in it?* (5:18-20)

Apparently Israel longed for a "day of the Lord," a day in which Yahweh would right all wrongs and deliver the righteous from the wicked.[16] For most, this day entailed the overthrow of the foreign nations (specifically Israel's enemies) and the exaltation of Israel once again to a position of supreme importance within the world community. For Amos, the day of the Lord would be a day when wrongs would be righted and the righteous would be vindicated; however, the wicked were none other than the wealthy and powerful within Israel, and the righteous were the poor and needy! Without a dramatic change in social behavior, disaster was inevitable, avoidance impossible.[17]

Amos 3-6 dramatically closes with a scathing denunciation of the social complaisance of the powerful and wealthy of Israel:

> *Alas for those who are at ease in Zion, and for those who feel secure on Mount Samaria, the notables of the first of the nations, to whom the house of Israel resorts! Cross over to Calneh, and see; from there*

---

[16] For similar imagery and language, see Amos 8:9-10. (Zeph 1:14-18 provides a helpful exposition of the day of the Lord.)

[17] The image is noteworthy. "Getting away" from God is likened to outrunning lions and bears and avoiding poisonous snakes. Amos returns to this theme in 9:2-4, where he masterfully reverses Ps 139. In Ps 139 the constant presence of Yahweh provides comfort and solace to the psalmist. An awareness of God's presence signals security and safety in the midst of ever-present dangers. Here, Amos presents a God determined to exercise justice through the punishment of the unjust. No arena escapes Yahweh's purview.

*go to Hamath the great; then go down to Gath of the Philistines. Are you better than these kingdoms? Or is your territory greater than their territory, O you that put far away the evil day, and bring near a reign of violence? Alas for those who lie on beds of ivory, and lounge on their couches, and eat lambs from the flock, and calves from the stall; who sing idle songs to the sound of the harp, and like David improvise on instruments of music; who drink wine from bowls, and anoint themselves with the finest oils, but are not grieved over the ruin of Joseph! Therefore they shall now be the first to go into exile, and the revelry of the loungers shall pass away.* (6:1-7)

To these mighty and influential who delight in their self-designated preeminence ("notables of the *first* of the nations"), Amos accords a different preeminence—they shall be the *first* to enter exile! Luxury and complaisance at the expense of others will no longer be tolerated.

Amos effectively exposes the core of Israelite society and demonstrates its failure to integrate its theology into its ethical behavior. Through his proclamation, the prophet articulates the implications of God's sovereignty for cultic activities and for ethical behavior toward the powerless and disenfranchised. Amos masterfully reverses Israel's cherished traditions and assumptions, re-aligning them with a proper theological vision of Yahweh's will and intent for his people. For Amos, recognizing Yahweh's sovereign claim upon all of life results in a community characterized by humility rather than pride, gratitude toward God rather than presumption, and a constant desire to implement justice and righteousness in every facet of life. Amos calls his community to "let justice roll down like waters, and righteousness like an everflowing stream" (5:24).

## Doom in Hosea: Shattered Covenant Relationships

While Amos addresses the social ills of his day against the backdrop of the sovereignty of God, Hosea utilizes the theology of covenant to proclaim God's word to that same audience. However, so that the true dynamic and timeless nature of the covenant is not missed, he personalizes the covenant through the use of powerful relational metaphors. Hosea employs three primary metaphors in his preaching—husband / wife; husbandman / vineyard; parent / child.

The book of Hosea divides unevenly between chapters 1-3 (Hosea's "story") and 4-14 (Hosea's oracles).[18] The marriage relationship dominates the first three chapters. Hosea 1 and 3 depict Hosea's marital relationship, first biographically (1) and then autobiographically (3). The children dominate Hosea 1; Hosea's marriage relationship is the specific focus of the third chapter. The opening of Hosea 2 leaves the brief impression that a discussion of Hosea's marriage continues, but this impression is quickly corrected. The marriage depicted in Hosea 2 is that of Yahweh and his spouse Israel:

> *Plead with your mother, plead— for she is not my wife, and I am not her husband—that she put away her whoring from her face, and her adultery from between her breasts, or I will strip her naked and expose her as in the day she was born, and make her like a wilderness, and turn her into a parched land, and kill her with thirst. Upon her children also I will have no pity, because they are children of whoredom. For their mother has played the whore; she who conceived them has acted shamefully. For she said, "I will go after my lovers; they give me my bread and my water, my wool and my flax, my oil and my drink." Therefore I will hedge up her way with thorns; and I will build a wall against her, so that she cannot find her paths. She shall pursue her lovers, but not overtake them; and she shall seek them, but shall not find them. Then she shall say, "I will go and return to my first husband, for it was better with me then than now." She did not know that it was I who gave her the grain, the wine, and the oil, and who lavished upon her silver and gold*

---

[18] Each chapter in Hos 1-3 has a similar structure – long doom oracle followed by a shorter hope oracle (1:2-9 |doom| > 1:10-2:1 |hope|; 3:1-4 |doom| > 3:5 |hope|; cf. 2:2-13 |doom| > 2:14-23 |hope|).

*that they used for Baal. Therefore I will take back
my grain in its time, and my wine in its season; and
I will take away my wool and my flax, which were to
cover her nakedness. Now I will uncover her shame
in the sight of her lovers, and no one shall rescue her
out of my hand. I will put an end to all her mirth, her
festivals, her new moons, her sabbaths, and all her
appointed festivals. I will lay waste her vines and her
fig trees, of which she said, "These are my pay, which
my lovers have given me." I will make them a forest,
and the wild animals shall devour them. I will punish
her for the festival days of the Baals, when she offered
incense to them and decked herself with her ring and
jewelry, and went after her lovers, and forgot me, says
the LORD.* (2:2-13)

The scene is graphic—Hosea portrays Israel as a wanton
paramour rejecting her faithful spouse and aggressively seeking
lovers so that she might be enriched. She persistently pursues
partners so that she might receive the "rewards of her labors."[19]
Her motivation is blatantly opportunistic. This amazing scenario
depicted by Hosea seems almost unimaginable. However, an
even greater surprise awaits the reader—Yahweh's response to
such willful disregard for the covenant! Rejecting the obvious
solution—severance of the relationship—Yahweh himself
chooses instead to block his people's every selfish move and
aggressively put Israel in a position to return to him.[20] The road
to return will neither be easy nor without danger. In response
to her consuming self-absorption, Yahweh withdraws all those
gifts Israel so desperately seeks. Her return will involve shame
and ridicule. However, *it is a return* rather than deserved
destruction. Yahweh's language is poignant—those very things

---

[19] "Bread, wool, water, and flax" were substances to be provided by the
husband (see Exod 21:10-11).

[20] The language is striking—"pursue" (*rdp*) suggests a determined chase;
"seek" occurs in the Deuteronomic Historian as a technical term for visitation
to a shrine. Clearly the underlying backdrop for the text is Israel's worship at
the Baal shrines.

Israel so brazenly sought and considered gifts from her worship of the Baals were in actuality gifts from the Lord himself![21]

The use of marital imagery powerfully portrays the polar approaches Yahweh and his people Israel have taken to the covenant relationship. On the one hand, Israel's approach to the relationship is consumed with self-absorption and opportunism. Israel envisions a divine–human relationship that is rooted almost solely in self-concern and profitability. For Hosea, this is the legacy of Canaanite thinking—religion that traffics in profitability and concern for oneself. In contrast, Yahweh stands forth as the faithful lover, the devoted spouse willing to care for and provide for a completely undeserving spouse. Yahweh demonstrates the ultimate love—giving gifts even when those gifts are attributed to another!

Although the marital relationship is the dominant and best-known relationship from the preaching of Hosea, it is not the only relationship he uses in his proclamation to personalize the covenant between Yahweh and his people. In Hosea 9-10, he uses the imagery of a vineyard owner and a vineyard.

> *Like grapes in the wilderness, I found Israel. Like the first fruit on the fig tree, in its first season, I saw your ancestors. But they came to Baal-Peor, and consecrated themselves to a thing of shame, and became detestable like the thing they loved... Israel is a luxuriant vine that yields its fruit. The more his fruit increased, the more altars he built; as his country improved, he improved his pillars. Their heart is false; now they must bear their guilt.* (Hos 9:10-11; 10:1-2a)

Though Hosea's imagery changes from marital to agricultural, his theology remains constant. The larger context of Hosea 9 portrays Israel past and present. The Exodus from Egypt and subsequent wilderness sojourn is depicted as Yahweh rescuing a defenseless vine or fig tree. However, this plant Yahweh intended for transplanting among the verdant hills of

---

[21] The triad "grain, wine, and oil" appears regularly in the Canaanite texts from Ugarit as elements under Baal's jurisdiction.

Canaan "rebelled" at Baal-Peor, before the transplanting could occur! This ancient tragedy is now matched by Israel's current stubborn refusal to embrace Yahweh in faithfulness.[22] Like Hosea 2, Yahweh refuses to abandon his people entirely; however, like Hosea 2, the road back to a right relationship will be demanding and fraught with anguish. Hosea sprinkles his language with futility curses;[23] every attempt of Israel to secure its own protection and future will be negated. The language is jolting—Yahweh turns Israel, the lovely palm, into a child murderer! Those "children" who *might* survive Yahweh himself will murder!

The language and imagery of Hosea 9-10 forces us to come to grips with two realities—first, like Israel, we often distance ourselves from a right relationship with God as we increase in prosperity; second, we often become what we worship. Hosea 10 sadly recounts the tragic reality that Israel's increased prosperity resulted not in an increased outpouring of gratitude and tightening of the relationship with Yahweh, but in a perverse tendency to increase in self-reliance and presumptuous independence. Hosea 9:10 reminds us that we "become what we love (worship)." Abandoning Yahweh for Baal, the people become shameful like the Baals they worshiped. Tragically, the call of "be holy, as I, the Lord your God, am holy" is overwhelmed by "become detestable, as the Baal you love is detestable!"

Hosea's final relational image occurs in Hosea 11:1-9:

*When Israel was a child, I loved him, and out of Egypt I called my son. The more I called them, the more they went from me; they kept sacrificing to the Baals, and offering incense to idols. Yet it was I who taught Ephraim to walk, I took them up in my arms; but they did not know that I healed them. I led them with cords*

---

[22] Hosea varies the picture slightly—he envisions Ephraim as a palm in a meadow (9:13).

[23] Futility curses occur in 9:14 ("miscarrying womb and dry breasts"); cf. also 9:16 ("their root is dried up, they shall bear no fruit").

*of human kindness, with bands of love. I was to them
like those who lift infants to their cheeks. I bent down
to them and fed them. They shall return to the land
of Egypt, and Assyria shall be their king, because
they have refused to return to me. The sword rages
in their cities; it consumes their oracle-priests, and
devours because of their schemes. My people are bent
on turning away from me. To the Most High they call,
but he does not raise them up at all. How can I give
you up, Ephraim? How can I hand you over, O Israel?
How can I make you like Admah? How can I treat
you like Zeboiim? My heart recoils within me; my
compassion grows warm and tender. I will not execute
my fierce anger; I will not again destroy Ephraim; for
I am God and no mortal, the Holy One in your midst,
and I will not come in wrath.*

Hosea 11 returns us to the world of Hosea 1-3. Hosea's
theology remains consistent; he simply changes imagery. Just
as Yahweh's love overwhelmed the grievous wrong his faithless
spouse committed in Hosea 2, so now his love for Israel
overwhelms the punishment that the recalcitrant child should
receive. Significantly, the imagery heightens the poignancy of
the wrongs committed by Israel, for both "offenses," the one
committed by the adulterous spouse and the other committed
by the rebellious child, are capital offenses warranting death
sentences. Hosea 11 graphically depicts a parental love for an
ungrateful child bent on self-destruction. Hosea's depiction of
Israel's rebellion remains constant—Israel repeatedly attributes
her "successes" to Baal and in turn bestows further gifts upon
Baal, creating a vicious cycle of infidelity and delusion. Like
Hosea 9-10, the road back to a right relationship with Yahweh
will be neither easy nor uneventful; it will lead through the
harrowing regions of Assyria and result in a tragic loss of life
for some. However, the destruction will not be total; the end
will not be final. Unlike the all-consuming destruction the Lord
wrought at Admah and Zeboiim (see Deut 29:23), the Lord will
withhold his full wrath in a last-ditch effort to win back the love
and devotion of his recalcitrant child.

Hosea, through his use of these powerfully personal metaphors, presents us with the true and living God. Our God's love is fiercely personal and intimate. He refuses to take the easy route and simply sever the relationship with his rebellious people. He rejects the option to exercise impersonal justice and retribution against the grievous wrongs his people have committed. Rather, he goes far beyond the second mile, bestowing his gifts, even when those gifts are received with ingratitude and credited to another!

The bulk of Hosea's doom oracles in chapters 4-14 alternate between documenting the grievous nature of the sins Israel commits and those leaders most responsible for initiating these sins. The people surely are sinners; however, their sins are the "logical" result of the perverse leadership they have experienced. Hosea caustically castigates the leaders of the land for a failure to instruct the people and embody for the people covenant loyalty. Hosea's opening oracles in chapter 4 capture the essence of his proclamation in chapters 4-14.

In Hosea 4:1-3, Hosea indicts Israel for serious breaches of covenant loyalty:

> Hear the word of the Lord, O people of Israel; for the Lord has an indictment against the inhabitants of the land. There is no faithfulness or loyalty, and no knowledge of God in the land. Swearing, lying, and murder, and stealing and adultery break out; bloodshed follows bloodshed. Therefore the land mourns, and all who live in it languish; together with the wild animals and the birds of the air, even the fish of the sea are perishing.

The covenant breaches are complete—the positive covenant virtues of faithfulness (*'mt*), steadfast love (*hsd*), and knowledge of God (*d't yhwh*) have been obliterated and replaced by crimes of social violence. Hosea cites the entire second half of the Decalogue! Not surprisingly, the land suffers grievously.[24]

---

[24] The language and imagery of Hosea reflect that of Deuteronomy. Like Deuteronomy, the land suffers the consequences of covenant infidelity. More than experiencing a simple drought, the land experiences a loss of vitality and returns to its primitive "unredeemed" condition.

Before the people can deny the charges or offer
counter-evidence, Hosea graphically exposes the real tragedy
in the people's wanton behavior:

> *Yet let no one contend, and let none accuse, for with*
> *you is my contention, O priest. You shall stumble*
> *by day; the prophet also shall stumble with you by*
> *night, and I will destroy your mother. My people are*
> *destroyed for lack of knowledge; because you have*
> *rejected knowledge, I reject you from being a priest*
> *to me. And since you have forgotten the law of your*
> *God, I also will forget your children. The more they*
> *increased, the more they sinned against me; they*
> *changed their glory into shame. They feed on the sin*
> *of my people; they are greedy for their iniquity. And it*
> *shall be like people, like priest; I will punish them for*
> *their ways, and repay them for their deeds. They shall*
> *eat, but not be satisfied; they shall play the whore, but*
> *not multiply, because they have forsaken the LORD to*
> *devote themselves to whoredom.* (Hos 4:4-10)

The true culprits in all this are none other than the teachers
of the covenant—the priests. However, rather than feed the
people, they feed *on* the people. Their sin is doubly tragic,
for rather than teach the people the proper response to God's
gracious acts, they seek profit from the sins of the people![25] The
delusions of the people are fed by none other than those leaders
responsible for providing the people with the true nourishment
of faithfulness, steadfast love, and knowledge of God. Without
proper priestly and prophetic instruction, the people are at the
mercy of the powerfully seductive Baal practices. Elsewhere
Hosea will charge the political leaders with a similar failure to
lead the people in the proper ways of the Lord.

A final scene from Hosea's oracles captures the extent
of the perversion of the relationship between Yahweh and
his people:

---

[25] For a suggestive parallel, see Ezek 34.

*I will return again to my place until they acknowledge
their guilt and seek my face. In their distress they will
beg my favor: "Come, let us return to the LORD; for it
is he who has torn, and he will heal us; he has struck
down, and he will bind us up. After two days he will
revive us; on the third day he will raise us up, that we
may live before him. Let us know, let us press on to
know the LORD; his appearing is as sure as the dawn;
he will come to us like the showers, like the spring
rains that water the earth." What shall I do with you,
O Ephraim? What shall I do with you, O Judah?
Your love is like a morning cloud, like the dew that
goes away early. Therefore I have hewn them by the
prophets, I have killed them by the words of my mouth,
and my judgment goes forth as the light. For I desire
steadfast love and not sacrifice, the knowledge of God
rather than burnt offerings.* (Hos 5:15-6:6)

The scene is tragic. Yahweh has threatened punishment
and waits longingly for his people to come in true repentance.
His people do in fact come, *mouthing repentance*, in fact a
repentance theologically and rhetorically compelling. However,
Yahweh responds negatively, for he knows this repentance
carries only rhetorical power; it has no behavioral modification
behind it. It is feigned repentance, repentance intended only to
assuage Yahweh's potential destructive anger, a repentance that
completely misses the true nature of the covenant relationship.
Yahweh, Lord of the universe, is no mere potentate seeking
flattery and lip service; this covenant partner desires an
intensely personal relationship with his undeserving people
that goes to the very core and every fiber of their being. Such
is the nature of the relationship Yahweh sought with his people
then *and* now.

## Doom in Micah: Addressing Systemic Sin

Micah's preaching reflects the varied social settings and
socio-economic groups of his day. Micah refused to become a

preacher speaking only judgment or grace.[26] To the powerful and self-confident, Micah could only proclaim judgment. Their confidence was misplaced, and their actions were misguided. Apparently the rich and powerful of Micah's day saw no injustice in initiating and implementing policies detrimental to the poor and oppressed within society.

Following the customary superscription, Micah 1:2-7 depicts the divine judgment attending Yahweh's arrival. Cast in the form of a covenant lawsuit,[27] Yahweh exits his heavenly palace and strides across the high places of the earth. Micah's opening charge addresses "all peoples." Yahweh's zeal to establish justice is universal. Yahweh's appearance has cataclysmic consequences. Mountains melt; valleys split open (v. 4).[28] The cause of such activity is next raised; Yahweh is responding in wrath to the "transgression" (pš') and "sin" (khtwt) of Israel and Judah. However, most revealing is v. 5b:

> *What is the transgression of Jacob? Is it not Samaria?*
> *And what is the high place of Judah? Is it not Jerusalem?*

The oracle concludes with a final announcement of punishment (vv. 6-7):

> *Therefore I will make Samaria a heap in the open country, a place for planting vineyards. I will pour down her stones into the valley, and uncover her*

---

[26] Although numerous scholars attribute the hope oracles of chapters 3-5 to a later editor, a compelling case can be made that these oracles are better understood as Micah's message to the beleaguered powerless of his immediate community, on whose behalf he speaks in Jerusalem. For a fuller discussion, see my "Micah and the Task of Ministry," *Restoration Quarterly* 30 (1988) 1-16, and "Micah and a Theological Critique of Worship," in *Worship in the Hebrew Bible. Essays in Honour of John T. Willis* (JSOTS #284). Eds. M. P. Graham; R. Marrs; S. McKenzie (Sheffield: Sheffield Academic Press, 1999), 184-203.

[27] For other covenant lawsuits, see Ps 50:1-7; Deut 32; Isa 1:2-20.

[28] Cf. Judg 5; Amos 1:2. For a striking liturgical parallel to Mic 1:2-7, see Ps 97.

*foundations. All her images shall be beaten to pieces, all her wages shall be burned with fire, and all her idols I will lay waste; for as the wages of a prostitute she gathered them, and as the wages of a prostitute they shall again be used.*

Although the opening call addresses "all peoples," it quickly becomes clear that the true focal point of the oracle concerns the people of Israel (and Judah). Micah 1:2-7 rhetorically functions somewhat akin to Amos 1-2. Though the nations are indicted, their eventual punishment is epitomized in the punishment rapidly enveloping Israel and Judah.

Noteworthy also is the source of Israel's sin. The message of Micah is consistent—the fundamental source of sin resides in the twin capitals of Samaria and Jerusalem.[29] These capital cities—symbols of power, authority, and security—are for Micah symbols of sin and transgression. The depiction of the punishment is graphic. Prior to the identification of the culprits, mountains melt and valleys burst open.[30] Once Samaria and Jerusalem are identified as the transgressors, the prophet delineates specific punishment; Samaria's sources of security and protection are "laid bare." Appropriately, her own mountainous walls will melt as foreign invaders roll the city's stones into the valley, exposing her foundations.[31]

The nature of the sin of these symbols of power resounds most eloquently in verse 7. If verse 6 elicits political securities, verse 7 envisions cultic securities. Idols and images are smashed and torched. Micah vividly articulates his contempt for such religious trappings—they are "whore's fees!" For Micah, these religious securities are none other than symbols of prostitution

---

[29] Micah regularly uses Samaria and Jerusalem where we might expect the more customary Israel and Judah.

[30] Interestingly, these capital cities, nestled atop or among mountains and hills, experience a flattening of the landscape. Later, Micah will envision a Jerusalem that experiences elevation through divine intervention (Mic 4:1-4).

[31] Yahweh's action is better understood as a military conquest than as an earthquake. The exposing of the foundation stones implies violation (cf. Pss 79:1; 137:7; Hos 2:10, 12; Lev 18:6-19).

gained through illicit activities.[32] Clearly, the reason for Israel's imminent downfall is her unfaithfulness to Yahweh.[33]

Suggesting the removal of cherished objects of security, whether military or religious, and attendant doom could only produce animosity and confrontation with the political and religious establishment. At least two pericopes manifest this conflict (2:6-11; 3:5-8, 11). Micah squarely sets himself against the wisdom of his day, challenging his contemporaries' understanding of the future and the divine word regarding that future.

Micah 2:6-11 is a notoriously complex passage, fairly bristling with textual and rhetorical difficulties. Determining speakers, identifying primary and secondary audiences, and location of possible quotation marks tax the interpreter. Although the historical relationship between Micah 2:1-5 and 2:6-11 is quite uncertain, in its present literary context, 2:1-5 serves as the rhetorical backdrop for verses 6-11.

Micah 2:1-5 portrays a blatant miscarriage of justice. Simply put, the rich have found effective ways (possibly legal!) to confiscate land from the defenseless and appropriate it for themselves. Micah excoriates this deliberate crime and pronounces Yahweh's impending judgment upon these land-grabbers. The rhetorical power of the oracle is dramatic. Through wordplay and thematic reversal, Micah declares that

---

[32] Idolatry is elsewhere regarded as whoredom in the prophetic literature (cf. Nah 3:4; Hos 2). Again, the importance of the capital city to Micah is implicit. Although Bethel and Dan were key northern religious sanctuaries, Micah considers Samaria the center of idolatrous worship and embodiment of the sins of the people (from Hillers, *Micah* [Philadelphia: Fortress Press], 21). Not surprisingly, Micah follows with a lament over the outlying villages impacted by these centers of sin (1:10-16).

[33] What Mic 1:2-7 states poetically and quickly, 5:9-14 (Eng., 10-15) elaborates and makes explicit: "In that day, says the Lord, I will cut off your horses from among you and will destroy your chariots; and I will cut off the cities of your land and throw down all your strongholds; and I will cut off sorceries from your hand, and you shall have no more soothsayers; and I will cut off your images and your pillars from among you, and you shall bow down no more to the work of your hands; and I will uproot your sacred poles from among you and destroy your towns. And in anger and wrath I will execute vengeance on the nations that did not obey."

the treatment the rich have dealt the powerless will be the treatment they receive. While the wealthy lie awake at night "devising wickedness and evil deeds" (*khšby-'wn wp'ly-r'*), Yahweh is "devising...an evil" (*kšb...r'h*). These powerful land-grabbers (v. 2) will find themselves robbed of their land by a more powerful foreign oppressor (v. 4); when exploited and abused, they will immediately cry foul!

For our purposes, this passage helpfully sets the stage for the ensuing discussion (vv. 6-11). To state the obvious, Micah 2:1-5 demonstrates that for the prophet Micah, the domain of prophetic critique includes commentary upon and evaluation of ethical practices. Micah, as God's spokesperson, apparently felt no hesitancy in challenging and denouncing current business activity. More significantly, however, is the manner in which he addresses the "problem." Micah condemns the practices through theological critique. For Micah, these unscrupulous activities involve nothing less than "coveting" (*khmd\**) a neighbor's "inheritance" (*nkhlh*).[34] The punishment Micah foresees for these nefarious "thieves" (*gzl\**) involves an ironic implementation of *jus talionis* — the land they have unethically seized will be similarly taken from them by a more powerful oppressor!

Against this backdrop, an apparent dialogue unfolds in 2:6-11. Although difficult, these verses seemingly contain a rejoinder to Micah by his opponents (vv. 6-7a),[35] Micah's

---

[34] Micah was quite concerned that his audience view actions, events, indeed life itself from a theological perspective. Such a concern cannot be overestimated. In 2:1-5, Micah excoriates the rich who plot against the poor to take their land and possessions. Most insightful is to note the language Micah uses to indict these land barons. His key term is "covet" (*hmd*; the only key term used twice in the Decalogue). Later, Micah announces the punishment upon these land barons – they will lose their own "inheritance" (*nkhlh*; another key theological term in the Old Testament). Not insignificantly, by employing such vocabulary, Micah is clearly stating that such atrocities are not merely "secular" misdeeds, but are in reality nothing less than "crimes against God!" These land grabbers deliberately and intentionally deprive (i.e., "covet") the powerless of their rightful gift from God ("inheritance"). Micah's use of "theological" vocabulary to critique the actions of his opponents is significant, for it shows clearly that Micah's social critique was informed by his theological understanding.

rebuttal (vv. 7b-10), and a final caustic caricature (by Micah) of the type of prophet his audience seeks.[36] Here Micah apparently quotes pious rejoinders from his opponents who feel secure in their religion. Micah caustically recites their crimes against society and then bitterly concludes with a caricature of a prophet who would pander to their every desire.[37] This paragraph implicitly contrasts Micah's preaching and that of the "prophets of plenty." In response, Micah's opponents may even be quoting Scripture to refute him.[38] For our purposes, the theological significance of this pericope is important: Micah's vision of the scope of the prophetic task differs vastly from that of his peer prophets; Micah, using theologically laden language, savagely critiques the social behavior of influential members of the community (2:1-5); in response to the appropriateness of such critique, Micah vigorously denounces those prophetic voices who would avoid such a message.

What 2:6-11 states implicitly, Micah 3:5-8, 11 makes explicit. In chapter 3, Micah unleashes an attack against injustice and abuse manifested among the political and religious authorities. Verses 1-4 concern the absence of justice in the courts, verses 5-8 concern the travesty of self-serving prophets, and verses 9-12 denounce the perverse nature of a community devoid of justice and integrity among its leadership.

---

[35] The precise identity of Micah's opponents is disputed. Three identifications are most common: 1) Micah's adversaries are the land-grabbers denounced in 2:1-5; 2) the opponents are the false prophets; 3) Micah's opponents are the false prophets speaking on behalf of the land-grabbers. The first identification seems most plausible (vv. 8-10).

[36] Micah's disdain for those who would preach primarily what their audience wants to hear is reflected in his reference "I will preach to you of wine and strong drink" (so NRSV [MT: *'tp lklyyn wlškr*]). The verb *ntp* may be implicitly derisive (see Amos 7:16). The reference to 'wine and strong drink' may be a metaphor for preaching only salvation (cf. Amos 9:13-14; Joel 2:24) or it may imply the self-serving nature of these prophets ("*for* wine and strong drink").

[37] Hillers, *Micah*, 34.

[38] Some scholars have suggested that v. 7 may contain an implicit quotation.

Significantly, Micah is not content simply to condemn specific crimes; rather, he also addresses the fundamental structures of a society that allow such iniquitous acts to continue. The language is graphic and terse; gripping images (e.g., cannibalism) and metaphors abound. The contrast Micah draws between the prophets of "profit" (vv. 5-7) and himself (v. 8) is most striking. In dramatic fashion, Micah declares that these prophets who primarily seek "profit" (v. 5) will suffer extensive "loss" (vv. 6-7). Micah graphically charges that whether these prophets proclaim weal ("peace") or woe (literally "sanctify war" [qdš mlkhmh*]) is dependent upon the payment they receive from their oracular recipients![39] Obsessed with "profit," Micah declares the imminent extent of their "loss." These prophets for hire will lose their "vision," finding themselves submerged in darkness. Blind seers, robbed of divination, will experience the ultimate humiliation for a prophet—they will have no revelatory word.[40] Congruent with Micah 2:1-5, the punishment fits the "crime." Just as 2:1-5 depicts landless land-barons, so here Micah depicts vision-less visionaries and speechless preachers.

In contrast, Micah characterizes himself and his ministry in verse 8:

> But as for me, I am filled with power and with the spirit of the Lord, and with justice and might, to declare (lhgyd) to Jacob his transgression (pš'w) and to Israel his sin (kht'tw).[41]

Unique among the prophets, this self-disclosure of Micah contrasts mightily with his prophetic opponents. In

---

[39] Put differently, Micah's opponents argued that politics and economic policy were not appropriate topics for preaching (or better—were areas of life unaffected by divine influence and vision).

[40] The judges receive a similar pronouncement of punishment (3:4). Cf. a similar scenario in Amos 8:11. The reference to "covering the lip" may intend either mourning (Ezek 24:17, 22) or perhaps leprosy (Lev 13:45).

[41] "Sin and transgression" hauntingly echo Mic 1:5.

contradistinction to their self-absorption, Micah's quintessential focus is justice. His polestar is declaring to God's people what they *need* to hear rather than what they *want* to hear.[42] His "fullness" accentuates their "emptiness."

The closing oracle of chapter 3 depicts Jerusalem's end, in language reminiscent of Samaria's end in 1:6-7: "Micah's word of judgment makes clear that a city built in sin will be destroyed in judgment."[43] At the heart of Jerusalem's transgressions stand her judges, priests, and prophets; tragically, justice, instruction in *Torah*, and the inspired word are for sale. Incredibly, these corrupted peddlers of God's word profess an unshakable trust in God. Corruption and greed permeate the political and religious establishment.

A final judgment oracle demonstrates poignantly the distance between Yahweh's desire from his relationship with his people and their (mis)understanding of the relationship. Micah 6:1-8, somewhat akin to a covenant lawsuit, captures the chasm between Yahweh and his people. Verses 1-5 provide a vision of who the God of Israel truly is; his nature is captured clearly in his deeds on Israel's behalf. Following a brief interlude that epitomizes the people's fundamental misunderstanding of the divine–human relationship, verse 8 concludes with a powerfully succinct statement of the appropriate human response to Yahweh.

In verses 1-5, Yahweh compellingly states his case and protests his innocence of any wrongdoing in his relationship with his people. Beginning with wordplay (vv. 3-4),[44] he quickly recites his redemptive deeds, from the Exodus out of Egypt to entrance into the promised land. Most tellingly, these "saving acts" (*tsdqwt*) of Yahweh demonstrate his right behavior towards Israel and the essence of his being.

---

[42] Accepting such a prophetic identity may generate unavoidable confrontation. It is perhaps significant that Micah uses the term *ngd* (Hiph.) for himself, a term which literally means "to stand opposite / against something."

[43] P. Miller, *Sin and judgment*, 34.

[44] 'O my people…in what have I wearied (*hl'tyk*) you? Answer me! For I brought you up (*h'ltyk*) from the land of Egypt.'

The transition from the recitation of Yahweh's saving
deeds (vv. 3-5) to the response of the people (vv. 6-7) is
abrupt.[45] Here the startling "with what shall I come before the
Lord…" (*bmh*) counters Yahweh's earlier questions ("What
have I done to you? In what have I wearied you? [*mh…mh*]").[46]
The response in verses 6-7 seems to imply that Yahweh is in
fact the problem! As a litany of possible "adequate" offerings
unfolds, the respondent moves rapidly from offerings indicating
total commitment on the part of the worshiper (whole burnt
offerings) to offerings of absurd proportions[47] to unthinkable
offerings (child sacrifice)![48] The place and purpose of sacrifice
in the divine–human relationship has been completely
misunderstood.

The "offering" Yahweh truly desires is powerfully
expressed in verse 8. It is neither new nor previously unheard
("he has told you").[49] The offering Yahweh "seeks" is "to do
justice (*ʿśwt mšpt*) and to love kindness (*ʾhbt khsd*) and to walk
humbly (*htsnʿ lkt*) with… God."[50] Cultic activity and worship,

---

[45] However, the tendency to locate rhetorical questions strategically is well
attested in the book of Micah (cf. 1:5b; 2:7; 3:1; 4:9; 6:10-11).

[46] Yahweh's questions in actuality function as assertions of innocence; the
opening rhetorical questions of v. 6 introduce a lame defense through the use
of absurdity.

[47] The rapid escalation from thousands to ten thousands couples with
astronomical measurements ('rivers of oil').

[48] It is noteworthy that the terms "transgression" (*pśʿ*) and "sin" (*khṭʾh*) again
appear (v. 7). Their presence is never distant for Micah; the human solution to
their presence is completely irrational. The movement to the absurd moves as
quickly as Yahweh's earlier recitation of his saving acts.

[49] Yahweh "declares" (*ngd**) his will (v. 8) just as Micah his prophet affirmed
his divine commission to "declare" (*ngd**) to Jacob his transgression and to
Israel his sin" (3:8).

[50] The first two elements of this triad (*khsd/mšpt*) are well known and need
not detain us, other than to emphasize the communal nature of both terms. Both
justice and steadfast love can only occur within the context of a community.
The third expression (*htsnʿ*) is best understood as "studied attention of another."
Heeding careful attention to the ways and will of Yahweh can only result in
the practice of justice and steadfast love. For a full discussion of the various
nuances of this expression, see especially P. Hyatt, "On the Meaning and Origin
of Micah 6:8," *Anglican Theological Review* 34 (1952), 232-39.

apart from ethical behavior pervading every facet of life, is worthless. V. Hunter captures the theological significance of this passage well:

> The good that Yahweh seeks in every person among his people is rooted in making justice and steadfast love the controlling interests in all of life, thereby fostering a relationship with Yahweh that is characterized by paying careful and judicious attention to honoring his claim on all of life. This is the offering Yahweh accepts.[51]

## Conclusion

The eighth century B.C. presented formidable challenges for Yahweh's prophets of doom. Amos, Hosea, and Micah had to struggle with the dilemma of preaching to the people what they *wanted* to hear or what they *needed* to hear. Criticizing cherished notions is never popular and often hazardous. Proclaiming such a message increases in difficulty when one's preaching peers conform their messages to the wants of the audience! Such a situation apparently existed in the days of Amos, Hosea, and Micah.

Faithful to a fault, these prophets of the Lord delivered his message powerfully. They refused to allow the people to place false confidence in misreadings of Yahweh's salvific acts on his people's behalf. They refused to allow the people to pervert the covenant promises and exploit them for their own selfish purposes. They refused to allow systemic abuses to continue, abuses that deprived the poor and powerless of the blessings God intended for them. Perhaps most importantly, they refused to allow God's people to disconnect their theology from their daily lives. Whether through a vision of the sovereignty of God, and its attendant concerns for social justice and righteousness, or through a vision of the covenant and its attendant concerns for faithfulness, steadfast love, and knowledge of God, these prophets faithfully proclaimed the word of the Lord to their

---

[51] V. Hunter, *Seek the Lord* (Baltimore: St. Mary's Press, 1982), 252.

overconfident and recalcitrant audiences. They ably applied the rich theological traditions of their relationship with Yahweh to everyday life issues. Refusing to become simply parrots of pious platitudes or harbingers of irrelevant oracles, they repeatedly called God's people to true repentance, a repentance that manifested itself in daily acts of faithfulness and steadfast love.

Such is the charge for today's ministers. In ministry, a perennial concern is the extent to which we are molders of theological vision, or are ourselves molded by societal values. Such activity is never a one-way street (i.e., we are both molders and molded). However, if we are faithful to the message of our ancient forebears, inculcating within our people a sense of theological perspective will result in justice becoming central in our lives and the lives of our audience. Such is the eighth century call of God to us through his prophets Amos, Hosea, and Micah.

# 3

# Theology, Ethics, and Homiletics in the Eighth Century Prophetic Oracles of Salvation

John Fortner

## Introduction

This essay explores the theological and ethical underpinnings that informed the formulation of the oracles of salvation in the eighth century prophets. It is central to our thesis that oracles of doom and salvation are conceptually of a piece. This unitary conception accords theologically with the view that God redeems what he has created. With regard to ethics, our thesis infers that the cosmos is value-laden and is thus the superlative habitation for moral and ethical formation.[1]

We will argue that as the eighth century prophets envisioned an era of renewal and well-being (šālôm) they (1) drew deeply on the biblical traditions of covenant, election, cult, ethics, and law; (2) were informed by wisdom traditions (including creation theology); and (3) understood that radical disjunction (a catastrophic end of political, social, and religious life in Israel) was predicated upon a radical conjunction (a divine purpose for Israel in history on the other side of catastrophe). In the course of our discussion, we'll note that the radical historical and theological disjunction which unfolded in the second half of the eighth century B.C. and which culminated in the events of 722

---

[1] For this view see William P. Brown, *The Ethos of the Cosmos: The Genesis of Moral Imagination in the Bible* (Grand Rapids: Eerdmans, 1999), 12 and our discussion below.

and 701 B.C.[2] served as a catalyst for an already developing theological synthesis of Israel's great historical and religious traditions. We will see how the eighth century prophets were among those who contributed to this synthesis by envisioning a radical historical and theological conjunction in a post-catastrophe era of divinely blessed *šālôm*.[3]

As we draw the essay to a close, we will discuss how the eighth century prophets regarded sapiential and creation traditions to be the underpinnings of a value-laden cosmos. We will argue that these prophets utilized such traditions and worldview not only to indict a faithless Israel and Judah but also to construct their visions of an era of covenantal, ethical, and environmental bliss. Finally, we shall draw some implications for contemporary Christian ministry and homiletics by placing Jesus of Nazareth within the canonical ebb and flow of theological radical disjunction and conjunction.

The classical or writing prophets of the eighth century B.C. were neither innovators nor lone misanthropes. We should not imagine that they emerged from the fringes of society or the perimeter of the wilderness to utter their oracles in an urban setting that was alien to them. For the most part, biblical prophets of all periods were members of the same constituencies and communities as those of their audiences. Some of them (such as seventh century Jeremiah) enjoyed a sympathetic support group;[4] others (Isaiah, it seems) inspired a cadre of disciples who may have developed a tradition of teaching in their names.[5] Their oracles reflect a wide spectrum of sophisticated learning. These prophets were equally at home in urban sprawl, temple courts, and palace antechamber.

---

[2] Primarily, we make reference to the siege and fall of Samaria in ca. 725-22 B.C. (2 Kgs 17). Secondarily we have in mind also the devastation of Judah and siege of Jerusalem in 701 B.C. (2 Chr 32 and 2 Kgs 18-20 // Isa 36-39).

[3] See Donald E. Gowan, "The Prophets as Theologians," in *Theology of the Prophetic Books: The Death and Resurrection of Israel* (Louisville: Westminster/John Knox Press, 1998), 1-21.

[4] See Jer 36:8-26 and 38:7-13.

[5] See Isa 8:16-20 and 30:8-9.

To such persons as these, the word of the LORD came with remarkable clarity and power.[6] Under the burden of the "word of the LORD," the prophets brought long-neglected theological and ethical perspectives to royal, cultic, and general public awareness. Thus, they formulated a powerful cultural critique against injustice and oppression. They delivered a blistering attack on the popular theology that Israel's leaders invoked to justify their injustices and oppression. From the oracles of indictment spoken against eighth century B.C. Israelite and Judean society, it's clear that the prophets didn't ground the ultimate authority of their messages in *themselves*. Rather, the authority of their oracles arose from an indisputable sense of divine call that informed their clear perception of the person and character of Yahweh. As a result, the eighth century B.C. prophets held Israel and Judah accountable to the highest standard of moral and ethical behavior. As God's covenant community, Israel was under a divine mandate to exhibit her knowledge of God through a dynamic religious ethic which was inextricably linked to Yahweh's nature. Israel's failure to realize this high religious ethos elicited a spectrum of prophetic responses in the name of Yahweh which ranged from ire, anguish, and pathos over what should have been to imaginative construals of what yet could be.

### Constructing a Baseline for Envisioning the Era of Šālôm

Donald E. Gowan correctly observes that "the OT vision of the future deals throughout with the world in which we now live."[7] While later apocalyptists envisioned different processes at work than did the classical prophets, both prophecy and apocalyptic classical prophecy envisioned an end to all evil.[8]

---

[6] For example, see Amos 5:21-24 and Mic 3:8-11.

[7] *Eschatology in the Old Testament*, 2nd ed. (Edinburgh: T & T Clark, 2000), 2.

[8] Ibid., as the *telos* of Israel's trajectory with her God.

Such a vision was neither monolithic nor monochromatic. It was dynamically evolving over time until its horizon encompassed "a new heaven and a new earth."[9]

The eighth century B.C. prophetic vision of the future stood in the strongest opposition possible to its contemporary religious and moral context. Ostensibly, if Israel would rectify the offenses against which the eighth century prophets inveighed, God would rescind his judgment of radical disjunction. It is important to note that such a rectified situation constitutes an ethos for God's people as well as for the physical world which approximates the prophets' visions of *šālôm*. The ideals upon which the prophets drew to construct their visions of the future were grounded in the same theological and ethical criteria that informed the prophets' indictments of contemporary eighth century society.

Of course, prophetic visions of the future don't represent what might be gained by playing a contemporary country song backwards (that is, one gets back his truck, dog, gun, and wife—in that order). Rather, beginning with Amos (ca. 760 B.C.), eighth century prophetic visions of future salvation expressed a complete reversal of current moral and religious conditions moving Israel toward divine wrath. By postulation a counterpoint for each item in Amos' "bill of indictments" against Israel (and Judah), we may establish a baseline for the prophetic vision of *šālôm*:

Disproportion of Goods & Influence: (3:12, 15; 4:1; 5:12; 6:4-6)
  REVERSAL: EVERY PERSON ON HIS LAND / EVERY FAMILY NAME PERPETUATED
Oppression of & Extortion from the Poor & Needy: (2:6-7; 4:1; 5:11-12; 8:4-6)
  REVERSAL: COMPASSION & MUTUAL REGARD
Abuse in the Courts: (5:7, 10, 15; 6:12)
  REVERSAL: EVERYONE'S PETITION IS HEARD AND ADJUDICATED JUSTLY
Violations of the Torah: (2:4, 12; 8:5-6)
  REVERSAL: TORAH IS UPHELD

---

[9] For which see Isa 65:17 and 66:22, but note also 42:9 and 48:6-7.

Complacency, Self-assurance, Self-indulgence: (4:1;
5:14, 18-20; 6:1, 4-6)
REVERSAL: RELIANCE ON GOD
Loss of Moral Bearing: (3:10; 5:13)
REVERSAL: LEADERS TEACH AN UNCOMPROMISING
ORIENTATION TOWARD GOD
The Environment Languishes: (3:7-11; 4:6-12; 5:16-17; 6:
12; 8:8)
REVERSAL: RENEWAL AND FECUNDITY OF THE EARTH
Loss of Geo-Political Viability: (3:11; 5:3; 6:14)
REVERSAL: RESTORATION OF POLITICAL INTEGRITY
& HEGEMONY
No Justice or Righteousness: (5:7, 21-24; 6:12)
REVERSAL: EQUITY AND COMMON WELL-BEING WHERE THE
WEAKEST VOICE IS HEARD
Worship Divorced From Ethical Imperatives: (5:14, 21-24;
9:1-4)
REVERSAL: WORSHIP AND LIFE REFLECT ETHICAL IDEAL
Greed: (2:6; 8:5-6)
REVERSAL: CONTENTMENT AND GRATITUDE
No Sense of Obligation or Accountability to Man or to
God: (3:1-2; 6:1-7)
REVERSAL: COMPASSION, DUTY, & RESPONSIBILITY ARE
RESPONSES TO DIVINE FAVOR
Corrupt Leadership: (6:1-3; 7:10-17; 8:11-12)
REVERSAL: RIGHTEOUS LEADERS IMPLEMENT GOD'S AGENDA IN
THE COMMUNITY
A "reign of terror" [šebet khāmās]: (6:3)
REVERSAL: THE KINGDOM OF ŠĀLÔM—THE REIGN
OF RIGHTEOUSNESS.

When taken together, these various reversals constitute
a conceptual baseline for God's *šālôm* that resembles in
several respects the utopian vision reflected in the rhetoric
of Deuteronomy.[10] Deuteronomy exhibits special concern
for those who are marginalized from economic and legal
recourse. The fatherless, the widow, the alien, and the poor are

---

[10] In this regard, note the striking similarity between Mic 6:6-8 and Deut 10:
12-13. Both passages present a conceptualization of the total relationship of
Israel with Yahweh.

indicative of such persons. At times, this concern is expressly
tied to Israel's own experience of alienation and oppression
in Egypt.[11] In Israelite society, concern for relational justice
and righteousness is to be expressed in additional ways. With
respect to Israel's leaders, note the stress upon uprightness and
integrity, often rooted in the integrity of Yahweh himself: (1)
in tribal and city judges;[12] (2) in elders at the gates;[13] and (3)
in an adjudicating and teaching role for the priests.[14] Among
measures designed to prevent disproportion of goods, power,
and property, note (1) the prohibition of false weights and
standards (25:13-16), (2) the third-year tithe (14:28-29;
26:12-15), (3) the seventh-year debt cancellation (15:1-11), and
(4) provisions for "brother-in-law marriage" (25:5-10). With
respect to sanctuary against the claim of blood revenge, there is
a provision for cities of refuge (4:41-43; 19:1-14).

The book of Deuteronomy purports to stem from the
prophetic mind of Moses.[15] With powerful homiletical rhetoric,
Deuteronomy expresses an ideal ethical, legal, and cultic vision
for God's covenant people in the land flowing with milk and
honey.[16] Deuteronomy casts an eye both to the past as well as
the future. Thus, contemporary Israel must embrace the full
scope of her relationship with Yahweh from Patriarchal times
as a prerequisite for a blessed future in the land of Canaan.
Moses charges Deuteronomy's second-generation covenant
community to perpetuate the relationship which God initiated

---

[11] Note these statements of concern at 5:12-15; 10:18-19; 14:28-29; 15:1-15;
16:9-12, 13-15; 23:7-8; 24:10-15, 17-22; 26:12-15 and 27:19.

[12] Deut 1:16-17; 10:14-19; 16:18-20; 17:8-13; 19:15-21; 21:1-9 and 25:1-3.

[13] Deut 21:18-21; 22:13-19 and 25:7-10.

[14] Deut 17:8-13, 18; 19:15-21; 21:1-9; 24:8 and 31:9-13.

[15] Scholars maintain a strong connection between Deuteronomy and the 7th-
century B.C. However, see now J. Gordon McConville, *Deuteronomy*. AOTC
(Downer's Grove, Ill.: Inter-Varsity Press, 2002 and Kenneth A. Kitchen,
*On the Reliability of the Old Testament* (Grand Rapids: Eerdmans, 2003),
283-307.

[16] See J. Andrew Dearman, "The Transformationist Vision of Deuteronomy,"
in *Religion & Culture in Ancient Israel* (Peabody, Mass.: Hendrickson
Publishers, 1992), 125-52.

in "loving the Fathers" and in nurturing Israel to this point.[17] It is critical to the flourishing of Israel in Canaan and to her role there as a witness to the nations that her ethos reflect Yahweh's character. There would have been no moment in the history of Israel in which the community of God were more in need of the rhetoric of grace and accountability with which Deuteronomy abounds than at this liminal juncture where Israel, camped in the Plains of Moab, is summoned to craft her future identity as Yahweh's witness in light of a past totally shaped by him.

Deuteronomy elegantly expresses the biblical perspective that both the prospect of blessing and the threat of catastrophe conceptually belong together. This conceptual linkage does not necessarily depend upon identifying Deuteronomy as a covenant document; neither is it necessarily dependent upon a strictly invoked doctrine of retribution. Rather, in Deuteronomy the theological ground for both grace (blessing) and accountability (judgment) are necessarily rooted in a dynamic relationship with God. Deuteronomy preaches a radical continuity of relationship with Yahweh to and for the new generation that will inherit the land (5:3). Yet despite this vision of šālôm, Deuteronomy contemplates the possibility of radical disjunction (note the blessings and curses of chapters 27 and 28, as well as the prospect of dispersion and return in 4:25-31 and 30:1-10). Indeed, an Israel whose *ethos* and *telos* are uniquely and publicly shaped by Yahweh may acquire a viable religious and ethical life only at the hand of both disjunction and conjunction.[18] Such a view accords with a Sovereign God who is ultimately committed to an engagement and relationship with humankind in which continuity (conjunction) triumphs over judgment (disjunction).

[17] See at 4:37-38; 7:6b-10; 8:1-5 and 9:4-6.

[18] A powerful rhetorical shape is given to Israel's *ethos* and *telos* in passages such as Deut 4:32-40; 6:10-25; 7:6-11; 8:1-5; 9:1-6; 10:12-22; and 11:26-28.

## Of Sovereignty and Continuity in the Eighth Century Prophets

### What's in a Name?

The oracles of Amos exhibit a rhetorically and theologically rich repertoire of names for Israel's God:

3:7-8 (see also at 6:8)
  "*the Sovereign LORD*" — '*ădōnāy yhwh*

9:5
  "*the Lord, the LORD Almighty*" —
  '*ădōnāy yhwh hatseba'ot*

4:13; 5:27
  "*Yahweh, God Almighty is his name*" —
  *yhwh 'elōhe–tseba'ôt š͑mô* [19]

3:13
  "*the Lord, Yahweh God Almighty*" —
  '*ădōnāy yhwh 'ĕlōhê–hatseba'ot*

5:16
  "*the Lord, Yahweh, God Almighty*" —
  *yhwh 'ĕlōhê tseba'ot 'ădōnāy.*

This repertoire of names is remarkable in two respects: (1) the names are magisterial in tone; (2) although similar epithets are found elsewhere, the frequency of these elevated and densely loaded epithets within such a brief span of text is unmatched in the canon.[20] Obviously, such a repertoire of names reflects an understanding of the deity that is transcendent and sovereign; yet, such a sovereign deity is remarkably relational.

---

[19] See also 5:14 and 6:8.

[20] Compare from the Psalter, 24:10; 46:7|8|, 11|12|; 59:5|6|; 69:6|7|; 80: 4|5|, 19|20|; 84:8|9|; 89:8|9|; from Isaiah, 3:1; 10:24; 19:4; 22:5, 12, 14, 15; 28:22; 37:16; 47:4; 48:2; 51:15; 54:5; and especially from Jeremiah, 2:19; 5: 14; 10:16; 15:16; 23:36; 28:2; 29:25; 31:35; 32:18; 38:17; 44:7; 46:10, 18, 25; 48:1, 15; 49:5; 50:25; 50:31; 51:5, 14, 19, 57.

Ironically, a 'doom only' interpretation, which still dominates Amos studies, calls into question the sovereignty of this Yahweh.[21] Set adrift from the oracles of salvation (9:11-15), the preponderance of Amos' oracles mandates an absolute end to the people of Israel. There is no prospect for a resumption of the rule of God over a remnant of his people in a post-catastrophe era.[22] Yet, as theologian and ethicist, Amos must be aware that a doom-only scenario would render Yahweh vulnerable to the ridicule of the very nations against which he inveighs (Amos 1:3-2:3).[23] Would not the God who brings about the absolute non-existence of his own people turn out to be a 'no-god' in the sight of the nations?

Furthermore, such a radical historical and theological disjunction precludes Yahweh from resuming an historical and theological relationship with a post-catastrophe remnant of Israel. Israel's historically rooted and covenant-based relationship with Yahweh formed a distinctive *ethos* and *telos* within her traditions, shaping her present and future identity. It is to Israel's memory of this covenant-based relationship which the eighth century prophets invoke that we now turn.

## What is Yahweh's Investment in Israel?

The oracles of the eighth century prophets reflect a familiarity with the ancient and rich historical traditions of Israel and Judah. By invoking Israel's memory of Yahweh's intimate engagement with Israel through the centuries, the

---

[21] Exceptions to a 'doom only' interpretation of Amos' prophecy with a survey of the relevant literature may be found in Shalom Paul, *Amos*, Hermeneia Commentary (Minneapolis: Fortress Press, 1991), 288-95 and in Gerhard Hasel, *Understanding the Book of Amos: Basic Issues in Current Interpretations* (Grand Rapids: Baker Books, 1991), 17-27, 105-20.

[22] Paul, *Amos*, 282-87 believes that 9:8-10 stipulates that only the sinners among the Israelites will die. Thus, the book ends with remnant teaching (see Gerhard Hasel, *The Remnant: The History and Theology of the Remnant Idea from Genesis to Isaiah* (Berrien Springs, Mich.: Andrews University Press, 1972), 175-79; 207-12; and idem. *Understanding Amos*, 105-20.

[23] Note the ridicule of Samaria's leaders and people which is anticipated from Egypt when the divine catastrophe descends (Hos 7:16).

prophets press the case that Israel and Judah are especially accountable to Yahweh for their covenant failures. In their oracles, the eighth century prophets have provided for us an array of allusions from which we may reconstruct a fairly full historical tradition that reaches back to the Patriarchs.[24] This reconstituted tradition includes allusions to the depravity of the cities of the plain; the patriarchal blessings and promises; the travails of Jacob; the Egyptian oppression; the exodus and its plagues and wonders under the leadership of Moses; the covenant and the giving of the Torah at Sinai; a forty-year desert travelogue; the crossing of the Jordan; the cultic and moral compromises in the conquest of Canaan; profound victory and dark depravity in the era of the judges; the initiation of kingship in Israel; David and his wars; and the phenomenon of prophetism through the centuries.

Such an historical memory of Israel's experience of Yahweh lends weight to the indictment of Amos at 3:1-2, based on Israel's election tradition:[25]

> Hear this word the LORD has spoken against you, O people of Israel—against the whole family I brought up out of Egypt. You only have I chosen of all the families of the earth; therefore I will punish you for all your sins.

It is noteworthy that the expression "of all the families of the earth" (*mikkōl mišp˘khôt hā'ǎdāmâ*) is attested elsewhere only at Gen 12:3 and 28:14, where Yahweh addressed Abraham and Jacob, respectively.[26] Thus, Amos 3:2 invokes the entire patriarchal cycle in order to accentuate the election status

---

[24] Consult Appendix: "Israel's Early History in Prophetic Memory" where these historical allusions are displayed. For historical allusions to early Israelite history in Hosea, see now Dwight R. Daniels, *Hosea and Salvation History: The Early Traditions of Israel in the Prophecy of Hosea*, BZAW 191 (Berlin: de Gruyter, 1990).

[25] Hasel' *Remnant*, 177-78.

[26] Consider also in this regard the Lord's reiteration of the promises to Abraham in Gen 18:18-19: ". . . all nations on earth (*kōl gôyê hā'arets*) will be blessed through him."

of Israel. The phrase "You only have I chosen (*yāda'tî*)..."[27] economically encapsulates the full trajectory of Israel's ancient and intimate relationship with her God. Since Yahweh made Israel the beneficiary of his constant care and attention, he held Israel particularly accountable to him: "therefore I will punish you for all your sins." This dynamic ebb and flow is the essence of a synergistic relationship generated between Israel and Yahweh which is more than the sum of its parts. This synergism (that is, *sum + x*) expresses itself in Israel's emerging teleology, eschatology, and theodicy. However, it also expresses itself in a popular but mistaken notion of privilege in eighth century Israel.[28] The prophets invoke this historically generated synergism as a justification for their declarations of radical disjunction (death) to Israel. As a predication for such declarations, however, there exists an ancient archetypal memory, not only of radical disjunction but also of radical conjunction, memory grounded in promise, grace, theodicy, and teleology.

## Working With Both Sides of the Equation: Radical Disjunction and Conjunction

### Memory as Archetype

The memory of a self-propelled descent into disobedience and of a divine gracious restoration at Horeb (Exod 32-34) was the foundation of Israel's tradition of election and accountability on the one hand and of her tradition of robust teleology on the other.

---

[27] On the other hand, 3:1-2 may be a reference to the exodus as at 2:10; 3:1; 9:7 (see also 5:25). For the relational aspects of *yd'* see Terence E. Fretheim, "---------(*yāda' I*)," in *New International Dictionary of Old Testament Theology and Exegesis*, ed. Willem VanGemren (Grand Rapids: Zondervan), 1997, 2:409-14.

[28] Israel's expectations from her doctrine of the 'Day of the LORD' (*yôm Yahweh* at 5:14 and 9:10) which Amos contravenes (2:16; 3:14; 5:8, 18-20; 6:3; 8:3, 9-10, 13-14) exemplify such a false notion. Attestations outside of Amos for the 'Day of Yahweh' are: Isa 13:6, 9; Joel 1:15; 2:1, 11; 2:31[3:4]; 3:14[4:14]; Obad 1:15; Zeph 1:7, 14; and Mal 4:5. However, see also Isa 2:10-22; 22:5; 34:8; Jer 4:5-17; 46:10, and Mal 3:2.

In the wake of radical disobedience at Horeb (Sinai), Yahweh mandated an annihilation of the tribes of Jacob (a radical disjunction). However, Yahweh provided an equally comprehensive solution to this decree of death (a radical conjunction). As we will see, the memory of this disjunction/ conjunction axis profoundly affected the dynamics of the synergism generated between Israel and Yahweh and thereby provided conceptual archetypes for the prophetic oracles of judgment and salvation.

In the history and tradition of Israel, there is arguably no greater transgression by Israel against Yahweh than her apostasy before the golden calf at the foot of Sinai. In many respects, it becomes the prototype of all her subsequent apostasy and faithlessness.[29] In the aftermath of Yahweh's decree to make a radical end to the community of Israelite tribes and to initiate a new plan through Moses' descendants alone, remarkably Moses refuses Yahweh's proffer. Horrified at Yahweh's proposal to make a radical end of the tribal community, Moses expresses concern for Yahweh's reputation among the nations. After all, by his singular power Yahweh has just liberated this desert community from the oppression of Egypt.

Now, in a "face-to-face" dialogue with God, Moses becomes the quintessential mediator for the people of God. He lays out the following case to persuade Yahweh to preserve this stiff-necked and faithless community (Exod 32:9-14):

- Israel is *your* (elect) people;

- You have delivered them from Egypt with great power and a mighty hand;

- If you make an end of all of them now, your reputation will be sullied by the Egyptians; they will malign your power, your motivation, and your character;

- You are a God who can (and should) relent of catastrophic plans and who can (and should) limit his anger;

---

[29] Note Exod 32:19-21; 30-35; Deut 9:7-10:11; Neh 9:16-18; and Ps 106:19-23. The installation of Jeroboam's calves at Dan and Bethel (1 Kgs 12:28) is hailed with a virtual quotation of Exod 32:4. For a lucid discussion of this apostasy at Sinai see Nahum Sarna, *Exodus*, JPS Torah Commentary (Philadelphia: The Jewish Publication Society, 1991), 202-17.

- You cannot renege on your promise and oath to the Patriarchs to multiply their descendants without limit and to give them the land of Canaan as a permanent inheritance (which, strictly speaking, couldn't be accomplished through Moses' descendants alone).

Moses' intercession procures an annulment of Yahweh's plan to make a complete end of Israel. Nevertheless, on account of this "great sin" (Exod 32:7, 21, 30-31), Yahweh retracts his proposal to place his Presence in the midst of the camp of Israel (Exod 25:8-9). The plans for construction of the Tabernacle (*miškān*) are shelved. Israel has "turned away from" the terms of the covenant—even before ratifying them! Thus, Moses shatters the tablets at the base of Sinai, thereby indicating that the entire covenant arrangement is in dire jeopardy (Exod 32:15-19). Because God recommits himself to fulfill his land promise to the Patriarchs, he ordains a proxy to lead Israel to Canaan. However, Israel will not enjoy the blessing of Yahweh's Presence in their midst along the way (Exod 32:34-33:3).

Moses is unwilling to leave Sinai with a mere nameless "messenger" as his guide. Thus, he doesn't relent from petitioning Yahweh to make good on his plan to dwell in the midst of his itinerant people. Moses reminds Yahweh (by implication) of his profound investment in the plan to create and shape a unique relationship both with Moses himself and with his people Israel (Exod 33:13b-16). On the basis of their intimate relationship, Yahweh finally accedes to Moses' petition.

Moreover, Yahweh now grants Moses' additional request for a limited visual perception of him to gain some concrete apprehension of God's weighty Presence (that is, his "glory" and "goodness"). As Moses stands before the LORD with two newly-hewn blank tablets, Yahweh reveals the covenant-relation content of his name (Exod 34:6-7). This seminal text constitutes a stunning template for the relational character of 'I AM.' Here we learn how Yahweh works with humanity in the face of the most severe covenant violations:

> [6]And he passed in front of Moses, proclaiming, "The
> LORD, the LORD, the compassionate and gracious God,
> slow to anger, abounding in love and faithfulness,
> [7] maintaining love to thousands [of generations],
> and forgiving wickedness, rebellion, and sin. Yet he
> does not leave the guilty unpunished; he punishes the
> children and their children for the sin of the fathers to
> the third and fourth generation."

This passage reveals in a startling way that humanity's relationship with Yahweh is possible only on the basis of what Yahweh's divine nature provides. Note that Israel is no more able to be obedient to Yahweh, recorded in Exodus 34, than she was earlier (32:10), when Yahweh was prepared to do away with her completely and start over again with Moses alone. However, being "slow to anger," "abounding in commitment and faithfulness," and "forgiving wickedness, rebellion, and sin" are among those characteristics that define the divine nature at its core (see also Micah 7:18-19).[30] The experience of this divine nature is now vouchsafed to Israel as a gift in the form of a continuing divine Presence in the community. Such divine attributes comprise the only means by which any relationship with Yahweh can be formed, maintained, and reformed.

As the eighth century prophets emphasize, punishment is a theologically necessary corollary to humanity's sinfulness, and it is especially appropriate in the case of disobedience by God's covenant people. Nevertheless, the scenario depicted in Exodus 32-34 makes it clear that divine wrath as a response to human sin is not among those attributes which form the essence of the divine nature; thus, when Isaiah reflects upon God's radical punishment of his people, he characterizes it as God's "strange work" and his "alien task" (28:21).[31] Divine virulent, intractable

---

[30] The attributes of Yahweh's nature which are catalogued in Exod 34:6-7 reverberate throughout the biblical corpus. The following citations are a sample of texts which contain 34:6-7 in whole, in part, or in echo: Num 14:18; Ps 86:5; Ps 103:8; Ps 145:8; Jonah 4:2; Joel 2:13; and Neh 9:17 (note also an authentic echo at John 1:14). Such an array of attestations and echoes confirms that Exod 34:6-7 touches upon God's fundamental nature.

[31] See also Isa 10:12. Note also the anguish of Yahweh at the contemplation of exercising his fierce wrath against Ephraim at Hos 11:8-9.

anger is incompatible with a divine-human relationship. In the
case of Israel, such anger cannot preserve the tribes of Jacob
long enough for them to inherit the Patriarchal promises!
Thus, Exodus 32-34 contains not only the archetype
of judgment upon apostasy but also the archetype of
reconciliation.[32] These archetypes in the tradition become
prototypes of the prophetic oracles of judgment and renewal.
Thus, judgment and salvation—disjunction and conjunction—
are theologically of a piece. The historically forged joining
of disjunction and conjunction that dotted the relationship
between Yahweh and Israel gave rise to questions of theodicy
and teleology, questions clamoring for answers. The eighth
century prophets were among those who probed the times
to construct a synthesis in which Israel could discern the
fingerprints and footsteps of a sovereign, yet relational, God.
As one expression of this developing synthesis, the eighth
century prophets balanced the theological equation by placing
visions of renewal alongside oracles of doom. The memory of
the events of Sinai, in which Yahweh and Israel discovered one
another once more, enabled these prophets to conceive of both
a coming catastrophe and a post-catastrophic era of renewal as
a conceptual unity.

### A Mutual Rediscovery

Israel first received her identity over against the oppressor
nation Egypt.[33] As a counterpoint to the memory of Israel's
election tradition (see Amos 3:1-2 above), Amos brings Israel's
growing sense of autonomy and immunity up short at 9:7:

"Are not you Israelites the same to me as the
Cushites?" declares the LORD. "Did I not bring Israel
up from Egypt, the Philistines from Caphtor, and the
Arameans from Kir?"

---

[32] Note that Ps 103:7-14 provides a commentary on Exod 33-34.

[33] See Gowan, *Eschatology*, 42-58.

Israel had perverted her understanding of election. To her surprise, Israel didn't fill the whole horizon of Yahweh's life! Yahweh has a 'history,' one that is not solely defined by Israel.[34] As Israel had gained an initial identity vis-à-vis the nations, so now a post-catastrophe re-emergent Israel would find herself and her God among the nations. The eighth century prophets defined Yahweh's relationship with the non-covenanted nations as follows: (1) he uses them as his instruments to accomplish his purposes; (2) he nevertheless holds them accountable to ethical standards which are woven into the fabric of the cosmos itself (thus, reflecting a theology of a value-laden created order); and (3) in a supreme paradox, Yahweh will parlay Israel's rich heritage with him into a coherent expression of salvation vis-à-vis the nations in the post-catastrophe era.[35]

Since the sovereignty of Yahweh encompasses the relational aspects of his nature as well, each side of the theological equation—the disjunction of judgment and the conjunction of renewal—complements the other and with it forms an integral unity. After all, in the view of the eighth century prophets (reflected also in the Deuteronomistic History), Yahweh himself mandates the destruction of the present generation of his covenant people. While neither before, during, nor after this decree of radical disjunction is Yahweh "found" by any other people, Yahweh himself *does survive* the destruction of his land, his temple, his cult, his people, and the royal Davidic House. Thus, after the fall of

---

[34] On the issue of Israel's misappropriated ideas of election with respect to the nations see especially Walter Brueggemann, "Exodus in the Plural (Amos 9:7)," in *Texts That Linger, Words That Explode: Listening to Prophetic Voices* (Minneapolis: Fortress Press, 2000), 89-103 where Brueggemann's term for this misappropriation is "mono-ideology."

[35] Throughout most of her existence, beginning with Exod 15, Israel found herself in an "over against the nations" relationship. Thus, in prophetic visions of salvation, the theme of Israelite hegemony over the nations looms large (Isa 49:23; 60:10-14; 61:5). Surprisingly, the nations are incorporated into some prophetic visions of *šalôm* (Isa 2:2-5 // Mic 4:1-5; Isa 49:22; and 60:4-9). Note the conversion of the nations in Isa 45:22-23 and Israel's role as a light to the nations in Isa 49:6; 60:2-3. See Brueggemann, "Always in the Shadow of the Empire," in *Texts that Linger*, 73-87.

Samaria and Jerusalem, respectively, some repatriates of Judah "find" this same Yahweh in a "resurrection" on the other side of the "death" of radical disjunction.[36] This mutual rediscovery of one another—that of 'Israel' and Yahweh—constitutes a radical conjunction in the course of their relationship. During the years of this mutual rediscovery, Israel's theology achieved a mature though variegated synthesis of theodicy, teleology, and eschatology through a variety of written genres which ultimately reaffirmed that a single divine will ruled the cosmos.[37] Such an intellectual, theological, and historiographical harvest would have been impossible apart from the pre-catastrophe seedbed that provided a matrix for such a synthesis. The eighth century prophets were among those who continued to weave the threads of the rich variety of Israel's ancient traditions into the tapestry of this maturing synthesis.

## The Eighth Century Prophets as Theologians and Synthesizers

### Values of the Past: Building Blocks for the Future

By 2800 B.C. in both Egypt and Mesopotamia, a conceptual linkage among cosmology, order, and kingship began to express itself in the structure of society, the cult, and in literature. The ideal implementation of this nexus into ANE (ancient Near Eastern) societies was known as justice (*mīšarum*) in Mesopotamia, as truth ('*ĕmet*), justice (*mišpat*), righteousness (*ts'dāqâ*), and equity (*mêšārîm*) in Israel, and as 'cosmic balance' (*ma'at*) in Egypt.[38] As part of the ambient cultural

---

[36] For the motif of "death and resurrection" as a way of conceptualizing the thought and outcomes of the classical prophets see especially Gowan, *Prophetic Books*, 1-21, 188-200.

[37] Ibid., 144-62.

[38] For background to these concepts as applicable to the king in the ANE and in Israel see Moshe Weinfeld, *Social Justice in Ancient Israel and in the Ancient Near East* (Jerusalem: Magnes Press, 1995), 25-74.

climate, this conceptual linkage influenced Israel primarily through (1) royal Egyptian ideology[39] and (2) Mesopotamian and Canaanite versions of the ancient Semitic combat motif.[40] As Israel established a monarchy in the 11th century B.C., this ancient nexus (in laundered form) supplied the socio-ethical-theological framework for an emerging synthesis of cherished Israelite values. Values that had been formed and nurtured in divine promise, law, covenant, epic, wisdom, cult, and prophecy now were integrated into the ideology of the Davidic dynasty and of Zion.[41]

At the same time, Israel's experience at the hands of the nations over a six-hundred year period (ca. 1000-400 B.C.) served as a catalyst to shape this emerging synthesis. The synergism thus created nurtured a multifaceted vision of what life under the rule of God should and could be like. The prophetic oracles of salvation are a primary expression of this vision in which the unilateral action of Yahweh achieves an historical continuity for the remnant of his people under his rule in an era of *šālôm*. Though this era comes at Yahweh's initiative, its fulfillment both requires and empowers humanity to be full partners through obedience to ethical and moral imperatives and through commitment to just and equitable relationships in community.

Through the centuries, Israel's creative minds bequeathed

---

[39] See the essays of Jacobus van Dijk, Erik Hornung, Herman Te Velde, and Leonard H. Lesko in *CANE*, ed. Jack M. Sasson, et al. (New York: Charles Scribner's Sons, 1995), 3:1697-1774.

[40] See the discussions of Susan Niditch, *Ancient Israelite Religion* (Oxford: Oxford University Press, 1997), 50-69 and Frank Moore Cross, *Canaanite Myth and Hebrew Epic: Essays in the History of the Religion of Israel* (Cambridge, Mass.: Harvard University Press, 1973), 112-44.

[41] Consult Dearman, *Religion and Culture*, 67-68; Bernhard Anderson, "Mythopoeic and Theological Dimensions of Biblical Creation Faith," in *From Creation to New Creation: Old Testament Perspectives*, OBT (Minneapolis: Augsburg Fortress Press, 1994), 75-96, and John Mauchline, "Implicit Signs of a Persistent Belief in the Davidic Empire," *VT* 20 (1970): 287-303. See also J.J.M. Roberts, "Zion in the Theology of the Davidic-Solomonic Empire," in *Studies in the Period of David and Solomon and Other Essays: Papers Read at the International Symposium for Biblical Studies, Tokyo, 5-7 December, 1979*, ed. Tomoo Ishida (Winona Lake: Ind.: Eisenbrauns, 1982), 93-108.

an oral and written inheritance of memory, theological reflection, and interpretation of her historical trajectory and covenant life as a vassal to Yahweh her suzerain. This inheritance provided the following components for an emerging synthesis which in turn continually shaped Israel's self-understanding:[42]

* CREATION THEOLOGY—Israel's unique expression of cosmology and its value-laden (didactic / relational / ethical) aspects (see discussion of Psalms 8 and 19 in this regard below);

* the NOACHIC COVENANT as an "eternal covenant" (b'rît 'ôlām) grounds the rhythm and blessing of life in the covenant faithfulness of God who is unconditionally committed to the physical world (Gen 8:21-22; 9:8-16);

* the PROMISES TO THE FATHERS concerning blessing (sufficiency), progeny (a name), and land (a future); referred to as an "eternal covenant" (b'rît 'ôlām) in Genesis 17:7;

* the issue of THEODICY—Israel's unique understanding of divine sovereignty, human freedom, and ethical responsibility;

* the memory of the EXODUS where Yahweh showed himself to be the divine warrior for Israel against the "anti-creational"[43] oppression of Egypt;

* Israel's taking upon herself the obligations of Torah as vassal to her suzerain Yahweh in the SINAI COVENANT (Exod 19-24);

* The promise of an enduring ('ad-'ôlām) DAVIDIC DYNASTY (2 Sam 7:11b-16).

---

[42] See Bernhard Anderson, *Contours of Old Testament Theology* (Minneapolis: Fortress Press, 1999), chps. 11-13, 17, and 23 for discussions of the various promises and covenants which formed the foundation of Israel's historical and theological identity.

[43] This well-chosen phrase is that of Terence Fretheim who in *Exodus*, Interpretation Commentary (Louisville: Westminster/John Knox Press, 1991), 27 and throughout develops this theme in a fine way.

Significantly, one can trace a literary trajectory of the synthesis of these components outside the eighth century prophets. For example, a convergence of some of these components in the person of the Davidic king and the locale of Zion emerges in several pre-exilic psalms. In Psalm 45:1-7[2-8], the responsibility of carrying out God's agenda to corral moral chaos on behalf of justice rests upon the ruling descendant of David. Political hegemony over the nations, while a reflex of the eternity of God's throne, can be realized only if the Davidic king "loves righteousness and hates wickedness." Psalm 72:1-4 opens with a prayer that the ruling descendant of David be endowed with the justice and righteousness of God. The king's burden is to judge rightly, to crush oppression, and to defend the cause of the afflicted and needy. In an echo of the Noachic covenant, justice will render the kingdom of David as enduring as the sun and the moon (vv. 5, 17). Royal implementation of righteousness is the key to fertility of the land, abundance of harvest, and security of the people from all oppressors (vv. 6-11, 16). All hopes for deliverance from oppression and violence are vested in the descendant of David, who vigorously adopts the agenda of the God of Israel (vv. 12-14). Finally, in an adaptation and reapplication of Genesis 12:3, the psalmist proclaims that the promise that all the clans of the earth will be blessed through Abra[ha]m will be realized through a Davidic rule, one that adopts the moral and ethical agenda of Yahweh (vs. 17).

A similar adaptation and reapplication of this promise to Abra[ha]m is found at Jeremiah 4:1-2, where the nations will be blessed through Judah's repentance and obedience! With a move of creative theological synthesis, Jeremiah links the survival of some descendants of Israel (31:35-37) and the continuity of the Davidic dynasty (33:14-26) to God's absolute commitment to the physical cosmos as expressed in the eternal Noachic covenant. Similarly, the eternal nature of the Noachic covenant is invoked at Isaiah 54:9-10 as an analogy for an enduring future for Zion, for the people of God, and by implication, for the Davidic king.

Religious and historical exigencies continually fueled Israel's intellectual and theological momentum toward a synthesis of her valued traditions. Events of the second half of the eighth century B.C. contributed monumental impetus toward the maturation of this synthesis. Amos was not only the first of the classical prophets to attempt such a synthesis, but his version of it also became paradigmatic for others who built upon his themes.

## Amos 9:11-15 as Prophetic Synthesis

The appearance of two prophetic oracles of restoration at Amos 9:11-15 (vv. 11-12 and 13-15, respectively), after more than eight chapters of unrelenting oracles of judgment, has caused many scholars to conclude that these oracles are not from the hand of Amos.[44] However, when compared with oracles of restoration in prophets who are known to date from later times than Amos, the expectations and descriptions in 9:11-15 of "that day" and of "the days that are coming" are decidedly brief and understated,[45] suggesting that the visions of 9:11-15 may be early prophetic formulations of what later evolved into more grandiose prophetic depictions of a historical future.[46] Thus, it is tenable to argue that many of the later prophetic oracles of salvation are rooted in the soil of Amos 9:11-15.[47]

---

[44] See notes 21-22 above for the relevant literature.

[45] For a full treatment of the introductory formulas to the salvation oracles see Claus Westermann, *Prophetic Oracles of Salvation in the Old Testament*, trans. Keith Crim (Louisville: Westminster/John Knox Press, 1991), 252-61.

[46] Nowhere in the eighth century prophetic oracles of salvation do the writers envision an absolute end to the historical process. That is, each of their portrayals of the future transpires within the horizon of time. As theological imagining develops more in the direction of apocalyptic, the "end of time" comes more and more into view: note Isa 24-27; 34-35; Ezk 38-39; Dan 12; and Zech 9-14.

[47] Th. C. Vriezen, "Prophecy and Eschatology," in *International Organization for the Study of the Old Testament: Congress Volume, Copenhagen 1953,* Supplements to Vetus Testamentum, 1, ed. Aage Bentzen (Leiden: Brill, 1953), 205 finds that "it is not impossible that the words [9:11-15] are authentic."
The interpretive history of Amos 9:11-15 is varied. See its use at Qumran: CD 7:15-16 and 4QHor i.11-13; in the New Testament: Acts 15:16-17; in early rabbinism: see Joseph Bonsirven, *Textes rabbiniques des deux premiers siècles chrétiens pour servir à l'intelligence du Nouveau Testament* (Rome: Pontifical Biblical Institute, 1954), §§ 695 and 2521 for discussion of Mishnaic and Talmudic references; and in Church Fathers of Late Antiquity, namely, Augustine, *The City of God* 18:28.

In the two juxtaposed oracles of 9:11-15 there are six themes that together form an ideal type for the earliest tradition of the oracles of salvation. Variations and elaborations of this ideal type appear in subsequent prophets, beginning with Hosea and extending through Ezekiel.[48] Since this ideal type of blessing and restoration is arguably among the earliest attempts in the biblical canon to produce a synthesis of the Noachic, Abrahamic, Sinaitic, and Davidic traditions, its texts and its themes invite close scrutiny:[49]

### ORACLE ONE

[11]"In that day I will restore David's fallen tent. I will repair its broken places, restore its ruins, and build it as it used to be, [12] so that they may possess the remnant of Edom and all the nations that bear my name," declares the LORD, who will do these things;

### ORACLE TWO

[13]"The days are coming," declares the LORD, "when the reaper will be overtaken by the plowman and the planter by the one treading grapes. New wine will drip from the mountains and flow from all the hills. [14] I will bring back my exiled people Israel; they will rebuild the ruined cities and live in them. They will plant vineyards and drink their wine; they will make gardens and eat their fruit. [15] I will plant Israel in their own land, never again to be uprooted from the land I have given them," says the LORD your God.

---

[48] See Hos 3:5; Isa 4:2-6; 11:1-16; Jer 3:14-18; 23:5-8; 30:3-10; 31:1-6, 23-28; Ezek 34:11-31; 37:15-28.

[49] The use of Amos 9:11-15 in Acts 15:16-18 is totally dependent upon the LXX which departs from the MT in several respects. For details, see Donald E. Gowan, *Amos*, in *The New Interpreter's Bible*, ed. Leander E. Keck, 7:426-31 (Nashville: Abingdon Press, 2001), 427-28.

*Thematic Analysis*

- The restoration of "David's tent,"[50] which has fallen or
  is about to fall involves "repairing its broken places,"
  "restoring its ruins," "building it as it used to be"—this
  is a reference to a descendant of David ruling over the
  twelve tribes of Israel (9:11);[51]

- There will be an extension of Davidic political
  hegemony beyond Israel and Judah to encompass once
  again Edom and all the nations of the old Davidic/
  Solomonic regime (9:12);

- There will be an unprecedented era of fruitfulness and
  fecundity (9:13);

- God will initiate the repatriation of his people Israel
  (9:14a);

- In sharp contrast to the judgment oracle at 5:11, the
  investment of labor in rebuilding, replanting, and
  cultivating will be rewarded as Israel lives in the cities,
  drinks the vintage, and eats the fruit of the gardens in
  security and *šālôm* (9:14b);

- The repatriated land that flows once more with milk
  and honey, as it were, is in reality God's own garden;
  it is now inhabited by Israel, and as in days of old,
  it is ruled by a descendant of David; God is Israel's
  guarantor of security in the land (9:15).

In this ideal type, Yahweh brings about a time of renewal
in the land of Promise and in all the earth in partnership with a
restored Davidic House that rules God's people. It is Yahweh's
own character, his commitment to the physical creation, and
his commitment to the creation of an ethos for his historically
shaped people Israel that will bring the vision to fulfillment.

---

[50] For similar depictions of the Davidic Dynasty see Isa 1:8; 16:5; and
33:20a.

[51] Isa 7:17 invokes the separation of Ephraim from Judah two-hundred years
prior as an appropriately dire precedent for the horror and trauma of destruction
soon to be wrought by Assyria upon Israel.

Although Amos 9:11-15 does not make an explicit linkage between this future era of *šālôm* and human expressions of justice and righteousness, the entire collection of his oracles to this point do just that (see further below). Each subsequent eighth century prophet elaborates upon this linkage between an unprecedented blessing upon Canaan and upon the entire earth with the practice of justice and righteousness in all interpersonal and societal relationships. This linkage reflects Israel's belief that the created order is essentially good and that the nature of the cosmos is value-laden. Such a viewpoint means that God has made the world to serve as a superlative habitation for moral education/re-education at both the personal and community levels.

## A Value-Laden Cosmos: The Ethos of Creation and Community

### Creation and Value in Israel

Israel's ethos of justice, righteousness, and equity was molded through the exigencies of history in a world created by Yahweh, a world that thereby reflects his nature. William P. Brown has demonstrated how each of several foundational creation theologies of the Hebrew Bible is grounded in the character of Yahweh.[52] His thesis is that the created order is above all a "habitation of moral agency."[53] Thus, the created order is not value neutral; rather, it is value-laden. Two familiar psalms corroborate this viewpoint.

---

[52] In discussing five major expressions of creation theology in the Hebrew Bible, Brown demonstrates that creation theology deeply influenced the intellectual, cultic, and moral life of ancient Israel. The foundational texts with which he works are: (1) Gen 1:1-2:4a; (2) Gen 2:4b-3:24; (3) Isa 40-55; (4) Prov 1-9, with special attention to 8:22-31; and (5) Job. For a summary of his conclusions about each one of these see *Ethos*, 381-96.

[53] Brown, *Ethos*, 12.

Psalm 8 reiterates humanity's role as God's vice-regent who is made in his image. With divinely delegated authority, humanity is to fill the earth and subdue and rule all created life (Gen 1:1-2:4a). By championing ethical values and moral behavior, humanity imitates God's actions of bringing order and light to the world. Since this good world has God's fingerprints yet upon it, replete with the majesty and glory of the God who made it, the cosmos thus brims with moral and ethical value. Humanity is the supreme moral expression of this God who has made humans rulers over such a value-laden cosmos. In Psalm 19, the silent cosmos has revelatory power as it speaks to humanity of the glory of God. The voice of God in the Torah complements the 'voice' of the cosmos. Both voices may be embraced by the human soul. The closing prayer of the psalmist gives voice to that inner person, a prayer that the human heart might sing in consummate rhythm and harmony with the voices of the cosmos and of the Torah.[54]

Since the warp and woof of the fabric of the physical world bear the fingerprints of God, the cosmos is a value-laden habitation capable of fulfilling God's moral and ethical purposes.[55] God proclaims the creation "good" seven times in the creation story of Genesis 1:1-2:4, good for the purposes God has in mind. At the center of those purposes is humankind whom God has crowned his vice-regent. Yahweh has neither turned away from his purposes nor has he rescinded this vice-regency. What may be drawn from this understanding of creation and value for our interpretation of the salvation oracles of the eighth century prophets?

---

[54] See the incisive comments on this psalm by J. Clinton McCann, *A Theological Introduction to the Book of Psalms: The Psalms as Torah* (Nashville: Abingdon Press, 1993), 28-30. In addition, Brown, *Ethos*, 248 states that Psalm 19 is a "clear example of the integral relationship between creation's ethos and human ethic.... The psalm establishes a natural connection between ethos and ethic. Law finds its home, its ground and integrity, in a thoroughly cosmic environment. Law has its dwelling in a cosmos in which divine *doxa* (glory) and *gnōsis* (knowledge) are transmitted by creation's non-verbal 'discourse'...."

[55] See Brown, *Ethos*, 1-33 and 381-410.

*Creation, Ethics, and Šālôm in the Community*

Although the oracles of indictment and doom of the eighth century prophets appear to flame with an apocalyptic-like aura, these prophets are not apocalyptists. They neither think of the "end of time" nor do they threaten or cajole with eternal punishments or rewards; rather, both Israel and her prophets inhabit God's good world in which there exists a commonwealth of community and environment. In such a commonwealth, immorality and disobedience have a corrupting effect upon the physical world, its inhabitants, and their communities.

The uniqueness of Israel's metaphysical conception among the nations of the ANE lies primarily in her postulation of a transcendent deity with a single divine will whose nature reflects moral and ethical consistency. As we have noted, Psalms 8 and 19 eloquently portray the cosmos as a value-laden habitation in which humanity plays a pivotal role in the maintenance of moral and ethical equilibrium. Thus, there are cosmological and creational underpinnings to the prophets' oracles that give coherence and authority to the moral imperatives that they speak in Yahweh's name. Clearly, not only Israel's sages but also her prophets were nourished from the fountainhead of creation theology.[56]

A linkage between the well-being of the physical world and the ethical behavior of its inhabitants is as old as Eden. Such linkage undergirds the biblical storyline in all its parts: (1) the days of Noah; (2) the cities of the Plain; (3) the liberation of Israel from Egyptian oppression; and (4) the fate of Israel in the land of Canaan. In the Noachic covenant (Gen 8:21-22; 9:8-17), God makes an unconditional commitment to the created order.[57]

---

[56] Thus, sages and prophets "share a common epistemological basis whose conclusions, in a Yahwistic society, are not unreasonably interpreted as an expression of God's standards of behaviour," for which see H.G.M. Williamson, "Isaiah and the Wise," in *Wisdom in Ancient Israel: Essays in Honour of J.A. Emerton*, ed. John Day, Robert P. Gordon, and H.G.M. Williamson (Cambridge: Cambridge University Press, 1995), 138.

[57] Bernhard W. Anderson, "Creation and the Noachic Covenant," in *From Creation to New Creation: Old Testament Perspectives*, Overtures to Biblical Theology (Minneapolis: Augsburg Fortress, 1994), 157.

By divine purpose, the life-ways of humanity are to constitute
a moral, ethical, social, and relational counterpart to this divine
commitment to cosmic stability. Indeed, humankind is to fulfill
the primordial command of the Creator to represent God's rule
and his will for *šālôm* upon the earth.[58]

In view of entering the Land of Promise, Leviticus links
secure and abundant living there with following God's decrees
and laws. Leviticus 18 enumerates the ways in which the
nations had already polluted Canaan as a warning to Israel
of the consequences of her own sin which would equally
pollute the Promised Land. In both instances, the land becomes
sick (vv. 24-28). Privatization of the Promised Land in any
absolute sense is forbidden, for the LORD decrees that "the
land is mine and you [Israel] are but aliens and my tenants"
(25:18-24).[59] This Levitical vision of the commonwealth of
environment and community accords fully with the platform
from which the eighth century prophets inveighed against
the pollution of society, religion, and politics in private and
public life.[60]

We may contemplate with the psalmist (Ps 46:2[3]) that
which is able to make "the earth give way and the mountains
fall into the heart of the sea" (that is, return the cosmos to a
pre-creation state of chaos). Note Jeremiah's vision of such a
scenario as he contemplates the moral and ethical perversion of
Judah (Jer 4:23-26):

> I looked at the earth, and it was formless and empty;
> and at the heavens, and their light was gone. I looked
> at the mountains, and they were quaking; all the hills
> were swaying. I looked, and there were no people;
> every bird in the sky had flown away. I looked, and
> the fruitful land was a desert; all its towns lay in ruins
> before the LORD, before his fierce anger.

---

[58] Ibid., 62-64.

[59] The land of Canaan is referred to as "the LORD's land" in the oracle of doom
at Hos 9:3.

[60] Note how falling away from God's covenant decrees is linked to the
languishing of the environment at Deut 29:19[18]-28[27].

Texts of the Torah, of the Prophets, and of the Psalter express a social and theological nexus of LAND, ETHICS, COMMUNITY *ETHOS*, and COMMUNITY *TELOS*. This nexus is a reflection of a value-laden cosmos in which Israel's sins are not only anti-Torah, they (along with those of the non-covenanted nations) are also anti-creational. Thus, regardless of the grandiose portrait of *šālôm* painted by the oracles of salvation, their realization may not be severed from an ethical walk that reflects the nature of Yahweh.[61] Below, we will note how the rhetorical strategies of the eighth century prophets Amos and Hosea were informed by this nexus.

## *Amos and the Ethos of Creation and Community*

Amos exhibits numerous texts that link the languishing of the physical environment to Israel's moral and ethical atrophy.[62] Moreover, the Creator unfailingly enlists the components of his created realm in an attempt to instruct, discipline, and punish Israel in her recalcitrance and her apostasies. The so-called 'doxologies' of Amos invoke the value-laden nature of the cosmos in the service of prophetic indictments against 'anti-creational' sins:[63]

> 4:13  He who forms the mountains, creates the wind, and reveals his thoughts to man, he who turns dawn to darkness, and treads the high places of the earth—the LORD God Almighty is his name:

---

[61] In Jeremiah's vision of the new covenant (31:31-34), the ethical 'gap' is conceptually bridged by the writing of God's law upon the heart and mind. The new day in the new covenant requires an inward transformation wrought by God. Perhaps what is depicted here is an inclination to obey and a disinclination to rebel. With such a receptive and penitent people, God is ready to forgive and remember sins no more.

[62] For example, see 1:2; 4:6-11; 5:18-20; 8:8-10; and 9:1-4.

[63] On the face of it, there is no reason to deny to Amos or to any other prophet either the use or modification of preexisting hymnody (such as Amos 4:13; 5: 8-9; 9:5-6 or Isa 2:2-5 // Mic 4:1-4) which would have been well known from participation in the daily and seasonal activities of the cult. The prophets were not in absolute opposition to the cult. Rather, they opposed its practice in isolation from the ethical requirements of Torah.

5:8-9 (he who made the Pleiades and Orion, who turns blackness into dawn and darkens day into night, who calls for the waters of the sea and pours them out over the face of the land—the LORD is his name— 9 he flashes destruction on the stronghold and brings the fortified city to ruin);

9:5-6 The Lord, the LORD Almighty, he who touches the earth and it melts, and all who live in it mourn— the whole land rises like the Nile, then sinks like the river of Egypt— 6 he who builds his lofty palace in the heavens and sets its foundation on the earth, who calls for the waters of the sea and pours them out over the face of the land— the LORD is his name.

These texts are cosmological and sapiential in character. As such, they brim with an ontological, epistemological, and hermeneutical richness that is nourished by the streams of creation theology.[64] For our purposes, we note that each of these liturgical pieces emphasizes a connection between heaven (the throne room of Yahweh) and earth (the realm of humankind, though deeply imprinted with Yahweh's footprints and fingerprints, as it were). Indeed, in these hymns the boundary between realms above and below has become porous. The God of these hymns is sovereign and transcendent; yet, in a fully relational and imminent way (4:13), he is 'hands on' with the demonstration of his presence and power.

As Shalom Paul among others has noted, the first and third of these hymn-like sections are strategically placed. The same may be argued for the middle 'doxology' (5:8-9). By an ancient convention of literary composition, the placement

64 Consult Samuel Terrien, "Amos and Wisdom," in *Israel's Prophetic Heritage: Essays in Honor of James Muilenburg*, ed. Bernhard W. Anderson and Walter Harrelson (New York: Harper & Brothers, 1962), 108-15. With respect to the interpenetration of currents of thought and tradition in the socio-religious world of Amos and others like him, Terrien rightly concludes "that various groups, such as priests, prophets, and wise men existed should not be denied. At the same time, such groups were not alien one from the others, and they lived in a common and mutually interacting environment" (115).

of the hymn at 5:8-9 is due to the catchphrase "to overturn" (√ *hpk*) in vv. 7-8.[65] Thereby, the point is made that "those who are guilty of social inversion shall now witness and suffer cosmic inversion."[66]

### Hosea and the Ethos of Creation & Community

Hosea 2:8-13[10-15] makes a transition from the prophet's personal marital experience to the sad realities that both he and Yahweh find in Israel. Note Yahweh's proprietary view regarding the source of grain, new wine, oil, wool, and linen:

> [8] She has not acknowledged that I was the one who gave her the grain, the new wine and oil, who lavished on her the silver and gold—which they used for Baal.
> [9] "Therefore I will take away my grain when it ripens, and my new wine when it is ready. I will take back my wool and my linen, intended to cover her nakedness.
> [10] So now I will expose her lewdness before the eyes of her lovers; no one will take her out of my hands.
> [11] I will stop all her celebrations: her yearly festivals, her New Moons, her Sabbath days—all her appointed feasts. [12] I will ruin her vines and her fig trees, which she said were her pay from her lovers; I will make them a thicket, and wild animals will devour them. [13] I will punish her for the days she burned incense to the Baals; she decked herself with rings and jewelry, and went after her lovers, but me she forgot," declares the LORD.

Here in Yahweh's name, Hosea unequivocally links the languishing of the cosmos with the moral and ethical failures of God's people.

In Hosea 4:1-3, Yahweh brings a charge (*rîb*) against his people which he grounds in the stipulations of the Decalogue:

---

[65] Each "doxology" punctuates Amos's indictments and is thus integral to the argument of the book as a whole, see Paul, *Amos*, 152-56.

[66] Paul, *Amos*, 168.

¹ Hear the word of the LORD, you Israelites, because the LORD has a charge to bring against you who live in the land: "There is no faithfulness, no love, no acknowledgment of God in the land. ²There is only cursing, lying and murder, stealing and adultery; they break all bounds, and bloodshed follows bloodshed. ³ Because of this the land mourns, and all who live in it waste away; the beasts of the field and the birds of the air and the fish of the sea are dying."

The erosion of the cosmos parallels the undoing of the Torah. The integrity of personal and community life is inextricably linked to the viability of a created order.

In a striking reversal of the contemporary situation, the prophet constructs a provocative narrative oracle of future blessing by reaching far into the past (2:14-23[16-25]). The prophet imaginatively revisits the earliest days of Yahweh's relationship with Israel. Yahweh lures Israel to the desert where he woos her with the language of love. From there he cedes to Israel once more the verdant Land of Promise. Now, however, there is no covenant violation in the camp (there is no "trouble" ['akôr], Josh 7:24-26). Rather, there is only yielding which creates a portal to a new day of hope (2:14-15[16-17]).[67]

The covenant of reconciliation which Yahweh will make in that day between heaven and earth will nourish šālôm between humankind and animals as well as among the nations.[68] What follows, however, is breathtaking. As the divine groom of a now disciplined and reeducated Israel,[69] Yahweh prepares to consummate the relationship by bringing to the renewal of the covenant—in contravention of cultural norms—the bride

---

[67] Note a similar use of the Valley of Achor tradition in the restoration oracle at Isa 65:8-10.

[68] This text has much in common with Isa 11:5-9 and 65:25 and their immediate contexts.

[69] The trajectory of discipline and remedial instruction is a prominent one in the book of Hosea; see 2:6[8], 9-17[11-19]; 3:3-5; 5:2.15; 6:4-5; 7:15; 10:11; 11:3-4; and 13:13. Consult also Gowan, *Prophetic Books*, 46-50.

price of righteousness, justice, commitment, compassion, and
faithfulness (2:19-20[21-22]):

> [19] I will betroth you to me forever; I will betroth you
> in righteousness and justice, in love and compassion.
> [20] I will betroth you in faithfulness, and you will
> acknowledge the LORD.

In this beautiful vision, the theological offspring of Exodus
34:6-7, Yahweh supplies what Israel cannot. Yahweh puts into
motion a chain of responsiveness and yielding: Yahweh to the
heavens; the heavens to the earth; the earth to the grain, new
wine, oil—all of which is a response to the 'sowing of God,'
that is, Jezreel (2:21-22[23-24]). In a reflection of the primeval
garden (Gen 2:8-25), Yahweh himself sows his people in the
land in compassion and in love and in familial relationship. The
covenant terms are spoken; heaven is once more knit together
with earth (2:23[25]).

It is clear that the eighth century prophets drew from
cultic and legal traditions and forms. However, their oracles
are also informed by wisdom traditions and their complement,
creation theology.[70] As theologians and ethicists, the prophets
employed every tool at their disposal not only to interpret
the contemporary scene but also to imagine a future in which
Yahweh and a remnant continuous with Israel from "the days
of old" might find one another again in an environment of
well-being that reflects the rule of God over the cosmos and
upon the earth. As contemporary theologians, ethicists, and
homileticians, what may we draw from this ancient nexus
of LAND, ETHICS, COMMUNITY *ETHOS*, and COMMUNITY *TELOS* for
our ministries?

---

[70] Brown, *Ethos*, has shown how extensively creation theology, whether
found in narrative, sapiential, or prophetic traditions, undergirds the ethical
vision of ancient Israel. See also Walter Brueggemann, "The Loss and
Recovery of Creation in Old Testament Theology," *ThTo* 53 (July 1996):
177-90 and Terence E. Fretheim, "Nature's Praise of God in The Psalms,"
*ExAud* 3 (1987): 16-30.

*Conclusion*

The "death and resurrection of Israel" is a useful interpretive grid for understanding the theological conjunction that underlies the oracles of disjunction in the pre-exilic classical prophets.[71] The prospect of taking such a hermeneutic seriously for our own time is both challenging and startling. As Christian theologians and homileticians, we may derive our most poignant and convicting illustration from the figure of our Lord and mentor as he prayed in the Garden of Gethsemane. There it became horrifyingly clear to him that as an obedient son he would have to quaff the contents of the cup of Yahweh's "strange work" and "alien task." Only through the experience of such a personal radical disjunction as awaited him at Golgotha could the resurrection power of the Father's kingdom fill the cosmos. Thus, the execution of a divine plan of radical disjunction became the means for allowing the divine plan of radical conjunction to become evident and efficacious.

In the incarnation, life, ministry, death, resurrection, and ascension of this Jew from Nazareth, who was at the same time a son from the heart of the Father, we come face-to-face with the personification of the Abrahamic Promises, the Torah, the Covenant, Israel, Canaan, the Davidic dynasty, Zion/Jerusalem, the Temple, and the *šᵉkînâ*. In him we stand in the presence of the very embodiment of Creation *and* Redemption, of Judgment *and* Salvation, and of *šālôm* itself.[72] The Eternal's singular plan came to exquisite focus in this Jesus wherein radical disjunction is forever eclipsed by radical conjunction.

In keeping with ancient Israel's most profound theological understanding, radical disjunction (the judgment of death) is predicated upon radical conjunction (the prospect of

---

[71] Gowan, *Prophetic Books*, 1-21. See also James A.Sanders, *Torah and Canon* (Philadelphia: Fortress, 1972), 117-21.

[72] Consult among others F.F. Bruce, *New Testament Development of Old Testament Themes* (Grand Rapids: Eerdmans, 1968); W.D. Davies, *Paul and Rabbinic Judaism: Some Rabbinic Elements in Pauline Theology*, 4th ed. (Philadelphia: Fortress, 1980); and P.W.L. Walker, *Jesus and the Holy City: New Testament Perspectives on Jerusalem* (Grand Rapids: Eerdmans, 1996).

resurrection). This understanding is consonant with a value-laden cosmos designed by the Creator to be a realm for instruction and re-education. Thus, any latent contradiction is resolvable when one regards the apparent polarity of disjunction and conjunction as two sides of a single coin. Such a polarity and its resolution finds its fullest reflex and most exquisite focus in the biblical narratives of the creation, the flood *and* the rainbow; the exodus, the golden calf, *and* the *miškān*; the conquest of Canaan, the exile, *and* the repatriation; the incarnation, the cross, *and* the empty tomb. When the transcendent sphere thus 'kisses,' as it were, our mortal clime (see Ps 85:10-11[11-12]), the 'rift' between heaven and earth is knit together, and all things are seen as new. As the eighth century prophets have shown us, however, there is a profound level at which any 'rift' within a value-laden cosmos is, after all, of a piece with the fabric itself.

# Appendix
## Israel's Early History in Prophetic Memory

| | AMOS | HOSEA | MICAH | ISAIAH |
|---|---|---|---|---|
| **PATRIARCHS** | | 1:10[2:1] | | |
| Abraham | 3:2 | | 7:20 | 29:22 |
| Isaac | 7:9, 16 | | | |
| Jacob | 3:2 | 12:2-14[3-15] | 7:20 | |
| Election | 3:2 | | | |
| Cities of the Plain | 4:11 | 11:8 | | 1:9-10; 13:19 |
| **EGYPT** | | | | |
| Return to Egypt | | 8:13; 11:5 | | |
| Plagues | 4:10 | | | |
| **MOSES** | | 12:13[14] | 6:4 | 10:26 |
| Aaron | | | 6:4 | |
| Miriam | | | 6:4 | |
| **EXODUS** | 3:1; 9:7 | 2:15[17]; 11:1; 12:9[10]; 13:4 | 6:4; 7:15 | 10:26; 11:16 |
| Wonders | | | 7:15 | |
| **COVENANT** | | 6:7; 8:1, 12 | | |
| Law | 2:4 | 8:12 | | |
| Decalogue | | 4:1-3 | | |
| Formulas | | 1:9[2:1]; 2:23[25] | | |
| **WILDERNESS** | 2:9-10 | 2:14[16]; 9:10; 13:5 | | |
| 40 years | 5:25 | | | |
| Balaam | | | 6:5 | |
| Balak | | | 6:5 | |
| Baal-peor | 9:10 | | | |
| **CANAAN** | | | | |
| Crossing Jordan | | 6:7 | 6:5 | |
| Land/Conquest | 2:9-10 | 2:15[17]; 9:3 | | 28:21 |
| Adam | | | | |
| Achan | | 2:15[17] | | |
| Gibeon | | | | 28:21 |
| **JUDGES** | | | | 1:26 |
| Gibeah | | 9:9; 10:9 | | |
| Midian | | | | 9:4; 10:26 |
| **KINGS** | | 8:4; 13:10 | | 7:17 |
| Saul | | 10:15 (?) | | 10:29 |
| David | 6:5; 9:11 | 3:5 | 5:2 | 29:1 |
| Mt. Perazim | | | | 28:21 |
| Omri | | | 6:16 | |
| Ahab | | | 6:16 | |
| Jehu | | 1:4-5 | | |
| **PROPHETS** | | | | |
| Precursors | 2:11-12 | 12:10[11] | | |

# 4

# Living in Hosea (1-3)

### Craig Bowman

***Contributor's Note***: This message was delivered amidst a community of believers. It is important to note the immediate public response. Several approached me in confessing that I had just told *their* stories by sharing *our* story. Many embraced Patti, expressing gratitude for her courageous presence during the disclosure of our failure and the witness of God's transforming grace. We, and others like us, who have experienced the healing power of God's mercy in broken marriages, have an essential witness within the Christian community. May we be faithful and discerning as we respond to the Spirit of Christ.

What does it mean to live in a biblical text, in this case a prophetic text, the eighth century text of Hosea? Much has been written about narrative theology and living within biblical narrative, but what about the prophetic world where the narrative element is more particularly the prophet's "call narrative"?[1] In the case of Hosea, where the call narrative is

---

[1] Walter Brueggemann, *Biblical Perspectives on Evangelism: Living in a Three-Storied Universe* (Nashville: Abingdon, 1993), 30: calls the decisive entry in the new world of the biblical text "lived appropriation," which has certain personal, social, communal, and theological implications for the person who enters. On the priority of experience as the entry point of the biblical text see Rebecca H. Weaver, "Access to Scripture: Experiencing the Text," *Interpretation* 52 (1998): 367-79. On the challenge of living in the biblical text, see also, Luke Timothy Johnson, "Hebrew's Challenge to Christians: Christology and Discipleship," *Preaching Hebrews* (vol. 4 Rochester College Lectures on Preaching; ed. David Fleer and Dave Bland; Abilene, TX: ACU Press, 2003), 11-28.

uniquely different—or even nonexistent—where does one enter, or how does one live in the textual story of this prophet? Most uninitiated audiences, like a freshman Bible class, laugh when the name of Hosea's wife Gomer is mentioned. A generation raised watching Gomer Pyle on TV (or TV Land reruns) finds the name of Hosea's wife laughable. But for those living in *this* biblical text, the story is anything but humorous.

The narrative world of Hosea's marriage to Gomer is so limited, so strange, so impossible. How can any preacher live in it? How could one craft an autobiographical sermon from it? What modern preacher would dare to obey the opening command Yahweh makes of Hosea—to marry a *prostitute*? The very difficulty of living in this text became a reality when I found myself alive in a similarly strange, unthinkable world—about as unpredictable as the Spirit throwing Jesus into the wilderness of the temptations. All of a sudden Hosea came true for me. I was unprepared for this move, for the glaring truth, and for the radical obedience necessary to keep my life within the story. Rather than a conscious, individual, or even accidental attempt to live in these chapters of Hosea, the unexpected experience of living in Hosea 1–3, although initially unwelcomed and unconscious, became providential and communal. I entered this text unexpectedly, but by divine intention.

One is to listen to this text parabolically in order to realize its Word of God for the community of faith. The clues for orienting our ears and hearts for this experience are found in the multifaceted rhetorical function of chapters 1-3. The parabolic form of Hosea 1-3 as a complex metaphor defies accurate historical reconstruction and accentuates a divine/ prophetic interplay, exposing and highlighting the breadth of Yahweh's impassioned character. What emerges from this prophetic parable is the critique of unwarranted assumptions and disrespectful attitudes regarding Yahweh's merciful *hesed*. As a parable, it emphasizes, more than any other detail, the incomprehensible and incomparable nature of a God who loves the unlovable with an illogical loyalty.

David Fleer asked me to present this paper to the 2003 Rochester College Sermon Seminar about living in Hosea 1-3 for several reasons. The primary one, known by close friends, was what also lies behind the writing of another recently-published article on Hosea 1-3.[2] Certainly on the basis of that article, one might conclude that I am qualified to speak about living in Hosea. But Fleer knows what lies behind it: why I wrote it, so to speak. And that is what brings us to this essay. There have been a couple of times in my marriage to Patti when we have found ourselves living in a chaotic-emotive world resonant of that of Hosea, Gomer, and Yahweh. It is because I've been there, and somehow by the grace of God, done that—doing what God commanded Hosea to do, loving again as God does—that Fleer asked me to write.

Inasmuch as I have lived several years within Hosea, recently I've also been immersed in the world of the Dead Sea Scrolls and the whole of The Book of the Twelve (the Minor Prophets). Each of these text-interpreting realms offers significant insights for understanding the narrative world of Hosea. The Righteous Teacher, in his typical way, quotes Old Testament prophetic verses that yield interpretive comments correlating the text with interesting contemporary historical references and eschatological allusions. In the *pesher*, a Hebrew word meaning interpretive commentary, on Hosea 1-3[3], he very clearly identifies the unfaithful who have been led astray, who by analogy are Gomer/Israel in the text of Hosea. This identification carefully distinguishes the Qumran community as the faithful over against any and all unfaithful—whether they be Pharisees, Romans, or all Gentile nations. As an introduction to The Book of the Twelve, Hosea 1-3 sets a tone and a rhythm for the rest of the whole, especially if the editor of the Book of the Twelve strategically ordered the prophetic books that follow Hosea around a cluster of key terms that are based in Hosea 1-3. If he did, then a reading strategy emerges, which when discerned clarifies the meaning of the Hosea prologue as a guide for reading all of the Minor Prophets together. Before exploring

---

[2] Craig D. Bowman, "Prophetic Grief, Divine Grace: The Marriage of Hosea," *Restoration Quarterly* 43 (2001): 228-42.

[3] 4QpHos[a]. On the Teacher of Righteousness, see Michael A. Knibb, "Teacher of Righteousness," *Encyclopedia of the Dead Sea Scrolls* (2 vols.; ed. L.H. Shiffman and J.C. VanderKam; Oxford: Oxford University Press, 2000), 2:918-21.

4QpHos[a] (the Qumran *pesher* commentary on Hosea from cave 4; fragment A) and The Book of the Twelve, let me address the reading praxis of Scripture and feminist hermeneutical issues related to Hosea 1-3. In each case, my intent is to surface needs, cautions, and urgencies related to reading and preaching Hosea in a postmodern, even post-liberal setting.

### *The Power of Prophetic Speech*

We don't know a great deal about Hosea's person, only that which we can deduce from reading his story. A man of distinction, a man of letters of a sort, he weaves words together like no other northern prophet; his metaphors, similes, puns, and rhymes reveal a passion for nature, life, God, and Gomer. The northern seductive syncretistic culture of Samaria hasn't squelched Hosea's allegiance to Yahweh, nor has it shriveled his ability to embrace it and critique it empathetically. As a preacher, Hosea seems to have enjoyed royal and religious independence. He is not owned by monarchical powers, nor is he associated with the religious practices that surround the king and his royal sanctuaries. All this to say that Hosea, as Yahweh's prophet in Israel during a time of political anarchy and religion gone awry, is a preacher whose words and actions together reveal his counter-cultural character. And he serves as a role model for us.

Some of us, though we are preachers of God's word, have lost the ease of crafting our sermons. Somehow our words just don't flow the way they used to. Somehow we've lost some of our passion for real life and for our real life with God. Our words come together but lack the kick, the connection, the life-creating passion they once had when we were compelled by a constantly clear sense of God's calling, with its compassionate commitment to the community of faith. We always knew that, in the midst of every demand, God's power was upon *us*, his preachers and prophets. We still put words together, exegetically based, from and in the text, but we've been beaten down over the years and our words don't have quite the excitement of the early days of ministry.[4] Hosea's ability with words reminds us of how it used to be. But his person and story also awaken in us a renewed sense of this contradictory void. Paradoxically, living in his story energizes our spirit, though we must be crushed by the realness of a broken marriage and spent emotions. We must lament before we can love again. With Hosea, we must cry to God before we can speak for God.

## Urged to Enter Cautiously

Feminist commentary on Hosea 1-3, particularly discussions of Gomer's character and identity[5] and patriarchal aspects of marriage in ancient Israel, alert us to potential problems as we enter the world of this text. Many feminist scholars naturally react negatively to the interpretations of female imagery in the text used to privilege men who are understood scripturally as the "True worshippers of the Lord... [as] good husbands and fathers...[while the] false ones [i.e., women] are like common whores."[6] Some male interpreters wrongly literalize metaphorical references to women directly

---

[4] Gordon Fee's stunning statement on the schizophrenic divide between exegesis and spirituality among scholars is pertinent. "The ultimate aim of exegesis is the Spiritual one—to produce in our lives and the lives of others true Spirituality, in which God's people live in faithful fellowship both with one another and with the living God" (276). See the title article (chapter 17) in his *To What End Exegesis? Essays Textual, Exegetical, and Theological* (Grand Rapids: Eerdmans, 2001), 276-89.

[5] See the standard critical commentaries and theological word dictionaries for the variety of ways the Hebrew *zanah* and its derivates are translated. Attempts to soften the offensiveness of this term and its synonyms are probably unfaithful to the original meaning of the word given its wide use by Israel's prophets, especially when their intent was clearly in some cases to arrest the attention of an apathetic wayward people who apparently could not have cared less (e.g., Ezek 16 and 23). For an in-depth treatment of *zanah* and derivative and related terms see, Phyllis Bird, "'To Play the Harlot': An Inquiry into an Old Testament Metaphor," in *Gender and Difference in Ancient Israel*, (ed. Peggy Day; Minneapolis: Augsburg Press, 1989), 75-94.

[6] Mary E. Mills, *Images of God in the Old Testament* (Collegeville, MN: Michael Glazier, 1998), 75.

and universally blame them for all that is seductive in the paternalistic prophetic context—and consequently in modern culture.

More positive constructive feminist readings of Hosea enable us to read the book as the Word of God and sustain us as we move through the offensive objections raised against female imagery. Representative are Gale Yee, Renita Weems, and Katharine Doob Sakenfeld. Yee sensitively concludes that

> For Hosea, Gomer is a "wife of whoredom," not because she is a prostitute, but because, according to the mores of Israel, she is blatantly licentious and wanton. In her sexual activity, Gomer is condemned as being "like a whore," although she is not a prostitute by profession. As a promiscuous wife, Gomer is more threatening to the social order than a prostitute—a woman marginalized but still tolerated in Israel.[7]

The intersection and the interruption of Hosea and Gomer's story by the particularity of Yahweh and Israel's story becomes paradigmatic for understanding how we too can live—in these chapters and out.[8] When readers of this narrative literalize the metaphorical description of God's punishment of his wife that she might repent as a means for legitimating dangerous acts of domestic violence, have they misread the text?

> Whereas Hosea 2 clearly describes the physical and emotional violence God inflicts upon his wife to punish her, Hosea 3 is selective in portraying the prophet's chastisement of Gomer: no descriptions of Hosea stripping and humiliating her, no reports of his

---

[7] Gale Yee, "Gomer," *Women in Scripture: A Dictionary of Named and Unnamed Women in the Hebrew Bible, the Apocryphal/Deuterocanonical Books, and the New Testament* (ed. C. Meyers, T. Craven, and R. Kraemer; New York: Houghton Mifflin, 2000), 85.

[8] Yee, "Gomer," perceptively writes, "The story of God's marriage to Israel interrupts that of Hosea's marriage to Gomer and becomes a paradigm for Hosea's treatment of Gomer in Hosea 3" (85). Convergence of the divine and prophetic marriages provides a unique context for understanding the spiritual dimensions for living in this text.

withholding her food and clothing, and no accounts of his physical mistreatment of her.[9]

How far does Hosea go in modeling Yahweh's acts of "love"? Chapter 3 implies that he instituted certain sanctions over Gomer's conduct. But the text is silent about any physical mistreatment by Hosea. Does this mean that the prophet beat his wife privately? Is chapter 2 a bit over the top, a prophetic-divine hyperbole to emphasize the severity of the crime and its appropriate punishment?[10] Certainly the narrative's silence and ambiguity invite speculation. On the other hand, what feminist scholars are reacting to is the way in which so many male commentators have unfairly stereotyped Gomer, without describing Hosea's flaws or their failing marriage with more modern understandings.

Frederick Buechner paints an imaginative portrait of Hosea and Gomer that balances the blame for marital difficulties.[11] His satirical characterization of Hosea as a doomsday, sandwich board-wearing fanatic whose marriage suffers under the pressure of his promising prophetic career subtly exposes a piece of the text that usually goes unnoticed.

What Buechner does with humor and wit, Renita Weems does with exceptional feminist exegesis. Weems suggests that chapter 2 reveals "that Hosea and Gomer's marriage was not as harmonious as chaps. 1 and 3 would lead us to believe. In fact

---

[9] Yee, "Gomer," 85.

[10] Patrick D. Miller, Jr. *Sin and Judgment in the Prophets: A Stylistic and Theological Analysis* (Chico, CA: Scholars Press, 1982), 7-20; reviews several passages in Hosea in which the conceptual, rhetorical, and correlational aspects of sin and corresponding punishment to demonstrate that "the prophet bears witness to the appropriate justice of God in his dealings with Israel" (7). Although Yahweh's response in punishment may be proper divine behavior, the ethical issue of the prophet or readers of Hosea modeling *all* of Yahweh's actions is not dealt with by Miller. On the complexity of Yahweh as a moral model for Old Testament ethics and other aspects of this difficult question see John Barton, "The Basis of Ethics in the Hebrew Bible," in *Understanding Old Testament Ethics: Approaches and Explorations* (Philadelphia: Westminster John Knox, 2003), 45-54.

[11] Frederick Buechner, *Peculiar Treasures: A Biblical Who's Who* (San Francisco: Harper, 1993), 47-49.

the threats and accusations of 2:4-15 show us the violent, highly erratic side of the otherwise obedient prophet."[12]

Not many commentators are as bold as Weems in characterizing Hosea's vulnerability within a metaphorical world, where his troubled marriage parallels that of Yahweh and Israel. Each has a historical reality, but each is related to the other metaphorically. In her words, "Does the fact that the marriage metaphor is 'only a metaphor' and the motif of sexual violence 'only a theme of the metaphor' insulate them from serious theological scrutiny?"[13] Metaphors work because two dissimilar items are related, the more familiar one used to give meaningful and instant insight into the other which is less familiar. Regarding the marriage metaphor of Hosea, Weems asks, What happens when "the reader becomes so engrossed in the pathos and details of the metaphor that the dissimilarities between the two are disregarded?"[14] What happens when the metaphor is taken literally, oversimplified, hinting that the husband act like God? One might ask, while reading Hosea, just how literally this prophet understood the metaphorical reality of his life? "In other words," says Weems, "to the extent that in our modern culture there are no circumstances under which physical violence [and verbal abuse] is acceptable in marriage,

---

[12] Renita Weems, "Gomer: Victim of Violence or Victim of Metaphor?" *Semeia: Interpretation for Liberation* 47 (1989): 96. See further Weems, *Battered Love: Marriage, Sex, and Violence in the Hebrew Prophets* (OBT; Minneapolis: Fortress, 1995) for a more complete discussion of the effects and implications of prophetic metaphors for unintended listeners and the surprising traits of Hosea's personality as a prophet.

[13] Weems, "Gomer," 100.

[14] Weems, "Gomer," 100. She founds her comments about metaphor on the work of Sallie McFague, *Metaphorical Theology: Models of God in Religious Language* (Philadelphia: Fortress, 1985). See also, J. Beekman and J. Callow, *Translating the Word of God* (Grand Rapids: Zondervan, 1979), particularly chapters 8 and 9 on metaphor and simile, 124-50.

the violent measures Hosea takes to chastise Gomer (should) pose a problem for the modern hearer."[15]

What are we to do with these feminist critiques and cautions about impending difficulties for living in Hosea 1-3, particularly the metaphorical tension related to God's sovereign behavior and its emphasis on sexual violence? A number of feminist Old Testament scholars have simply abandoned any attempt to stay very long in this text. They reject the male image of an inadequate god prone to sexual violence as one shaped by human attitudes and patriarchal cultural values. They charge us to find an image of God set free from these earthly trappings.[16] Is it possible to free the text of these problems or are we stuck?

Katharine Sakenfeld, in her now classic book on *hesed*, articulates the positive side of the marriage metaphor as employed by the prophet Hosea, particularly within the context and concerns of covenant loyalty. The emphasis in the metaphor, according to Sakenfeld, is on

> the everlasting loyalty of God the divine husband, whose ways are not like human ways, who is free to let go of Israel and start again, has not and will not let go. Here is the quintessential exercise of loyalty. The One who is forever free chooses to remain bound to this

---

[15] Weems, "Gomer," 101. On the challenges of preaching this text, see the outstanding contribution by Jeffrey Rogers, "Women in the Hands of an Abusive God? The Trouble with Hosea 2," in *Interpreting Hosea for Teaching and Preaching* (KC: Cecil P. Staton, Jr., ed.; Macon, GA: Smyth & Helwys, 1993), 33-45; and the entire issue of *Review and Expositor* 90 (1993) on Hosea.

[16] J. Cheryl Exum, *Plotted, Shot, and Painted: Cultural Representations of Biblical Women* (Sheffield: Sheffield Academic Press, 1996), whose comments on Yahweh as Israel's husband in Hosea are contained in a chapter called "Prophetic Pornography." She claims that even the sexual language used in Hosea has been toned down by most translators. At the other end of the theological spectrum is Raymond C. Ortland, Jr. *Whoredom: God's Unfaithful Wife in Biblical Theology* (Grand Rapids: Eerdmans, 1996), who responds to the feminist objections by dismissing most as deconstructionist attempts to find offense, where there is none, in the biblical text, and by calling gender-nuanced deconstruction cultural imperialism of Scripture (177-85).

weak and needy people, that they may bear witness
before all the nations that Yahweh alone is God. [17]

As we seek to live in this narrative, she cautions against
abusing the gender inequity of the metaphor and also points
out that men as well as women break marriage vows and that
wives as well as husbands are apt to demonstrate astonishing
loyalty. Certainly the imbalance created by a fixation on the
unfaithful wife in the prophetic marriage metaphor must be
corrected by the extraordinary aspects of Yahweh's emotively
gracious redemptive action and the biblical examples of female
faithfulness and devotion found in the book of Ruth and other
places. Just like the ancient characters, Hosea, Gomer, and
Israel, only by Yahweh's *hesed* can we reside in this story.

### Qumran Commentary on Hosea

There are at least two ancient ways of reading this text that
are instructive in light of the previous discussion for our effort
to live in Hosea 1-3. The first is 4QpHosea[a] from the Qumran
Scrolls and the second is a consideration of the dynamic strategy
established by Hosea 1-3 as the prologue for reading The Book
of the Twelve. Each of these sections will briefly introduce a
few ideas that further inform our reading before returning to a
more personal word about my living in Hosea.

Among the largest group of exegetical writings found
at Qumran are the biblical commentaries which, while
fragmentary, offer an idiosyncratic verse-by-verse interpretation
of selected prophetic books. In each case, the mysteries revealed
by the Old Testament prophets are brought to bear directly on
the history and circumstances of the Qumran community. The
Commentary on Habakkuk[18] describes the revelatory process,
from text to sermon:

And God told Habakkuk to write down the things that
are going to come to pass upon the last generation, but

---

[17] Katharine Doob Sakenfiled, *Faithfulness in Action: Loyalty in Biblical Perspective* (OBT; Philadelphia: Fortress, 1985), 68-70. See also the reprint *The Meaning of Hesed in the Hebrew Bible: A New Inquiry* (Eugene: Wipf & Stock, 2002)

[18] 1QpHab 7.1-5a.

the fulfillment of the period He did not make known to him. And when it says, "so that he can run who reads it," its interpretation concerns the Righteous Teacher, to whom God made known all the mysteries of the words of his servants the prophets.[19]

Thus, the Righteous Teacher interprets the lines he quotes from Hosea 2:6-12 in accordance with his divine charge. His commentary emphasizes a peculiarly biased description of the unfaithful, using words like blind, bewildered, treachery, led astray, forgetful, and disgraceful. On the other hand, the members of the Qumran community are characterized as already having turned from sin and wickedness. In their repentance, they are devoted to the teaching of the Righteous Teacher whose job, in addition to revealing the mysteries of God, is to preserve this faithful remnant community while it remains in the midst of the wicked world.

At the center of this interpretation is the identity and cause behind those who have been led astray,[20] a theme that receives considerable attention in the other prophetic commentaries in addition to those we find on Hosea. The blind and confused who have been led astray are, according to the other commentaries, enticed by a certain Man of the Lie or the Spouter of the Lie, who causes many to err, worship falsehood, and revile God's elect.[21] In other words, the reason for going astray is tied directly to the apparent opponent of the Righteous Teacher. While the chapter in Hosea offers no logical explanation for

---

[19] For translation and introduction to the Qumran Pesherim, see Maurya P. Horgan's work in *Pesherim, Other Commentaries, and Related Documents* (ed. James Charlesworth; vol. 6B in *The Dead Sea Scrolls: Hebrew, Aramaic, and Greek Texts with English Translations*, ed. James Charlesworth; Tübingen: Mohr Siebeck, 2002), 113-193.

[20] Although "being led astray" is explicitly stated in Hos 2, its concepts of harlotry, unfaithfulness, and abandonment of God, appear in a cluster in 4:12 that accentuate the cause and consequences of straying from God. The Qumran commentary on Hos 4 is not extant, but the Teacher of Righteousness may have associated these chapters as is suggested by his interpretive comments on chapter 2.

[21] 1QpHab 10.9; cf. 1QpHab 2.1-2, 5.10-11; 4QpPsa frgs. 1-10 1.26, 4.14; CD MS B 20.15.

Gomer/Israel's having gone astray, seeking other lovers, or her refusal to recognize Hosea/Yahweh's goodness, the Righteous Teacher's *pesher* interpretation clearly does. Both those who have gone astray and the Man of the Lie are opposed not only to him but to God (cf. Hos 7:13). Therefore they are blamed and destined to receive God's harshest judgment.

Unfortunately, the fragmentary condition of the Qumran Commentary doesn't include the second half of Hosea 2, which precludes a more balanced reading of this text. The Teacher's interpretation, however, is consistent with most of the other apocalyptically-oriented writings of Qumran and separates the community on the basis of purity and faithfulness from the rest of the world by establishing clear lines of division.[22] Consonant with this view, anyone led astray—for whatever reason—permanently plays the role of the unfaithful spouse, Gomer, an unrepentant sinner forever excluded from God's mercy. This reading also depicts an extreme position for the Qumran community, people who have already turned away from sin, as if they are the final remnant securely saved forever. There will be no second chances; expect only judgment for those who did/do not return. Indeed the age of God's wrath was imminent, but they had repented. According to the Qumran Commentary on Habakkuk, this is the authorized and true interpretation. But are we to live in the text of Hosea *this way*?

### *Hosea as a Preface to the Minor Prophets*

For another alternative, we turn to the group of Old Testament books recognized as the Minor Prophets, or to what I have mentioned above as The Book of the Twelve.[23] These are the prophetic books, beginning with Hosea and ending with

---

[22] On the apocalyptic worldview and religious ideas of the Qumran community see Geza Vermes, *The Complete Dead Sea Scrolls in English* (New York: Penguin Books, 1997), 67-90.

[23] On the range of issues and details of the discussion, see James D. Nogalski and Marvin A. Sweeney, eds., *Reading and Hearing the Book of the Twelve* (SBLSymS 15; Atlanta: Society of Biblical Literature, 2000).

Malachi.[24] Although there has been favorable scholarly debate about treating these twelve prophetic books as a single, unified biblical volume, none of the major commentaries on Hosea regard the first three chapters as having an introductory function beyond the book itself. Moreover, the majority of introductory books on The Book of the Twelve proposes for this collection various "catchword" schemes like "the day of Yahweh" but ignore what may work as a more persuasive unifying formula. Given these two observations, I contend that the book of Hosea serves a significant and intentional rhetorical function in its position at the beginning of The Book of the Twelve.

I object to the thematic phrase "day of Yahweh" holding these books together simply because the phrase is not found in the lead book Hosea. Immediately Amos, Joel, Zechariah, and Malachi come to mind—where Yahweh's day is either expected or threatening—but not the book of Hosea. Why would the compiler of The Book of the Twelve, if we can posit that there was someone who intentionally grouped them, begin with Hosea (specifically with Hosea 1-3) when this main theme is absent?[25] If there is an editorial intention behind the anthology of the Twelve, what is it and can it be found in the opening chapters of Hosea? Can it be found throughout the whole, and specifically, is it present in the closing verses of the concluding book, Malachi? Finally, if these elements can be discerned and articulated in a convincing way, might they help locate the focus and function of The Book of the Twelve for later audiences like us?

The opening line in Hosea, following the superscription

---

[24] On the canonical order and variation between the Masoretic Text and the Septuagint and the chronological order of composition see the helpful discussion and bibliography in Douglas Stuart, *Hosea-Jonah* (WBC 31; Waco, TX: Word, 1987), xlii-xlv.

[25] Gerlinde Baumann, "Connected by Marriage, Adultery and Violence: The Prophetic Marriage Metaphor in the Book of the Twelve and in the Major Prophets," (*SBLSP*; Atlanta: SBL, 1999), 552-69; promises more than she delivers by suggesting that the marriage metaphor is central in an explicit way to the structure of The Book of the Twelve. In the end, she dismisses it as integral to The Twelve and moves on to discuss the metaphor in Isaiah, Jeremiah, and Ezekiel.

in 1:1, reads as follows: "When Yahweh first spoke to Hosea, Yahweh said to Hosea, "Go, take for yourself a promiscuous wife and have children of promiscuity, because the land has turned from Yahweh in gross promiscuity."[26]

Although the word for turning is not used in this verse, it is implied—on the basis of its centrality, both in its positive and negative aspects throughout the book of Hosea. Indeed, in Hosea, the Hebrew word *shub* (meaning "to turn, return, repent") is used twenty-two times.[27] Its first occurrence is in 2:7 [Heb 2:9] where, like the prodigal son, Gomer/Israel may realize just how much better things were/will be when she returns to Hosea/Yahweh. The initial ideas of turn and return are repeated several times in the book and set up the final double plea in Hosea 14:1-2: "Return, O Israel, to Yahweh your God, for you have stumbled because of your iniquity. Take with you words and return to Yahweh; say to him 'Take away all iniquity; accept us graciously, for we offer the sacrifice of our lips.'" Even though, in 11:7, Israel is described as a "people bent on turning away," Yahweh declares that his own heart is turning against itself because he cannot bring himself to destroy his beloved nation (11:8).[28] In Hosea 14, Yahweh invites return and even choreographs the way it can take place. Moreover, in verse 4 he says, "I will heal their faithlessness; I will love them freely, for my anger has turned from them."

Elsewhere in The Book of the Twelve, the reciprocal nature of this concept of mutual return as restoration of covenant

---

[26] Translations of the biblical text are mine.

[27] William L. Holladay, *The Root SUBH in the Old Testament* (Leiden: Brill, 1958). The limits of this paper preclude a full display of the data and its discussion regarding the other key words that form a cluster that undergirds the central importance of *shub* in The Book of the Twelve. Additionally are *biqqesh* and *darash*. Rolf Rendorff, "How to Read the Book of the Twelve as a Theological Unity," in *Reading and Hearing the Book of the Twelve*, 86; mentions these significant words in passing related to a discussion on the "Day of the Lord," without pursuing broader connective implications.

[28] Heart imagery in Hosea is a significant structural and connective thread throughout the entire book: Hos 2:14; 4:11; 7:6, 11, 14; 10:2; 11:8; 13:6, 8. For this insight I am indebted to Royce Dickinson, whose sermon on Hos 1-3 "Heartbroken for the Heartless," appears elsewhere in this volume.

loyalty, rather than the enactment and fulfillment of covenant curses, is found in Zechariah 1:3 and Malachi 3:7: "Return to me and I will return to you, says Yahweh Sabaoth." Evidence of a faithful return to Yahweh lies in the outpouring of sincere speech—confession, praise, and a proper seeking after God that gratefully acknowledges who Yahweh has been and is within the covenant—and faithful, just action in demonstration of *hesed* both to God and to people.[29]

In the whole of The Twelve, the only book that explicitly lacks the word *shub* is Haggai. Nonetheless, one can argue, within the historical context of postexilic temple rebuilding, that the idea of reciprocal return is *the* pressing issue for the prophet Haggai, whose initial prophecy may have prompted the repentance of the people and returned them to the priority of building Yahweh's temple. If that is the case, it seems all the more appropriate that when Zechariah comes on the scene he uses the formulaic "Return to me and I will return to you" (Zech 1:3) "to remind the community from the outset that their repentance toward Yahweh was a prerequisite for his return to them."[30]

Haggai and Zechariah reminded postexilic Israel that return to the land didn't automatically and simultaneously mean a return to Yahweh. The Hebrew word for land is also one of the more significant words used within each book.[31] Remarkably, the opening verse in Hosea and the closing verse in Malachi, the bookends of this prophetic collection, refer to the land in a negative way, in close proximity to *shub*. First, Yahweh announces to Hosea that the land has turned from him in gross promiscuity. Finally, in Malachi, comes the declaration that Yahweh is sending the prophet Elijah as a forerunner to the great and terrible day of Yahweh's imminent destruction

---

[29] Hos 3:5; 5:15-6:3; 10:12; 12:6;14:1-7; Joel 2:12-29; Amos 9:11-15; Mic 6: 8; 7:18-20; Zech 7:8-14.

[30] Janet E. Tollington. *Tradition and Innovation in Haggai and Zechariah 1-8* (JSOTSS 150; Sheffield: Sheffield Academic Press, 1993), 203-5.

[31] Although *'eres* has been overlooked in attempts to justify a unified reading of The Twelve, it is used seventy-three times. Obadiah is the only book without it, using *sadeh* twice instead.

so that this prophet might reconcile (*shub*—turn/return) the hearts of the fathers to their children lest he smite the land with a curse. Often in The Twelve, the fate of the land is directly connected to Israel as people whose covenant fidelity or infidelity (turning faithfully to or from) determines whether it yields blessings or manifests a curse. Perceptively, Walter Brueggemann includes the land within the marriage imagery in Hosea, claiming that the prophet entwines "fertility images to speak of *covenantal* realities. And he announces by that odd and inventive combination of form and substance that the covenant is ended. It is voided, and with it the covenant gift, the land, is also forfeited. And the payoff is landlessness" (Hos 2:3).[32]

Faithful return to Yahweh not only turns away punishment and the threatened destruction of the land (and people), it may also restore the devastated land to conditions better than ever before (Hos 2:18-23; cf. 2:12 and 4:1-3). The consequence of covenant violations require Yahweh to take away his gift and cut off Israel.[33] The ebb and flow of Israel's history from the eighth century into the postexilic period, reflected across the span of The Book of the Twelve, focuses on charges of covenant infidelity and the landlessness of exile. Yahweh's recurring summons through these prophets is for Israel to return to him, a theme dramatically set forth in the opening book of Hosea and its prologue chapters 1-3. It is forcefully and finally spoken as a still open condition in the last verse of the last book. Apparently the change of loyalty on the part of Israel, demanded expectantly by Yahweh that he might return to her in mutual reconciliation, had not fully happened in Malachi's day. The contingent nature of this repentance and allegiance was more than even the postexilic community could actualize—despite the prophetic warnings that filled Israel's heritage.

---

[32] Walter Brueggemann, *The Land* (OBT; Philadelphia: Fortress, 1977), 104.

[33] It is questionable whether Yahweh really ever abided strictly by the so-called rules and consequences of the covenant, particularly given His emotional outbursts interspersed throughout the extended covenant lawsuit of Hos 4-14. In these specific places Yahweh as the magistrate prosecuting his people becomes the loving outspoken parent guilty of contempt of court. The same dynamic is found in chapter 2 where a sudden rhetorical shift takes place between judgmental threats and promise of renewal.

Among other things, The Book of the Twelve declares that
Yahweh's sovereignty as Israel's God of the covenant, who
judges even the Gentile nations according to his covenantal
justice, must be universally accepted and acknowledged.
This is particularly true for those in covenant relationship
with Yahweh. Israelites who claim covenant benefits must
reciprocate Yahweh's *hesed* in humility and justice. Yahweh's
promise to return to a wayward people is predicated on their
willingness to return to him first on his terms.

## My Life in the Text of Hosea

Allowing Hosea 1-3 to establish this message within the
book of Hosea and the Book of the Twelve changes the way one
lives in the narrative. Suddenly we are not siding with Hosea as
a flawlessly faithful husband who somehow matches Yahweh's
level of perfection as the Holy One of Israel. Nor are we
blatantly blaming or excluding those who have gone astray or
legitimizing private bouts of spousal abuse by making Hosea or
Yahweh a self-serving moral model. The rhetorical function of
Hosea 1-3 situates Yahweh—and us—in a much larger context
and opens the way for understanding the marriage metaphor
as one among many, but entirely rooted in and elevated to a
Yahwistic ideal for marriage: "in righteousness and in justice,
in *hesed*, and in mercy... in faithfulness" (Hos 2:19-20).[34] Have
you ever heard more lofty and more empowering marriage
vows than these?

<hr>

[34] In Hosea this list is preceded by the abolishment of war, and by extension
within the marriage metaphor, prior domestic violence, and is followed by a
covenant renewal ceremony equal to the exchange of wedding vows. The
list has certain affinities to the list of core adjectives that describe Yahweh's
character in Exod 34:6-7, which is repeated in various forms throughout The
Book of the Twelve and elsewhere in the Old Testament (Joel 2:13;Jonah 4:2;
Nah 1:3; Jer 32:18; Num 14:18; Pss 85:10-13; 86:5, 15; 103:8; 111:4; 112:4;
116:5; 145:8; Neh 9:17, 31; 2 Chr 30:9). See Walter Brueggemann, *Theology
of the Old Testament: Testimony, Dispute, Advocacy* (Minneapolis: Fortress,
1997), 215-28.

What if we fast-forward to the end... to read the final words of Hosea[35]... to gain perspective from the wise one who responded to the invitation of Yahweh to return... maybe it was only Hosea or maybe it included Gomer, and the kids... maybe... must we demand integrity and perfect obedience of prophets and preachers? Aren't our words wiser than our actual lives most the time?

As Hosea looks back over his life, where do the opening chapters of this prophetic book fit? In the end, did he cherish Gomer or hold a grudge against Yahweh for the commands to marry and to love? Does he mourn, over and over, the loss of the nation that he and God loved again in vain? Or was it really in vain? Did his kids gather round his deathbed to receive his blessing—or perhaps to bless him? Were they faithful in the end? Was Gomer faithful after 3:5? Did they flee together as a family in 721 B.C., retreating to Judah so Hosea could peacefully edit his prophetic memoirs?[36] Maybe it wasn't so peaceful after all. Did Hosea add the wisdom postscript to the end of his book in the later or last stages of his life as a reflective conclusion, an indication that in hindsight he could fully accept the will of God for his family and his nation? While his heart may have found peace finally in the infinite wisdom of God, he knew that Yahweh's heart would always turn upon itself in love for heartless people who tended to turn away from him in foolishness.

---

[35] C.L. Seow, "Hosea 14:10 and the Foolish People Motif," *CBQ* 44 (1982): 212-224; persuasively, and correctly, argues that the theme *foolish people* in Hosea is Hoseanic and central to the proper interpretation of the book. He also establishes irrefutably that the final verse belongs to Hosea. See further Seow, "Hosea," *Anchor Bible Dictionary* 3:291-97.

[36] A post-Samarian scenario that places the prophet Hosea in Jerusalem might also explain the Judean glosses throughout the book. See discussion by Hans Walter Wolff, *Hosea* (Hermeneia; Philadelphia: Fortress, 1974), 210-11; 224; and A.A. Macintosh, *Hosea* (ICC; Edinburgh: T&T Clark, 1997), lxx-lxxiv.

As I fast-forward my life to the end to look back reflectively with theological perspective, what will I see? I identify closely with Hosea's backward look: A man of letters who turns phrases... a man of passion and pathos who wears the heart of God on his sleeve... a man whose life is broken by the will of God... a fallible husband in a failing, topsy-turvy marriage... the father of three children whom he loved.

Only a handful of people know the details of my life. And it is not so much that you, the reader, need to know all the particulars. What is important to know is the fact that when I was ready to dissolve my marriage, I was immersed in Hosea, researching, writing, and teaching. In the midst of that study, although my life was not in sync with the prophet's, his words of lament allowed me to express my rage and confusion, and opened the way for reconciliation.[37] The resounding imperative "to love again," to love as God loves, became my directive for renewal. For days I fought the correlation. I resisted the idea that my life was mirrored in Hosea. I steeled my heart to the voice of God, the pathos of God, and the action of God in Hosea.[38] How could God be calling me to do such an illogical thing as forgive when I was the one wronged? Even my kids struggled with what I was willing to do. By the power and pathos of God,

---

[37] Dorothy Soelle, *Suffering* (Philadelphia: Fortress, 1975) 76, makes the point that one afflicted must find words to "express and identify his suffering." No one else can voice another's suffering, but where a person finds words to speak about the affliction does not matter. Hosea found words to express his anguish in those given to him by Yahweh, who voiced His own suffering through the prophet. Soelle claims that it is not enough for one to enter into dialogue with oneself, even though that will still take place. Thus, prayer, and specifically lament, have tremendous value for one to verbalize the experience of suffering in the process of liberation. For Hosea, this seems to take place in and through his delivery of the oracles to the nation; otherwise, Yahweh would not have commanded him to love Gomer again.

[38] Abraham Heschel, *The Prophets* (2 vols.; New York: Harper and Row, 1962), daringly suggested that God himself is capable of emotion, and in fact is more emotionally sensitive than human beings. In Heschel's words, "He is moved and affected by what happens in the world, and reacts accordingly" (2:4). Thus, "The prophet is guided not by what he feels, but by what God feels" (2:94). On the ontological necessity of prayer, see Heschel's *Quest for God: Studies in Prayer and Symbolism* (New York: Crossroad, 1987).

I loved Patti again. I didn't have to buy her out of bondage, and I didn't force restrictions on her life. Those pieces of the Hosea-Gomer story certainly don't apply. Neither did I cast her out into the wilderness, but there was a time of separation, seeking refuge, and existing in exile before her return. The whole experience was costly in every respect, but it seems that God somehow covered the expenses, even the emotional ones. All the anxiety of who knew, what they knew, and how they found out, all the ramifications and embarrassment surrounding the circumstances of teaching in a small Christian college and with friends in several churches, all that emotional uncertainty—God handled it all, when we could not. So many true friends emerged to support us and to encourage our life together. These important details, missing in the Hosea-Gomer story, are central to my living in their story. Surrounded by a strong community of faith— certainly not the case for Hosea and Gomer—proved to be essential for our relationship to survive and thrive in resurgence. We had spiritual mentors who exhorted, guided, and opened us to the therapeutic presence of the Spirit of God. The community context for our living in this story was essential.

Living in Hosea allowed me to embrace the call of God to love again and to embrace Patti in new ways; we didn't ignore our 27 years together but deepened our relationship with newfound commitment, respect, and loyalty. The breakdown was long in coming, and the precursors were there from the beginning. The issues were deep and complex, exploding destructively at the worst times. The healing process has been a divine one, of equal depth and complexity, but enriching and fulfilling, making the last few years the best. We didn't welcome the downfall, and we never anticipated how wonderful recovery would be.

Thus, Patti and I feel that it's wholly appropriate within this community of faith to share unashamedly this personal experience of living in Hosea 1-3, to bear witness to the powerful pathos of God in theological reflection of call, lament, and praise.

### A Personal Reflection on the Call of God

I heard God say "It is not good for you to be alone. I have called you to marry Patti, your dearest friend, that you and she may learn to love one another as I love, with a love full of compassion, loyalty, and forgiveness. You and she will be tempted and your love tried. Though I haven't told you yet, she struggles with self-esteem, commitment, and faithfulness. Her love will be intense; however, it will also be distracted, self-directed, and scattered. You are to love her as I love, that you and she may mature and be perfected in your experience of divine love. All this that you may know, with confidence and commitment, that I AM the God and Father of Jesus Christ who has called you and Patti to this marriage, to be one flesh, united in person and spirit. As you marry, your friends will remind you both of what covenant means through wedding songs and prayers, and through the exchange of vows. The words of pledge and promise will become words of purpose and possibility. Blessing and curse, fulfillment and failure await your marriage. Awake to the realities of a challenged relationship, one characterized by divine *hesed* at its core, but tested by the constant tug and torment of the real world. Shallow romance will turn to ruin overnight or over the course of twenty years. It will happen to you, but remember that I am with you, the model and source for the love necessary to be faithful, true, and steadfast. Look to me to endure the strain. Rest assured that I have struggled in my love for ancient Israel. You are not alone."

### A Lament for a Renewed Spirit (A prayer based on Hosea 1-3)

Remember, O Yahweh, how your servant has
been scorned.
Remember, O Yahweh, what has befallen me;
See my disgrace and weep.

I have been betrayed, but you command me to
love again;

I have been rejected, but you call me to redeem.
Your word goes out; it falls on ears and hearts
  that are dead.

My eyes are weary from watching in vain;
My lips are still because none will listen.
My heart is faint with crying to you.

Hear my prayer, O Yahweh,
Listen to my cry, for I call to you.

Remember my affliction and bitterness,
The spirit of my life is crushed within me.

My spirit is reduced to ashes;
Love has no soil in which to grow.

You are the ground upon which we stand.
You are the rain that soaks the hard earth.
Send forth nourishment to our spirits, broken and
  burdened.

Feed us with your love.
Then will I again love Patti, but our hearts
  are hard.
Then will love grow where there is no soil.

For you, O Yahweh, we wait.
Pour forth your *hesed*;
I know that your mercy does not fail.

Renew my spirit that I may hope again;
Restore my being for my hope is founded
  upon you.

Though Patti was unfaithful, I too have failed
  and am afraid.
And grief has overwhelmed me; grieving
  has beset us.

Can we again become faithful to you?
May we receive each other anew, as at first.

O Yahweh, my God, be our strength;
Continue your *hesed* to those who seek you,
    To those who seek you
To those who seek to do what is right.

Praise be to God for his marvelous grace!

### Conclusion

The scandalous claim of Hosea 1-3—its invitation to partner in prophetic pathos with the God who bears his heart, its emotional capacity that far exceeds ours, and its invitation of reciprocal return—requires us to love the same heartless, unlovable people to whom God has committed himself, including us. What you have read here, you know from experience. We have listened and learned from several interpreters, who as the called of God, attempted to live in this text for the sake of community. From feminists we understand why we cannot manipulate metaphors to legitimize our actions as if we ourselves have the sovereign freedom of the Holy One. From them we discovered that the parabolic key to understanding this text is Yahweh's extreme loyalty, his hesed, which is to be reciprocated if healthy lasting relationships are expected. By counter-example, we learned from the Righteous Teacher at Qumran not to read this text as justification to blame or exclude others in such a way as to distance them from God's redemptive love. We know that even those who go astray can be redeemed ultimately and that no one exceeds the reach of the God who ever calls us and seeks to love us to his own hurt. Now we are aware that the marriage metaphor of Hosea 1-3, and its emphasis on the transformative potential of mutual return, opens a wider rhetorical door to The Book of the Twelve. From that enlarged theological and historical context, we have insight into the pressing need to make this truth reality—urgently, personally, and communally. In sharing my marital pilgrimage into the depths of Hosea 1-3 and the pathos of God. I urge you to take seriously the claim of the text that we who would proclaim the gospel of redemptive love from Hosea must first accept God's call and with God to enter the painful expression of lament, which always seems to be an essential part of prophetic life.

# 5

# *Re-imagining the Future:*

## Past Tense Words in a Present Tense World

Timothy Sensing

The question of how to preach eighth century prophetic literature is a hermeneutical question involving how we understand the Bible as Christian Scripture on behalf of the church. The following proposal re-examines preaching eighth century prophets by exploring how the Bible itself interprets older prophetic literature for the community of faith in a new generation, particularly how one sixth century prophet, Zechariah, appropriated and preached the eighth century tradition to address his present situation in order to shape his audience's future. Zechariah's hermeneutical and homiletical practices—using the past to speak to the present and alter the future's possibilities—can serve as a model for our own preaching. Using Scripture's theological re-appropriation of itself as a prototype for our own preaching is an act of taking the Bible seriously. We respect Scripture, as Richard Lischer puts it, by "proclaiming the gospel in texts, by means of texts, and in faithfulness to texts."[1]

Lischer proposes that preachers exchange the existential and individualistic language event[2] and embrace community

---

[1] Richard Lischer, *A Theology of Preaching: The Dynamics of the Gospel* (Durham: The Labyrinth Press, 1992), 5, 14. See also, Walter Brueggemann. "The Social Nature of the Biblical Text for Preaching," in Arthur Van Seters, *Preaching as a Social Act: Theology and Practice* (Nashville: Abingdon, 1988), 128 and Richard Hays, *Echoes of Scripture in the Letters of Paul* (New Haven: Yale University Press, 1989), 66.

[2] See also, Charles L. Campbell, *Preaching Jesus: New Directions for Homiletics in Hans Frei's Postliberal Theology* (Grand Rapids: Eerdmans, 1997).

formation. Likewise, preachers should leave behind illustration, welcoming narrative that gives an identity and mission to God's people. Finally, preachers should discard the hermeneutical metaphor of translation[3] and recover the performance nature of Scripture enacted in worship and witness. Lischer's proposal accords with The Second Helvetic Confession,[4] *the preached word of God is the Word of God.* Preaching is the Word of God in that it participates in God's purpose, is initiated by Christ, and is supported by the Spirit within community and in the world. The Word creates, transforms, establishes, and preserves the people of God.[5]

However, the proverbial gap[6] between the world of the Bible and our world has enticed biblical preachers to attempt to bridge the gulf by using various historical-critical methods without regard to how Scripture functions normatively in the life of the church or how biblical authors themselves normatively used scripture. Historical analysis of texts has only caused the gap to widen.[7] As a viable means to traverse the hermeneutical

---

[3] David H. Kelsey, *Proving Doctrine: The Uses of Scripture in Modern Theology* (Harrisburg, PA: Trinity Press International, 1999), 185-192. Similar critique could be given to the metaphor "bridge." If not translation or bridge, then what models or metaphors best describe the hermeneutical enactment between text, preacher, and congregation? Utilizing multiple models and metaphors keeps the process dynamic. I have utilized "enactment", "horizons", "spirals/helix", "contextualization", "dialogue", "triangulation", "critical correlation", "transaction", "witness", and "trifocals" to name a few.

[4] "The Second Helvetic Confession," *The Book of Confessions, The Constitution of the Presbyterian Church (USA), Part I* (Louisville: The Office of the General Assembly, 1996), 5.004, 55.

[5] Nicholas Lash, "Performing the Scriptures," in Richard Lischer, *The Company of Preachers: Wisdom on Preaching, Augustine to the Present* (Grand Rapids: Eerdmans, 2002). See also Stephen E. Fowl & L. Gregory Jones, *Reading in Communion: Scripture & Ethics in Christian Life* (Grand Rapids: Eerdmans, 1991), 62.

[6] George A. Lindbeck, "Scripture, Consensus and Community," *The Church in a Postliberal Age*, ed by James J. Buckley (Grand Rapids: Eerdmans, 2002), 211.

[7] Fowl & Jones, *Reading in Communion*, 61. Their proposal that "discontinuities are not historical but moral and theological" rings true for Zechariah's community that is still dealing with the nature of true fasting as it relates to social justice and the inbreaking of God's Kingdom.

divide, Zechariah embraces the performance of Scripture in conversation with the past, present, and future.

## The Prophets as Interpreters

God sent prophets because of unprecedented upheavals in the political, military, economic, and social situations in Israel, especially those connected to a series of catalysts (722, 587, 538 B.C.). As Israel progressively moved from God's covenant to worship other gods, religious upheaval grew. Finally, shifts in population and national boundaries led to constant unsettled conditions. Israel's pre-understandings of the nature of their covenant and position in the land came under scrutiny by their experiences. The people needed a Word from the Lord, a reminder, so that God's covenant society could be preserved. If the society would not respond to the message, then God would punish them for violating the covenant. Even then, God would not leave them, for he would reestablish his covenant in the future.

The prophets were conditioned by the old traditions of the Torah. They re-interpreted these traditions by applying them to their present times. The prophets modified the traditions because of the new situations within which they found themselves. New situations opened up fresh possibilities of understanding old traditions. Subsequently, the message of the prophets emerged as a forging interplay of three factors: (1) the ancient covenant traditions of Israel's election and land promise; (2) God's new word for Israel today; and (3) the concrete realities of some particular situation.[8]

Prophets exhorted reformation not innovation, confrontation not creation, revival not change. Therefore, preservation of the tradition was central as they reapplied the covenant to new situations, re-envisioning the present in light of the past in order to ensure future fidelity. The prophets saw God doing a new thing in the land. Prophets were not interested in the future generally, but rather focused on the activity of God in the present. Torah

[8] For a fuller argument see, Tim Sensing, "A Call to Prophetic Preaching," *Restoration Quarterly* 41 (Third Quarter 1999): 139-154.

traditions were not timeless truths abstracted out of context but rather expressions of God's past and future activity among his people. The new action of God in the land revolved around a restoration of his original intent for his community.

The capacity of the text to communicate a message to the community creates an enactment rather than a translation. An enactment is more than just explaining or reiterating the texts at hand or correlating the text by analogy to experience; instead, it allows these texts to speak a present tense word. Thus, Zechariah recalled the Torah, the old traditions of Israel's faith, and the words of "former prophets" as he addressed present situations in order to create a possible new future. When the Word of God comes alive, a change of existence for the community is possible, enabling the listening community to move from unbelief to faith.

When preachers today face the pressing issues of the congregation and the larger society, they can preach a similar prophetic Word. Prophetic preaching has the potential to transform the lives of people as they struggle to face the everyday challenges in a swirling society. To accomplish transformation, however, the sermon must first be rooted in the tradition of the congregation's historic faith. Next, the message must be theologically informed. Furthermore, present issues must be interpreted in the context of faith and theology. Finally, the preacher will envision for the audience God's intended future that can be presently realized. In other words, the prophetic sermon disorients the status quo by addressing present issues with a Word of God so that a new orientation (reality) can be created in the lives of people. The new and future Word will faithfully represent the old Word in the turbulent present. Preachers, who presume to do more—or less—lose their credibility if not their authority. Properly understood, prophetic preaching will be as demanding, threatening, rebuking, encouraging, and promising today as it was then.

Zechariah's sermon in chapters 7 and 8 is used below as a homiletical model. Although any of the Twelve could have been chosen, for they all rely intertextually on former traditions in Scripture, Zechariah was chosen due to his explicit references to the "former prophets." Zechariah didn't invent the process of using older texts in order to address his community;[9] he inherited this hermeneutical tradition. And I propose that Zechariah serves as a model of how the Bible itself provides its own interpretive framework. I am adapting Craddock's famous line, "The question is not how to preach the Bible, but how does the Bible preach?" by asking, "The question is not how do we interpret the eighth century prophets for preaching, but how does the Bible itself interpret these texts?" So, how then can we let these texts interpret us? How can we preach eighth century prophetic literature? Let us look to a sixth century interpreter and preacher, Zechariah, and see how he did it.

### Zechariah's Gospel (Zechariah 7-8)

Have you seen the McDonald's shake commercial? The little daughter won't quit chattering until mom and dad buy her a McDonald's shake. You've been in that car, haven't you? Remember traveling down the highway, keeping time to a chorus of voices, "Are we there yet?" It is the constant question of a people traveling on a journey: "Are we there yet? What town is this? When will we get there? How long has it been?"

Zechariah partners with Yahweh to assist bringing about the new community fit for the new age promised by the earlier prophets. Zechariah believes that the return from exile and the rebuilding of the temple will inaugurate God's eschatological future. Zechariah looks back at an earlier era, the time of the former prophets. He understands the exile to have been the fulfillment of their words and declares that he and his fellow Jews now stand at the threshold of the new era.

> The Lord was very angry with your forefathers. Therefore tell the people: This is what the Lord Almighty says: 'Return to me,' declares the Lord Almighty, 'and I will return to you,' says the Lord

---

[9] Rex Mason, *Preaching the Tradition: Homily and Hermeneutics After the Exile* (Cambridge: Cambridge University Press, 1990), 203, 290, fn17. See also Michael Fishbane, *Biblical Interpretation in Ancient Israel* (Oxford: Clarendon, 1985), 7.

Almighty. Do not be like your forefathers, to whom
the earlier prophets proclaimed: This is what the Lord
Almighty says: 'Turn from your evil ways and your evil
practices. But they would not listen or pay attention to
me,' declares the Lord. Where are your forefathers
now? And the prophets, do they live forever? But did
not my words and my decrees, which I commanded
my servants the prophets, overtake your forefathers?
... Are these not the words the Lord proclaimed
through the earlier prophets when Jerusalem and its
surrounding towns were at rest and prosperous, and
the Negev and the western foothills were settled? ...
They made their hearts as hard as flint and would not
listen to the law or the words that the Lord Almighty
had sent by his Spirit through the earlier prophets. ...
You who now hear these words spoken by the prophets
who were there when the foundation was laid for
the house of the Lord Almighty, let your hands be
strong so that the temple may be built. (Zech 1:2-6b;
7:7, 12; 8:9)

The paralleling phrases "my words," "decrees," "law,"
"words that the Lord almighty sent," and "words spoken" imply
that the prophetic word was now regarded as authoritative
teaching on a par with Torah. Zechariah alludes to Hosea and
Joel and echoes Amos and Micah.[10] Zechariah has a Bible, a
canon, a body of Scripture that functions as an authoritative
and reliable tradition. The tradition acts as testimony to a faith
and practice that allows the emergence of a new understanding
of his present context. He is not translating the text from then
to now, correlating the text by way of analogy, or explaining
the former prophets. Rather, he proclaims the former words

---

[10] Specifically, allusions to Hos 14:1-4 and Joel 2:12-13 are in Zech 1:3 and
echoes of Amos 2:6; 3:14; 5:5-6 and Mic 6:8 are found in Zech 7:8-10. Mason
examines Zechariah 7 finding from the former prophets allusions and common
verbal images in Hos 13:3; Jer 3:19; 19:4; 23:19; 25:32; 44:3; Am 1:14; Ez 32:
9; Isa 29:6; Deut 29:25; 32:17; 2 Chron 29:8; 30:7. (Mason, *Preaching*, 218).
Zechariah's references to the former prophets meets all seven of Hays' criteria
to identify and interpret intertextual echoes. (*Echoes*, 29-31).

as his word in order to reshape his community. Even though Zechariah's and the former prophets' message are the same, the contexts are different, the intents are different, and the responses are different. The former prophets' words bring devastation; Zechariah creates hope.

Israel's exile ended with the return of God's people from Babylon. Soon after, during the temple rebuilding, Zechariah receives night visions full of hope and promise concerning what God is already doing in the new age at hand.

> The riders of the horses proclaimed, "We have gone throughout the earth and found the whole world at rest and peace." And God declared, "I will return to Jerusalem with mercy, and there my house will be rebuilt ... my towns will again overflow with prosperity, and the Lord will again comfort Zion and choose Jerusalem." "Jerusalem will be a city without walls because of the great number of men and livestock in it. And I myself will be a wall of fire around it," declares the Lord, "and I will be its glory within." "Shout and be glad, O Daughter of Zion. For I am coming, and I will live among you," declares the Lord. (Zech 1:11b, 16; 2:4-5, 10)

But the question persists, WHEN? Are we there yet? When will peace and prosperity come again to the land? The first night vision raises the question of the delay of the promise: "How long will you withhold mercy from Jerusalem and the cities of Judah, with whom you have been angry these seventy years" (Zech. 1:12). WHEN? The world Zechariah envisions doesn't correspond to the reality the people experience.

The tension of WHEN runs throughout Scripture. In the life of Abraham and Sarah, wondering about not only when would their offspring be like the stars of the sky, but when would they have even one child? And in the days of Judges as they asked, "When will we get a king?" The Psalmist and Habakkuk both sing the chorus, "How Long, O Lord, How Long?" The woman at the well expresses the tension when she says, "I know the Messiah is coming. When he comes, he will proclaim everything to us" (John 4:25). And in the early church, scoffers say "Where is this 'coming' he promised? Ever since our fathers died, everything goes on as it has since the beginning of creation" (1 Pet 3:4). The tension of WHEN is felt when those under Roman persecution cry out "Maranatha, Come Lord Jesus!"

Are We There Yet? We know the tension of WHEN—

• Each time a baby cries in a neonatal intensive care...

• Each time a husband calls the shelter stalking his wife...

• Each time a mother receives a visit from the White House about her child who died for peace...

• When hospice takes up residence in the next room...

• Job contentment, marriage satisfaction, a rebellious child...

• And in the church, when the gospel falls on deaf ears, when a community suffers a natural disaster and the church has no hands to help, when one speaks falsely about another, or when grumbling overtakes rejoicing.

We know the tension of WHEN. When will rest, peace, and the joy of our salvation return? When? Such a simple question—the same question Zechariah asks, "Should I mourn and fast in the fifth month, as I have done for so many years?" (7:3)

According to 2 Kings 25:8-9, Jerusalem falls in the fifth month. For 70 years, the lamentations and fasting beseech the throne of God on behalf of the land, Jerusalem, and the people. And during their exile, the prophets proclaim a coming age of grace, a time when a remnant of the people will return to the land. Now with the return of the prophets Haggai and Zechariah, the temple itself is under reconstruction. And in the second year of that reconstruction process, about halfway through, a delegation comes asking "Should I mourn and fast in the fifth month, as I have done for so many years?" Or deeper still, "Is rebuilding the temple the dawning of a new age?" If the temple is being rebuilt, then why are we still suffering the consequences of God's judgment? Shouldn't we be seeing God's restored kingdom with a son of David on the throne? But we see no evidence of God's action. "How long, O Lord, how long?" Such a simple question, "Are we there yet?" WHEN? Lingering underneath the surface is a complexity of issues.

When we ask the question "WHEN?" we believe God's Word still speaks. The oracles of Zechariah refer repeatedly to the "former" or "earlier" prophets. In the former days, during periods of prosperity, when Jerusalem and the surrounding towns were at rest, the prophets spoke. But the question "Shall we mourn?" is about the present life of the community of faith. The question asks whether the present is determined by the past.

The delegation's question affords Zechariah the opportunity to interpret the past, present, and future of God's intent for his people. He reminds them of the words of Torah spoken by the former prophets: "Render true judgments, show kindness and mercy to one another; do not oppress the widow, the orphan, the alien, or the poor; and do not devise evil in your hearts against one another" (Zech 7:9-10). However, the people didn't listen in those former days. The God of the past who had brought prosperity also brought judgment. Consequently, the land of prosperity became desolate. Zechariah continues:

> They refused to listen, and turned a stubborn shoulder, and stopped their ears in order not to hear. They made their hearts adamant in order not to hear the law and the words that the Lord of hosts had sent by his spirit through the former prophets. Therefore great wrath came from the Lord of hosts. Just as when I called they would not hear, so, when they called, I would not hear, says the Lord of hosts, and I scattered them with a whirlwind among all the nations that they had not known. Thus the land they left was desolate, so that no one went to and fro, and a pleasant land was made desolate. (Zech 7:11-14)

Their problem is not exegetical, but moral.

Formerly, in the eighth century, they rejected the instruction of grace that would have created a healthy and whole community, a community of shalom. Why? Why would they reject instructions concerning compassion, hospitality, fairness, and mercy? Incredible! Both then and now, concern for the widow, the orphan, the stranger, and the poor has always been part of God's covenant. Anyone should be able to recognize that a community's well-being is dependent upon the health of all its residents, from the least to the privileged. It's almost unbelievable that people both then and now reject justice, mutuality, and forgiveness. That's what makes its rejection all the more reprehensible.

Nineteen times throughout the sermon in chapters 7 and 8, either the messenger formula ("thus says Yahweh of hosts"), the revelation formula ("the word of Yahweh came to ..."), or the oracle formula ("Says Yahweh") constitutes Zechariah's understanding of the continuation and authority of the prophetic tradition to interpret the present in light of the past to reorient the future. Zechariah speaks prophetically; he speaks as a prophet by quoting the prophets:[11] "For thus says the Lord of hosts: Just as I purposed to bring disaster upon you, when your ancestors provoked me to wrath, and I did not relent, says the Lord of hosts, so again I have purposed in these days to do good to Jerusalem and to the house of Judah" (Zech 8: 14). Zechariah's words are not a reiteration of the words of old, but a reversal. The shalom of old is restored; God's future begins now.

And the message of the earlier prophets now becomes his message. For Zechariah, *The preached word of God is the Word of God*. The old call of Torah to the ancestors to live in the future as God's intended covenant community still lives in the present tense, calling Zechariah's church into that same named future. Zechariah's words are performative, in that they create a reality not yet experienced.

---

[11] Ben C. Ollenburger, *The Book of Zechariah*, NIB vol. VII (Nashville: Abingdon, 1996), 793.

Although the former prophets passed from the scene, God's Word remains alive. Rex Mason states, "The whole passage illustrates the fact that later dependence on earlier prophecy sprang not from slavish imitation but from living faith in the continuing relevance and vitality of the word of God."[12] The Word of God by the former prophets continues to speak to them about what God has done, was doing, and will do. Zechariah preaches the Word of the former prophets because that Word is still alive. Their words still have power. It still speaks to God's people. New occasions demand new interpretations, not repetition but re-appropriation. Zechariah reshapes the issues to address a new time.

Mason continues, "Such a homiletical practice serves at least three purposes. It explains why the promises of the prophets have not yet been fully experienced; it puts the stress on moral regeneration which is where the preacher believed it must be; and it serves to keep hope and faith alive in face of any temptation to despair and disillusion."[13]

So when we ask "WHEN?" and "Are we there yet?" we recognize we're asking the question that people in covenant community with God, who have been traveling that road, on that journey, have been asking a long time. And his Word of grace and judgment still speaks authoritative words to us. It is a Word that is still living, active, and speaking today. Therefore, as a response to God's grace,

> This is what the Lord Almighty says: 'Administer true justice; show mercy and compassion to one another. Do not oppress the widow or the fatherless, the alien or the poor. In your hearts do not think evil of each other.' ... These are the things you should do: Speak the truth to each other, and render true and sound judgment in your courts; do not plot evil against your neighbor, and do not love to swear falsely. I hate all this, declares the Lord. (Zech 7:8-10; 8:16-17)

---

[12] Rex Mason, *The Books of Haggai, Zechariah and Malachi* (Cambridge: Cambridge University Press, 1977), 33.

[13] Mason, *Preaching*, 224.

A response to God's coming creates a community that practices authentic justice, exhibits mutuality and compassion, does not defraud the socially vulnerable, and does not plot each other's harm. "Love is patient, love is kind. It does not envy, it does not boast, it is not proud." Love does not discount people because of the language they speak or the gray in their hair. "It is not rude, it is not self-seeking, it is not easily angered, and it keeps no record of wrongs." Love does not honor one gender over the other and keeps no record of one's economic value. Love protects the child and the disabled. "Love does not delight in evil but rejoices with the truth. It always protects, always trusts, always hopes, and always perseveres." And love is strong, strong enough to bend at the knees and strong enough to extend the hand of welcome and of grace. Love never fails.

God's grace calls us "to be strong" (Zech 8: 10, 13c). As Zechariah calls his people "to be strong and not afraid" and not to interrupt the journey of rebuilding the temple but to continue to strive to join in God's salvation, so too God's Word calls us to partner with God's activity in the world to bring about his kingdom reign on earth as it is in heaven.

These social practices give us, the community of God, the opportunity to respond in kind to the grace God extends to us. As God's community, the church, we become a neighbor, mother and father, brother and sister, to the citizens of this larger society. However, if we reject practicing shalom, we reject the grace that lies at the heart of God and in so doing become a people of desolation.

So finally comes the answer to the question asked by the delegation—or in reality not an answer but a reversal. Fast days of mourning will become seasons of celebration: "Once again men and women of ripe old age will sit in the streets of Jerusalem ... The city streets will be filled with boys and girls playing there. ... The fasts ... will become joyful and glad occasions and happy festivals for Judah. Therefore love truth and peace" (8:4-5, 18-19). In the past, God's Word involved a reversal from prosperity to adversity, but now the future involves a reversal from fasts to feasts! God's return to Jerusalem inaugurates the beginning of the future *now*.

Can you imagine what such a community would look like?
How would the people around us respond? A vision of God's
coming reign is like a public park where old men and women
can sit together, talk, and bask in the sun. And little children
can play in safety with nothing to threaten them, no one lurking
in the shadows to lure them with candy, no drug dealer waiting
to peddle his poison to innocents, no child bruised or warped
by abusive parents, no people stunted by poor nutrition or
inadequate education, not even a bully among the group to
terrorize the younger and weaker.[14]

A child peacefully at play in a park—of such is the Reign
of God. This is a picture of this world made new by the coming
of God—its goodness confirmed and restored to that wholeness
that its creator intended for it from the beginning. And when we
think to join cause with God's purpose for his earth, we need to
ask ourselves if we are constructing a place where little children
may play. God's kingdom will not have come on this earth until
its streets are fit for its children. But by the same token, it will
not have come until its children are fit for its streets.

Maybe, just maybe our neighbors would join us on the
journey. Listen to Zechariah envision what God's reign would
look like in the future.

> Thus says the Lord of hosts: Peoples shall yet come,
> the inhabitants of many cities; the inhabitants of one
> city shall go to another, saying, "Come, let us go to
> entreat the favor of the Lord, and to seek the Lord
> of hosts; I myself am going." Many peoples and
> strong nations shall come to seek the Lord of hosts
> in Jerusalem, and to entreat the favor of the Lord.
> Thus says the Lord of hosts: In those days ten men
> from nations of every language shall take hold of
> a Jew, grasping his garment and saying, "Let us go
> with you, for we have heard that God is with you"
> (Zech 8:20-23).

Imagine people coming to us and asking "Come, let us go
to entreat the favor of the Lord, and to seek the Lord of hosts."

---

[14] The image of the park comes from Elizabeth Achtemeier. *Nahum-Malachi*
(Atlanta: John Knox, 1986).

As a result of God's restoration in Christ, we are renewed, and we become the light unto the nations. A true sign of the age to come is for a people who love truth and live for peace to be a blessing to the nations. And those around us would know we are Christians by our love as we live such inviting lives that people long to receive with us the blessings of the kingdom. And as they see us traveling the roads of the kingdom, they will want to travel with us. Not to be with us, but to "entreat the Lord and seek the Lord Almighty."

And no one will ask, "Are we there yet?" For the road itself will be a kingdom journey. And we will realize that it has always been more about the journey than the destination. Eternal life is an ongoing life, not a stopping place. The reign of God to come is already coming, and is now here—a dynamic place open to possibilities.

I know a church, a church that participates in feeding homeless folks and victims of HIV. I know a church, a church that nurtures and challenges, through support groups, those addicted to the clutches of sin. I know a church, a church that provides shelter to unwed mothers and to families without a place to lay their heads. I know a church, a church that cares for children from MOPS to scouts, from clubs to classes. I know a church, a church that reaches out with the gospel on mission trips, to prisons, apartment complexes, and by the airwaves. I know a church, a church that provides mentoring couples to newlyweds, pastoral care in abundance and prayer everywhere one turns. I know a church, a church that gathers each Sunday to praise God, bless children, baptize believers, and feast at his table.[15]

"Are we there yet?" Not just yet. But God's kingdom is very near, closer than ever before. When will God pour out his blessings? Look around! The future is now. The kingdom of God is among you. As we gather every Sunday, around the Lord's Table, he opens his hands wide, saying "This is not a table of fasting, but a feast of grace. A table where everyone is

---

[15] This concretization comes from a sermon preached at the Highland Church of Christ, Abilene, TX, July 28, 2002. The ministries described in the paragraph mirror Highland's ministries.

welcomed without partiality until he comes." And people will say, "Let us go with you, because we have heard that God is with you."[16]

---

[16] The explanation of what Zechariah is doing hermeneutically with the eighth prophetic literature has now been fully transformed into a present tense message for the 21st century. This essay attempts to conclude by doing homiletically what was discovered exegetically that Zechariah did.

# 6

# Exploring Preaching's Voices from Ex Cathedra to Exilic

Robert Stephen Reid

As Walter Wangerin, Jr. shares the memory in *Miz Lil &
the Chronicles of Grace*, the matriarch of the congregation was
before him in the Sunday morning greeting line when he got
up the nerve to ask the question. What had she meant with her
distinctions between Sundays "you say I teach" and Sundays
"you say I preach?"

> Now Miz Lillian was holding my hand in hers, which
> was work hardened, her little finger fixed forever
> straight, unable to bend. "When you teach," she said,
> instructing me, "I learn something for the day. I can
> take it home and, God willing, I can do it. But when
> you preach—" She lowered her voice and probed me
> deeper with her eyes. "God is here. And sometimes
> he's smiling," she said, "and sometimes he's
> frowning surely."[1]

Miz Lillian was keenly aware, probably even more than her
preacher, of the different *voices* he assumed when he stepped
to the pulpit. Initially, he was pleased with her response until
her husband, Douglas, stepped before him and, as if to soften
the blow, shrugged out the words apologetically, "Just one o'
them things."

---

[1] Walter Wangerin, Jr., *Miz Lil & the Chronicles of Grace* (San Francisco:
Harper and Row, 1988), 37.

Wangerin thought he preached sermons. Miz Lillian had just informed him something more significant was occurring. Some sermons are just that—sermons that provide answers and insights that help her to learn. Other sermons facilitate encounters with God. But Douglas' embarrassment catches up with this minister and all who preach in its judgment. Sometimes God comes approving of the way the sermon names God and names grace; other times God comes saddened with the sermon's meager potential for grace and faith. Wangerin thinks he's preaching sermons, but this day he learns that sometimes the voice with which he preaches is his only, sometimes it has the potential to be the voice of God, and yet other times it's something less than the voice of God. So he was learning—learning how to speak the language of faith and grace for the life of this inner city Christian community.[2]

Obviously, I am using the word *voice* to describe something more than mere homiletic articulation in delivery[3] or the preacher's ability to write and speak for the listener's ear.[4] This notion of *voice* has to do with *identity*—who is speaking— and the identity of the group that *voice* constructs as its implied listeners—who is responding.[5] Literary critics employ the term to name the implied identity of the author who tells the story. *Voice* describes a dialogic experience of identity creation between author and audience, sometimes embedded more in the experience than the expression of the story. It answers the

---

[2] Observant readers might question this reading of Miz Lil's words, but Douglas' apologetic alerts us as it does Wangerin, that God's 'frowning' may have multiple layers of meaning. As will become apparent in what I have to say, I choose to explore the ambiguity of her words to redescribe the possibilities of conceiving what counts as her experience of his authenticity in preaching.

[3] See Charles L. Bartow, *The Preaching Moment: A Guide to Sermon Delivery* (Dubuque: Kendall/Hunt, 1995).

[4] See G. Robert Jacks, *Just Say the Word: Writing for the Ear* (Grand Rapids: Eerdmans, 1996).

[5] For differences in voice as male or female preached identity see Catherine Agnes Ziel, "Mother Tongue/Father Tongue: Gender-Linked Differences in Language Use and Their Influence on the Perceived Authority of the Preacher," Ph. D. diss., Princeton Theological Seminary, 1991.

question 'who speaks?' regardless of the point-of-view of any characters within a tale. Applied to the present context, *voice* is embodied in three dimensions of preaching identity. First, it becomes embodied in the identity assumed by the one who speaks—the preacher. Second, it becomes embodied in the way this *voice* calls listeners into its confidence—the constructed identity of the responding listeners. And, third, as Miz Lillian reminds us, that embodiment can be experienced as so authentic, it can become a third identity—the embodiment of *voice* as Word of God.[6]

Voice matters. Whether the preacher adopts the voice of one who speaks an authoritative answer *ex cathedra* or speaks with the voice of an exilic prophet daring to offer "decentered truths for decentered people," authenticity of voice involves a negotiation of assumptions about the nature of language and the nature of authority. Of course, voice can be examined as a negotiation of the intersection between other tensions such as the sermon's "divine expression" versus its "scandalous fleshiness."[7] Or it can be examined as a dimension of the sermon's bases of persuasive appeal, its strategy of communication, its homiletic theology. All are relevant to understanding voice. They also tend to be treated as dimensions of the general art of preaching in other homiletic resources. My argument is that authenticity of voice is more likely to be experienced by listeners if preachers learn to turn an intuitive understanding of voice into an explicitly employed rhetorical resource.

In what follows I begin to differentiate the emergent post-liberal approach to preaching from New Homiletic and other, more established conceptions of the task. My examination of these approaches reveals that they are grounded in different assumptions about the natures of language and authority. Four voices that represent preaching options in contemporary North

---

[6] David Buttrick, *A Captive Voice: The Liberation of Preaching* (Louisville: Westminster/John Knox, 1994), 32.

[7] Andre Resner, "At Cross Purposes: Gospel, Scripture and Experience in Preaching" *Preaching Autobiography: Connecting the World of the Preacher and the World of the Text,* David Fleer and Dave Bland, Eds. (Abilene: ACU, 2001), 47-74.

American homiletics are identified. Then, in keeping with the current Rochester Seminar's interest in preaching the eighth Century Prophets, I provide analysis of four exemplars of these voices based on sermons from Amos.

## Beyond the New Homiletic

David Fleer, Jeff Bullock, and I published a brief essay canvassing contemporary options in what we termed the "New Homiletic" in 1995.[8] It offered a survey of the homiletic practice of Craddock, Lowry, Mitchell, and Buttrick with a view to discovering the productive unity of their approaches to preaching. We concluded that these methods shared a common attention to the interpretive experience of listeners, what Thomas Long had already described as a "listener-driven" approach to preaching that invites "listeners to get in on the act and to join with the preacher in the creation of meaning."[9] Gene Lowry challenges our conclusion, claiming that sermon "shape" (the *strategy* by which a sermon is configured by a plotted sequence), rather than the listener's experience of a narrative or imaged sermon, was the productive unity of the New

---

[8] Robert S. Reid, Jeffrey Bullock, and David Fleer, "Preaching as the Creation of an Experience: The Not-So-Rational Revolution of the New Homiletics," *The Journal of Communication and Religion*, 18, no. 1 (1995): 1-9. <http://www.cios.org/jcr/djvu/v18n1/a01/djvu/p0007.djvu> (29 May 2002). The phrase "new homiletic" originates with David Randolph who, in 1969, called for a "new homiletic viewed against the background of the new hermeneutic" (17). The phrase was picked up in 1987 by Richard Eslinger who differentiated the "old homiletic" from the "new homiletics" (13). There is, however, a verbal quality to the usage of this phrase in both of these writers that our original essay treated as a fiat. By 1995 the New Homiletic was the term that had come to define this collection of methods though Eslinger argues that the term should be continued as a plural; Richard Eslinger, *The Web of Preaching: New Options in Homiletic Method* (Nashville: Abingdon, 2002) 288n2. See David James Randolph, *The Renewal of Preaching* (Philadelphia: Fortress, 1969); Richard Eslinger, *A New Hearing: Living Options in Homiletical Method* (Nashville: Abingdon, 1987).

[9] Thomas G. Long, "And How Shall They Hear? The Listener in Contemporary Preaching" in *Listening to the Word: Studies in Honor of Fred B. Craddock*, Ed. G. R. O'Day and T. Long (Nashville: Abingdon, 1993), 170.

Homiletic.[10] He believes that the genius of the New Homiletic
is its relocation of sermon strategy from Aristotle's rational
ordering of form in the *Rhetoric* to that of narrative plotting
found in the *Poetics*.[11] Of course, there is little question that
the last quarter century has witnessed an explosion of attention
to form, but our interest was to name the *experience* of "Aha!"
that seemed to be implicit in the various efforts of shaping
designs for preaching in the New Homiletic.[12] Specifically, we
wanted to locate homiletic's notion of the listener's experience
of coming to an "Aha!" of insight in the hermeneutical theories
of Paul Ricoeur and Hans Georg Gadamer, both of whom view
interpretation as an experience of being overcome by an event
of meaning. We concluded "This privileging of the individual's
experience of narrative and imagination over rational argument
is conceptually the essence of what we believe is the emerging
paradigm shift in homiletic theory."[13]

In a subsequent essay, David Fleer, this time in conjunction
with Dave Bland, continued the argument that the New
Homiletic—whether the methods of Cradddock, Lowry or
Long—attends to the narrative quality of experience both
in the biblical text and in the ways that preaching allows a
congregation to be taken up into the preacher's own process
of hermeneutical insight.[14] I would agree that it is this dual

[10] Eugene Lowry. *The Sermon: Dancing the Edge of Mystery* (Nashville:
Abingdon. 1997), 20-28.

[11] Lowry. *The Sermon*, 42.

[12] See Ronald J. Allen, Ed., *Patterns of Preaching: A Sermon Sampler* (St.
Louis: Chalice, 1998). "Aha!" was the climactic point-of-turning in Lowry's
original formulation of sermon design in *The Homiletic Plot: The Sermon as
Narrative Art Form* (Atlanta: John Knox, 1980). Allen draws attention to this
experience of "Aha!" as essential to what the listener experiences as "meaning"
in this approach to preaching (94).

[13] Reid, Bullock, and Fleer, 7.

[14] David Fleer and Dave Bland. "Tensions in Preaching." *Preaching From
Luke Acts*, Eds. David Fleer and Dave Bland (Abilene: ACU, 2000), 28-29.

attention to preaching's listeners and the confluence of narrative theology's initial efforts of articulation that join many of these different homiletic methodologies into a movement that should properly be termed the New Homiletic. Attention to narrative and concern about over-simplifying it would eventually eclipse the attention to listeners in the emergence of post-liberal preaching. Because of this, it is worthwhile to explore briefly what is meant by an attention to the narrative center of preaching and its relationship to narrative theology.

In the *Eclipse of Biblical Narrative,* published in 1974, Hans Frei concluded that the power of the biblical narrative is lost when an interpreter relocates its meaning in thematized propositions, ideals, and doctrines derived as abstractions from the text.[15] For Frei, these rational abstractions should never replace the way in which biblical narratives interpret experience and theological reflection about it. In Frei's narrative theology, the story of Jesus found in the biblical texts invites those who experience it to enter into the world of its story as incomplete because "Jesus *is* his story." It is an unfinished story because it brooks no division between Christology and eschatology. He argues that Gospel stories provide incomplete clues to the rest of Scripture and ambiguous clues to the experience of history that invite an audience, whether readers or listeners, to envision being taken up into and joining their story with the story unfolded in the world of the text.[16] It is in this sense that Paul Ricoeur writes "The whole of contemporary exegesis has made us attentive to the primacy of the *narrative* structure in the biblical writings."[17]

---

[15] Hans Frei, *The Eclipse of Biblical Narrative: A Study in Eighteenth and Nineteenth Century Hermeneutics* (New Haven: Yale University, 1974).

[16] Hans Frei, "Remarks in Connection with a Theological Proposal," in *Theology and Narrative: Selected Essays,* George Hunsinger and William Placher, Eds. (New York: Oxford University, 1993), 43.

[17] Paul Ricoeur, "Naming God," in *Figuring the Sacred: Religion, Narrative and Immagination,* Mark Wallace, Ed., David Pallauer, Trans. ( Minneapolis: Fortress, 1995), 224. It is in this sense that Bullock, Fleer and I argued for the importance of understanding the issue of the *experience* of listeners as central to the various approaches we termed the New Homiletic. We originally suggested this argument by way of reference to Stephen Crites seminal essay "The Narrative Quality of Experience," *Journal of the American Academy of Religion,* 39 (1971): 291-311.

Without negating the New Homiletic's functional attention to form, I would still argue that its genius and its productive unity derives from its interest in permitting listeners to be taken up with and included in the eschatological implications of the unfinished Christological story. In its desire to have listeners experience the preacher's own "eureka" of insight (Craddock), to experience the "aha!" of a sudden shift where a profound gospel simplicity overtakes previous confusion (Lowry) or to have listeners experience theological thinking translated into an image system of lived experience (Buttrick), New Homiletic preaching privileges the ability of listeners to experience finding themselves *included* in the narrative center of a gospel reality. And it is this concern for narrative knowing, coupled with attention to the listener, that eventually shapes the methodological boundary of what constitutes the New Homiletic.

The potential problem with such approaches is that transcendence is grounded in the experience of narrative form rather than in the character of Jesus, the subject of the gospel stories.[18] Thus, if "shape" or "form" is the defining center of the New Homiletic, then Charles Campbell's critique of the New Homiletic matters because it is not enough to attend to the narrative center of Scripture. Narrative theology certainly challenges objectivist ways of knowing with more interpretivist ways of appropriating understanding from the text.[19] For Campbell, the latter cannot be accomplished to the exclusion of the community that has been shaped by its continuing involvement with this narrative.[20]

---

[18] See Richard Eslinger's survey of approaches that assume the experiential-expressive model of preaching in *Narrative and Imagination: Preaching the Worlds that Shape Us* (Minneapolis: Fortress, 1995), 14-19.

[19] On the distinctions of this hermeneutical divide see Sandra M. Schneiders, *The Revelatory Text: Interpreting the New Testament as Sacred Scripture.* 2nd Ed. (Collegeville: The Liturgical, 1999) 11-26.

[20] "Faithful preaching thus enacts on behalf of the entire church an interpretive performance of the story of Jesus. In the practice of preaching, the preacher enacts the way of Jesus in the world—the way of nonviolent engagement with the powers;" Charles Campbell, *Preaching Jesus: New Directions for Homiletics in Hans Frei's Postliberal Theology* (Grand Rapids: Eerdmans 1997), 216-17.

Campbell's critique would be equally challenging to those who would privilege the listener's experience over that of "preaching Jesus." As Fleer and Bland noted in their essay, post-liberal preaching argues that human experiences are not the common bond for a congregation.[21] Christian formation and, therefore, Christian identity does not flourish when we begin with contemporary culture and try to help listeners relate to the biblical world. For post-liberal preaching, the question is not what biblical texts "meant," it is what they "mean."[22] William Willimon writes, "We come to a biblical text, raising questions about its relevance to our present daily lives, only to find that the text questions us about our relevance to the way of Christ."[23] The biblical world is the "real world" and preaching is the occasion by which a Christian community forms itself through the language of its own distinctive speech.

For post-liberal preachers, the sermon instructs listeners in the use of their own language by performing it with them as an act of moral obedience to the way of Jesus.[24] In this approach to preaching, the flow of traffic on the hermeneutical bridge between Scripture and culture is reversed by the preacher, who invites listeners to step out of the world of contemporary culture into the real world of their part in the *unfinished* story of Jesus in Scripture.[25]

Post-liberal preaching challenges the presuppositions of New Homiletic preaching with regard to how this experience of faith occurs, but both of these approaches to preaching accept the fundamentally indeterminate nature of their preaching

---

[21] Fleer and Bland, 30.

[22] Gail O'Day, "Bible and Sermon: The Conversation Between Text and Preacher," in *Sharing Heaven's Music: The Heart of Christian Preaching*, Ed. Barry Callen (Nashville: Abingdon, 1995), 70-72.

[23] William Willimon, *Pastor: The Theology and Practice of Ordained Ministry* (Nashville: Abingdon, 2002), 131.

[24] Charles Campbell, *The Word Before the Powers: An Ethic of Preaching* (Louisville: Westminster/John Knox, 2002), 79-80.

[25] Fleer and Bland, 32.

because it is a participation in the "unfinished" nature of narrative theology. They stand in opposition to approaches to preaching that tend to thematize text into propositional meaning and ascribe transcendence to the nature of this *truth*. If we ask whether the more indeterminate approaches place too much of transcendence's weight on language and the narrative dimension of texts, Ricoeur poses much the same question by asking whether Christian preaching pre-supposes the language of its own truth claims and responds,

> The presupposition of listening to Christian preaching is not that everything is language; it is rather that it is always within language that religious experience is articulated.... More precisely, what is presupposed is that faith, inasmuch as it is lived experience, is instructed—in the sense of being formed, clarified, and educated—within the networks of texts that in each instance preaching brings back to living speech.... I can name God in my faith because the texts preached to me have already named God.[26]

Post-liberal preaching may have opened up the debate between plot and character for interpretivist (or indeterminate) approaches to preaching, but Ricoeur reminds us that the language of religious experience and the nature of truth are also in tension in current debate.[27]

What is interesting to me at this point is that indeterminate preaching in either the New Homiletic or the post-liberal modes are substantive alternatives to homiletic method that treats the text as a fixed object and a finished story.[28] Where the

---

[26] Ricoeur, "Naming God," 218. See William C. Placher, *The Domestication of Transcendence: How Modern Thinking About God Went Wrong* (Louisville: Westminster/John Knox, 1996), 184-5n8.

[27] On the debate between plot and character see Eslinger, *The Web*, 93-98.

[28] Schneiders observes, "The point of H.-G. Gadamer's masterwork, *Truth and Method*, is that when method controls thought and investigation the latter may lead to accurate data, but it does not lead to truth. Method, understood as a pre-established set of procedures for investigating some phenomenon, in fact not only attains its object but creates its object. In other words, it determines a priori what kind of data can be obtained and it will consider relevant. If, for example, my method of investigation is a ruler, the only scientifically reliable datum that can emerge is linear dimension;" *The Revelatory Text*, 23.

former approaches tend to be grounded in the indeterminacy of narrative, or interpretivist knowing, the latter approaches tend to operate with a "hermeneutic of distillation" that seeks to tease a summarizing "Big Idea" or a rational conceptualization of the meaning from the text.[29] They treat meaning as if it's fixed in a finished text rather than constantly contextualized within an ongoing tradition of interpretation in an *unfinished* story.[30]

In their Rochester presentation, Fleer and Bland succinctly identify the traditional conception of the expository sermon, which seeks to explicate the meaning of the text, and the newer seeker sermon models of preaching, which respond to the felt needs of the culture with principles for living, as the dominant examples of these fixed-meaning, rationally-centered approaches to preaching.[31] These two orientations to the preaching task tend to make their appeal to listeners based on either the integrity of a specific tradition of interpretation/doctrine, or they may make the appeal by turning that tradition into a set of palliative applications to remediate the felt needs of listeners. In either case, determinative answers are provided to listeners through a hermeneutic of distillation.

The present discussion should make it obvious that some of these approaches share similar concerns about the basis of the sermon's appeal in the nature of language but differ concerning their assumptions about a sermon's orientation to the nature of authority. Other approaches share assumptions about the focus of authority but differ concerning the assumptions about

---

[29] Eslinger, *The Web*, 152. A recent example relevant to Old Testament preaching is Steven Mathewson, *The Art of Preaching Old Testament Narrative* (Grand Rapids: Baker, 2002), 79-90. Mathewson writes, "The preacher wants to do more than make a point. He or she wants to let various elements of the story—a certain scene, a conversation, a theological idea—form in the minds of the hearers. The goal is to plot out the movements in the preaching of the story: "First I need to tell them this. Second, I need to tell them this. Next, I plan to tell them this" (126). Mathewson's verb's of "tell them" never really allow him to move out of the propositional, big idea centered approach to a true narrative approach to preaching.

[30] E.g., the Restoration Movement functions as an ongoing tradition of interpretation in the way I am using this term.

[31] Fleer and Bland, 22-27.

the nature of language in the basis of their appeal. In the next section, I suggest that the degree to which a preacher is able to make a unified conception of the sermon's intention—in its basis of appeal through language, whether persuasively determinate or indeterminate, and its basis of appeal through authority, as addressed either to corporate or personal faith—is the primary resource available to a preacher who wishes to control the rhetorical potential for authenticity in his or her preaching voice.

## Preaching's *Voices* as Preached Identities

Well-crafted sermons seek to accomplish something. Whether the sermon's purpose serves the function of 1) explanation or 2) a desire to facilitate a personal encounter with the holy or 3) a personal exploration of meaning or 4) dialogical engagement of a tradition of corporate belief, the sermon should be structured by its intentions of persuasive appeal in its assumptions about the nature of language and authority. Some homileticians have argued that persuasion has no place in preaching, but effective speaking always has some intentionality associated with it. The classical Ciceronian intentions taken up into homiletics by Augustine were to teach, delight, and move. We can think of other purposes, such as rouse to action, gain assent, elicit insight, or facilitate spiritual formation, but good sermons are self-consciously up to something.[32]

All sermons begin with some implicit assumptions about the corporate or personal nature of truth, as assumptions about the way language orients a locus of authority for the congregational consciousness. They also begin with implicit assumptions about the determinate or indeterminate nature of language and the way this usage constitutes what counts as reality. If we bisect the corporate-personal tension of

[32] The author of one of the most influential textbooks in contemporary public speaking claims that the purpose of all speech-making is to effect a desired response from listeners. Stephen Lucas, *The Art of Public Speaking*, 7th Ed. (New York: McGraw Hill, 1995), 98.

preaching with the determinate-rational vs. indeterminate-narrative tension across a continuum of controlling intentions, four primary voices emerge: Teaching, Encouraging, Sage, or Testifying.

1. **Determinate-directive preaching concerned to affirm corporate truths.** The intention of this kind of preaching is to *Explain* meaning, to speak *ex cathedra* concerning agreed-upon teaching or truths the preacher wishes the listener to affirm. Haddon Robinson describes one version of this kind of preaching as "the communication of a biblical concept, derived from and transmitted through a historical, grammatical, and literary study of a passage in its context, which the Holy Spirit first applies to the personality of the preacher, then through him to his hearers."[33] This is preaching controlled by a *Teaching* voice.

2. **Determinate-directive preaching concerned with personal truths of existential self-awareness.** The intention of this kind of preaching is to facilitate the listener's *Encounter* with Grace/God/Spirit/Truth based on that listener's awareness of his or her own existential need. The preacher speaks as one who encourages the listener to experience the personal meaning of the truths made apparent. Ian Pitt-Watson writes, "Preaching is God speaking through us who preach."[34] Thus, "Instead of telling people what to do, authentic biblical preaching helps people to do it. Authentic biblical preaching is about action enabled by insight, imperatives empowered by indicatives, ethics rooted in theology, 'what we ought to do' made

[33] Haddon Robinson, *Biblical Preaching: The Development and Delivery of Expository Messages* (Grand Rapids: Baker, 1980), 20.

[34] Ian Pitt-Watson, *A Primer for Preachers*, (Grand Rapids: Baker, 1986), 14.

possible by what God has done."[35] This is preaching controlled by an *Encouraging* voice.

3. **Indeterminate preaching concerned with personal truths of existential self-awareness.** The intention of this kind of preaching is to incarnate truth by way of a homiletic conversation, obliquely inviting individuals to *Explore* meaning through a *gestalt* of insight. Fred Craddock writes that the sole purpose of this kind of preaching is to engage listeners in ways that permit him to "think his own thoughts and experience his own feelings in the presence of Christ and in light of the Gospel." In speaking in this oblique manner, the preacher takes on the role of a *Sage* whose concern is "to communicate with people who after the sermon is over will have to continue thinking their own thoughts, dealing with their own situations and being responsible for their own faith."[36] This is preaching controlled by a *Sage* voice.

4. **Indeterminate preaching concerned to affirm corporate truths.** The intention of this kind of preaching is to offer de-centered speech as *Testimony* that seeks to *Engage* listeners in a dialogue with the language of their theological tradition, directing "the faithful into the implications of their own redemption in Jesus Christ."[37] Walter Brueggemann argues that this kind of preaching "is analogous to preaching to exiles. More broadly, biblical preaching is addressed to a particular community of believers committed through baptism to the claims of biblical faith

[35] Pit-Watson, 22, 66.

[36] Fred B. Craddock, *As One Without Authority: Revised and with New Sermons* (St. Louis: Chalice, 2001), 124.

[37] Richard Lischer, "Preaching as the Church's Language," in *Listening to the Word: Studies in Honor of Fred Craddock,* Ed. Gail R. O'Day and Thomas G. Long (Nashville: Abingdon, 1993), 126.

addressed to the community of the baptized in order to articulate, sustain, and empower a distinctive identity in the world."[38] This is preaching controlled by a *Testifying* voice.

Lucy Hogan and I have already suggested specific strategies of sermon arrangement that would be relevant to each of these divisions.[39] When taken together, the preached identities implied by these homiletic assumptions as bases of persuasive appeal represent distinctly different preaching intentions, each of which is represented by a voice appropriate to its presuppositions.[40] These voices can be represented in the following matrix of Preaching Voices.[41]

|  | Corporate Truth | Personal Truth |
|---|---|---|
| **Persuasively** **The Nature** **of Language** | **Testifying Voice** engages listeners in a formative coversation | **Sage Voice** explores meaning through a gestalt of personal insight |
| **Persuasively** | **Teaching Voice** explains truth of tradition/doctrine/ text | **Encouraging Voice** facilitates encounter with Grace/God/ Spirit/Truth |

[38] Walter Brueggemann, *Cadences of Home: Preaching Among Exiles* (Louisville: Westminster/John Knox, 1997), 78.

[39] Lucy Lind Hogan and Robert Reid, Connecting with the Congregation: Rhetoric and the Art of Preaching (Nashville: Abingdon, 1999), 113-36.

[40] Preaching voices clearly have some overlap with David Kolb's learning style of converger vs. diverger and assimilator vs. accommodator. Kolb's Learning Style Inventory (LSI) is used in a variety of educational and business settings. David A. Kolb, *Experiential Learning: Experience as the Source of Learning and Development* (Englewood Cliffs, NJ: Prentice-Hall, 1984). The LSI instrument is distributed by McBer & Company.

[41] Jackson Carroll's "Conceptions of Authority" matrix provides a productive parallel for the proposal I offer; Jackson W. Carroll, *As One with Authority: Reflective Leadership in Ministry* (Louisville: Westminster/John Knox, 1991), 57.

To be experienced as authentic, the voice a preacher takes up should be consistent with the preaching intention's assumptions about the nature of language and authority. A preacher, whose intention is to *explain* meaning, will likely speak authoritatively on behalf of a tradition of interpretation. A preacher whose intention is to *facilitate an encounter* with the holy will likely speak encouragingly with solutions directed toward listener's felt needs. A preacher, whose intention is to create an event of meaning in which listeners can *explore* insight, will likely speak as a knowing sage who can guide listeners on a journey of self-awareness. A preacher, whose intention is to *explore* confessional identity in ways that permit listeners to come to terms with who they are in Christ, will likely testify with the voice of the church in contrast to the voice of secular culture.[42]

Of course, in every sermon a preacher is, in turn, likely to speak as one who teaches, one who encourages, as a sage, and as one who testifies. As with the classic notions of questions of fact, policy and value all occur in a speech, but only one should control the intention of the presentation. All four voices are usually along for the ride in preaching, but only one of them should be behind the wheel. The alternative is a sermon with no clear voice that leaves listeners equally confused by what is expected of them in response to having heard the sermon. Consistency of voice does not mean exclusivity of voice. It means that the assumptions about the natures of language and authority of one voice control what the preacher desires to have happen as a result of people listening to the sermon.

---

[42] Of course preaching is never one thing, quantifiable in a neat matrix. There are other aspects of voice that are not immediately apparent in this kind of construal. For example, a preacher who approaches the sermon process primarily from a theological orientation is likely to assume that preaching is rightly viewed as an occasion of the spoken Word of God. Such a preacher would likely begin with the assumption that the "efficacy of faith's activity" is the most important aspect of any occasion of the preached Word. On the other hand, a preacher who approaches the process of creating a sermon with an implicit rhetorical orientation would likely be listener-centered and implicitly begin with the assumption that the "person of the preacher" functions as the most persuasive aspect in the rhetorical situation of Christian proclamation. Andre Resner. *Preacher and Cross: Person and Message in Theology and Rhetoric* (Grand Rapids: Eerdmans, 1999), 137-38.

I am suggesting that authenticity of voice is correlated to a consistent and congruent negotiation of the sermon's bases of appeal. Whether the preacher chooses to adopt the voice of one who speaks an authoritative answer *ex cathedra* at one end of the spectrum of contemporary homiletic options or the voice of an *exilic prophet* daring to offer "decentered truths for decentered people" at the spectrum's other end, the ring of authenticity begins with clarity of purpose in negotiating these options. Our preaching voice is actually a preaching of our faith identity. Its witness will either be experienced as clear and credible or the expression of a confused identity, a witness to faith somewhat adrift. Control of these factors is the first step in creation of the kind of authenticity of voice that invites listeners to acknowledge the possibility that God was present in what was spoken.[43]

## Preaching's Voices in Praxis

In keeping with the current Rochester Seminar's interest in preaching the "Cry of the Eighth Century Prophets," I want to explore the distinctive expression of these voices as they might be developed for a sermon from Amos 5:18-27.[44] The following analysis represents an attempt to identify the distinctive qualities of these voices as found in published sermons/sermon briefs preached by Elizabeth Achtemeier, Lloyd Ogilvie, William Willimon, and Barbara Brown Taylor.

### Sermons in a Teaching Voice

The distinctive element of the *Teaching* voice is its assumption that the purpose of the sermon is to affirm truths

---

[43] Wangerin, 37.

[44] The first three sermons examined are based on this text. The sermon from Barbara Brown Taylor is based on a related text in Amos.

for a community of faith in a persuasively determinate fashion. Sermons in this *voice* may still end by calling for a response of some kind. But whatever is said, the controlling intention throughout the sermon is one that invites listeners to affirm the ideas presented.

Various organizing patterns serve this voice: topical, doctrinal, expository, verse-by-verse, indicative-imperative, as well as Puritan plain style and Thesis-Antithesis-Synthesis arrangements.[45] Sermons offered in this voice present an authoritative interpretation of a text/topic/contemporary thematic. By virtue of position and/or training, preachers assuming a *Teaching* voice speak *ex cathedra*—on behalf of the church. They speak as one who has been certified to explain meaning authoritatively.[46] This is why the controlling intention of this voice would have listeners affirm the explanation offered even when some action is invited at the sermon's end.

For example, in a sermon brief for Amos 5:18-27 in *Preaching from the Minor Prophets*, Elizabeth Achtemeier suggests preaching the theme "The Inseparable Pair." Her title is clearly a play on this famous pairing of justice and righteousness, "[L]et *justice* roll down like waters, and *righteousness* like an ever flowing stream (5:24). But Achtemeier observes that the text also declares that love of God, manifested in worship, must be inseparably matched with love of neighbor. Jesus tells us that these two commitments are inseparably yoked when he was asked to name the greatest commandments (Mark 12:28-31). Key to Achtemeier's orientation to this voice is her belief that the preacher must determine a big idea that frames his or her approach to interpreting and explaining the meaning of a text/topic/problem. Achtemeier urges preachers to listen to texts on behalf of the congregation and then to pair Old Testament texts with their echoes in the New Testament.[47] For Amos 5, she

---

[45] The strategies of sermon arrangement here and in what follows draws largely on the patterns of preaching identified in Ronald Allen, *Patterns of Preaching: A Sermon Sampler* (St. Louis: Chalice, 1999).

[46] For the rhetorical concept that implicit theories of communication structure the *persona* a speaker assumes see Roderick P. Hart, *Modern Rhetorical Criticism*, 2nd Ed. (Boston: Allyn and Bacon, 1997), 211-20.

[47] Elizabeth Achtemeier, *Preaching From the Old Testament* (Louisville: Westminster/John Knox, 1989), 54-59.

divides her sermon brief equally between her exposition of this topic in Amos and its subsequent thematic development in the New Testament. Analogically, she assumes that there is little difference between the prophets' demand that worship must be consonant with covenant obedience in Israel and the same for Christians today.

The big idea framing this sermon on the inseparable pair would be "To reject others is to reject our Lord (Matt 25: 41-46) [since] worship and practice cannot be separated."[48] Achtemeier's sermon structure is a basic indicative-imperative design. Her theological assumptions about the nature of authority and language are clearly communicated in her assertion, "To be sure, we do not work our way into God's favor or earn our deliverance and salvation at his hands. He redeems and will save us for his eternal kingdom solely out of the pure grace of his mercy and love toward us. In the end, that is the reason he will save Israel too, and neither Israel nor we are ever worthy of that salvation."[49]

The *teaching* voice has been employed across a vast array of theologies and perspectives. Fundamentalist and Old Liberal draw on it as a resource equally. This approach can as readily lend its voice to a Womanist theology as it can serve the Dispensationalist or Achtemeier's Reformed perspectives. Sermons in a *Teaching* voice are distinguished by the controlling intention of helping listeners affirm or reaffirm a faith identity as part of the larger faith identity embodied in the theology of the sermon.

### Sermons in an Encouraging Voice

The distinctive element of the Encouraging voice is its assumption that the purpose of the sermon is to affirm truths directed to the person in a persuasively determinate fashion. Encouraging preachers shape sermons with the intention that

---

[48] Achtemeir, *Preaching*, 44.

[49] Achtemeir, *Preaching*, 44.

listeners feel renewed hope, stronger faith, and a desire to recommit. They view preaching as an event in which listeners have the opportunity to meet the living God, have an encounter with grace, an encounter with the Holy, or renew their zeal to let the Spirit of God be released to affect some work of grace in their lives. Paul Scott Wilson writes that "Since this encounter affects a new relationship with God of reconciliation and empowerment, we may also acknowledge preaching as a salvation event. Hence, Preaching is an event of encounter with God that leaves the congregation with stronger and deeper faith commitment to doing God's work."[50]

Harry Emerson Fosdick's Problem Solving approach and its updated version in Lloyd Ogilvie's Evangelical Motivated Sequence design are examples of the Felt-Need expressions of this voice.[51] The classic Law-Gospel sermon design serves the intention of calling listeners to accept the grace named in the sermon. Yet again, one could locate Jigsaw sermons, Journey to Celebration sermons, and Four Pages of the Preacher sermons as additional design strategies conducted in this voice. The distinctive element shared by all of these strategies of composition is their assumption that the persuasive intention of preaching is to facilitate an encounter between the listener and God/Grace/Spirit/the Holy. Whether felt-need or celebration of grace, the preacher's ability to speak on behalf of his or her own experience of life and faith is a basis of appeal that authorizes authenticity in these approaches.

---

[50] Paul Wilson, *The Practice of Preaching* (Nashville: Abingdon, 1995) 21.

[51] On Ogilvie's Evangelical Motivated Sequence design see the "Five 'I'" design in Hogan and Reid, *Connecting*, 125. The Evangelical Motivated Sequence design is a variation on public speaking's Motivated Sequence strategy of arrangement. It consists of five divisions: Identification move, Interpretation move, Implications move, Implementation move, and Inspiration move. For Ogilvie's perspective on preaching that addresses felt-needs see Lloyd John Ogilvie, "It's Time to Listen," *Reformed Liturgy and Music* (now *Worship*) 21, no. 2 (1987): 92-96. On the relationship between the Introductory "Identification" move and the effectiveness of preaching see Ogilvie, "Introducing the Sermon," *A Handbook of Contemporary Preaching*, Ed. Michael Duduit (Nashville: Broadman, 1993), 175-87; rprntd. in *Preaching* 8 (March.-April 1993): 16-22.

I suggested above that the felt-need approaches to preaching Fleer and Bland identify as popular in seeker-centered preaching often draw upon this *voice*. Lloyd Ogilvie, the recently retired chaplain of the United States Senate is one of its more effective exemplars. He offers a sample sermon of this type on Amos 5:18-27 in his *Communicator's Commentary* entitled "No Place to Hide."[52]

The sermon begins by offering Harry Houdini as an illustration of a man who never entered a situation in which he wasn't in complete control. Ogilvie then posits the fact that "Houdini Christians" are like this. They appear to be committed to God, but always keep their escape options open.

With this provocative identification established, Ogilvie moves to an interpretation of the text noting that Amos describes Israel as a people who, in the day of the Lord, will try to escape, running from God and running from repentance. Yet, according to Amos, they will discover that they have run right into the God who was tracking them all the time.

From this tailored interpretation, Ogilvie derives several implications. First, "We are all escape artists when it comes to God.... We can try to run from God, but we can't hide. Running from him is like being in a hall of mirrors—everywhere we turn we see not our face but his!" Second, "There is no escaping the inescapable God ... no place to go where He will not be there waiting for us." Third, there is no more seemingly effective way to hide from God than in religion.... [But] Yahweh was tracking down his people. What was happening in their lives and their society was directly related to their escape into false religion. The forms of their religion were keeping them from him."

Next, Ogilvie derives an application that invites listeners to consider what God wants to have happen as a result of hearing this message. He writes, "The same thing happens to us when ... our gods of success, affluence, materialism, popularity, political loyalties, and even religious work compete for first place in our lives." Ogilvie tells us that just as Amos' day of the Lord will

[52] Lloyd John Ogilvie, *The Communicator's Commentary: Hosea, Joel, Amos, Obadiah, Jonah* (Dallas: Word, 1990), 317-23. All subsequent quotations are from this text.

be as if someone fled from a lion only to be met by a bear (Amos 5:19), so it is that the Lord starts tracking us while we go from lion to bear, thinking we have God in a box from which we can escape. But God tracks us down because God "wants to remold our character, reshape our personalities, and reorder our priorities."

From hearing what God desires from listeners, Ogilvie shifts the sermon with an inspirational move that encourages listeners to believe that this God is indefatigably pursuing them as well. He claims that "Life's greatest disappointment, the most monumental despair would be to think God would let us escape." Amos argues that we only think we're fleeing from the dangers of bears, lions, and poisonous snakes. When we stop running and take time to look, we discover that God has replaced the face of these vicious beasts with another—the face of the Lamb of God. This one who takes away the sin of the world "had always been there if we would only stop running long enough to see."

The big idea for this sermon would likely be expressed, "Run and hide in all the ways we will, there is no escaping the fact that we are loved by an inescapable God."[53] Ogilvie would have preachers distill biblical principles from the prophetic text and analogically apply them to Christians today. Through his or her interpretive expertise and personal authority, a preacher who adopts an *Encouraging* voice seeks to move people to experience grace or to employ the biblical principles derived from the text to address the need they have in their life. Sermons in the *Encouraging* voice invite listeners to experience reconciliation with and empowerment by God.

### Sermons in a Sage Voice

The distinctive element of the Sage voice is its assumption that the purpose of the sermon is to affirm truths directed to

---

[53] Though the present focus suggests how this text could be explored in response to felt needs, the basic design is just as readily employed by approaches that could be described as framing the concerns of liberation theology. For example, the five moves of Ogilvie's approach with the similar moves in the sermon on Joshua 17:13-18 by Carolyn Ann Knight, "If Thou Be a Great People" in Allen's *Patterns of Preaching*, 225-30.

the person in a persuasively indeterminate fashion. Strategies in this voice include variations on New Homiletic approaches to preaching, such as plotted sermons (both conventionally and through indirection), imaged sermons, "From First to Second Naiveté" sermons, and personal journey sermons. The distinctive element shared by these strategies of composition is their assumption that the persuasive intention of preaching is to take listeners through an experience of the meaning to discover a gestalt of new meaning. Sermons in this voice invite listeners to journey with the preacher and co-discover new possibilities of understanding and personal applications of faith.

Will Willimon obviously is a leader in defining the emerging *Testifying* voice of post-liberal preaching, but along the way to this place he was also once one of our finest exemplars of the New Homiletic's *Sage* voice. It is in this voice I suggest we understand his preaching intention for his sermon "The Day of the Lord" in *Preaching to Strangers*.[54]

He begins the sermon purposefully from the perspective of contemporary culture: What makes Sunday worship in Duke "good worship?" Along the way, he names personal and probable prejudices for himself and those gathered with him. Before long the question intrudes, "Yet how often have we asked, What does God like about worship?" Yet quickly, perhaps not quickly enough for listeners, he draws them back to a reassuring discussion of what makes the experience of worship in Duke Chapel so satisfying. He locates the worship and then dislocates it. Over against Duke's order that too easily becomes the affirming, confirming, ordering that locates the "grand procession of the eternal verities" comes the dislocating word of the prophet Amos. "We ask What do we want? Amos asks What does God want?"

Here the sermon shifts to unpack the biblical text. Willimon deftly restates Amos' vitriolic indictment of Israelite worship and the Day of the Lord. They too were "busy affirming, confirming, ordering, locating" and the Lord despised it. "You

---

[54] William Willimon and Stanley Hauerwas. *Preaching to Strangers: Evangelism in Today's World* (Louisville: Westminster/John Knox, 1991), 91–97. All subsequent quoted references are from this text.

know what I like on Sunday morning?" Willimon asks. "A joyous chorus from Handel, a clear trumpet, sounded from our organ.... That's what I like. You know what I love on a Lord's day?" says the Lord. "Justice rolling down like Niagara, righteousness flowing like the Mississippi, that's what I like," says the Lord. Willimon then takes listeners back to Sinai. Here a contemporary Moses ends up asking God which one of the worship war styles is his true preference. "You know what I like?" says the Lord. "I like the kind of worship where you shall have no other gods before me. You do not kill. You do not steal. You don't commit adultery. That's my idea of a good time on Sunday. The ethical linked to the liturgical."

The remainder of the sermon juxtaposes two images. "What we want is Sunday as a time of stability" where we all sit in a line of bolted-down pews. Stability. Order. "What we are provided is a prophetic, linguistic assault on the establishment.... The known, fixed, royal world is disrupted by prophetic, poetic speech about the end of the world. Disruption. "Humph!," Will Campbell mumbles upon seeing the beauty of the Duke Chapel, "He's come a long way from Bethlehem."

With the exception, perhaps, of the final movement, this is classic New Homiletic indirection. Willimon begins with the congregation where they are, but the goal was to get the nod of recognition before the shoe drops for the shock of recognition. "Yes... Yes...," the listeners say. This is what we like about Duke worship. And "Yes... Yes... we like to hear Amos tell those others off." Oh, my. Have we really turned beauty into security, the status quo into enduring worship? Is God really saying 'Hear no evil, see no evil, smell no evil?' Is our worship that far off? What do you mean we have substituted the liturgical for the ethical? Have I? What do you mean failed obedience is failed worship? Is mine? Have I lost my way this far? What will I do with this? Provocatively, Willimon's sermon leaves listeners in Amos' dark day of the Lord, in the disarray of judgment. Like a sage, Willimon leaves us to ponder what we will do with the remainder of the journey through which he has led us. Like a sage, he leaves us the work of discovering what obedience requires of us to be brought back into community.

The focus statement would likely have been, "As the people of God, our worship can too easily substitute the liturgical for the ethical unless we permit the disruptive word of God to challenge our ordered, bolted-down practices." The sermon design is a journey through indirection, what Craddock describes as the art of crafting a self-consuming artifact. Willimon is our sage, taking us into the territory of this text as one who knows the way and will guide us to the point where we must choose for ourselves how we will respond.[55] The basis of the appeal is persuasively indeterminate, but the focus of truth is personal. The goal is to lead the individual to the shock of recognition.

### *Sermons in a Testifying Voice*

The distinctive element of the Testifying voice is its assumption that the purpose of the sermon is to engage a community of faith's corporately held truths in conversation in a persuasively indeterminate fashion. Unlike the Teaching voice, sermons in this mode refuse to mount a hierarchy privileging one reading of the biblical text. This voice implicitly acknowledges the plurivocity of any reading of the biblical text or our contemporary situation. It invites listeners to engage in a conversation with their tradition, their contemporaries, and the Holy Spirit, with the intention of furthering the formation of faith.[56] In this voice, any interpretation of preaching's Word is understood as a 'coming to terms' that occurs as dialogical engagement within the proclamation community.

---

[55] With indirection, the goal of each sermon move is like the rung on a latter the primary purpose of which is simply to assist the listener's move to the next rung. See Fred. B. Craddock, *Overhearing the Gospel: Preaching and Teaching the Faith to Persons Who Have Heard it All Before* (Nashville: Abingdon, 1990), 130-32.

[56] André LaCocque and Paul Ricoeur, *Thinking Biblically: Exegetical and Hermeneutical Studies*, trans. David Pellauer (Chicago: University of Chicago, 1998), *xv*.

One finds post-liberal, Revisionist, and Conversational/ Roundtable preaching conducted in this voice.[57] Bi-polar and Quadrilateral preaching are more traditional patterns that also invite practitioners to assume this voice. Preaching in Testimony's voice resists reduction to specific strategies of composition, preferring the notion of sermon as improvisation on the language of Scripture and tradition playing out our own stories as "counter-imagery, as counter-speech that challenges contemporary cultural imagery of domination and subordination."[58]

Barbara Brown Taylor's "Famine in the Land" sermon on Amos 8:4-12 can serve as an exemplar for this voice.[59] Brown Taylor begins by juxtaposing Amos' lament about the rapacious economic policies of the rich and contrasts them with testimony of contemporary examples in which she delves into the problem of the poor and powerlessness in our own cities. As she reflects on the way in which Israel had lost its way, where language grounded in belief in Yahweh no longer shaped its ethical reality, she moves to express her own hunger to be shaped by the word of God. With humility she names her own experience of a famine of hearing the words of the Lord (Amos 8:11-12).

---

[57] If post-liberal preaching would have the community of faith revise their understanding of the world from the perspective of the gospel, Revisionist preaching is equally willing to invite the community of faith to allow the interpretation of its inherited, Christian tradition to be revised from the perspective of contemporary insight. See Allen, *Patterns of Preaching*, 237; Ronald J. Allen and Gilbert L. Bartholomew, *Preaching Verse by Verse* (Louisville KY: Westminster/John Knox, 2002), 8. McClure's Roundtable preaching represents a third effort to recognize the plurivocity of textual interpretation and the plurality of understanding that may abound within a congregation. McClure invites listeners to engage the question of how a particular tradition of faith that gives rise to a congregation's religious identity can continue its work of spiritual formation contextualized by sensitivity to its diverse expression within a particular congregation; John McClure, *The Roundtable Pulpit: Where Leadership and Preaching Meet* (Nashville: Abingdon, 1995).

[58] Campbell, *Preaching Jesus*, 219.

[59] Barbara Brown Taylor, "Famine in the Land," *Home By Another Way* (Cambridge: Cowley, 1999), 180-86.

She acknowledges that such words are rare: "Most of what we hear sounds like noisy gongs and clanging symbols. And yet, every now and then, divine words do break through—clear notes emerging from a background of static.... The question is how do you know? With so many words coming at you, how do you know which ones are God and which ones are not?" Note how Brown Taylor frames the essential indeterminacy (the plurivocity) of this response as a coming to terms her listeners are invited to join with her in acknowledging.

"The time is surely coming, says the Lord God, when I will send a famine on the land; not a famine of bread, or a thirst for water, but of hearing the words of the Lord" (Amos 8:11). How can we discern what may feed this hunger for a divine word? Brown Taylor offers her own tentative suggestions. She listens for the way God's word is expressed. Does it yank our secure supports away or serve arrogantly to undergird them? Does it frighten us for fear's sake or make us stop in our tracks keenly to become aware? "I guess the best way to combat the famine of hearing the words of the Lord," she writes, "is to speak them ourselves—never with arrogance, never to coerce or frighten, always with understanding that they are like nitroglycerine in our mouths...." And we speak these words in community. We are not called to stand alone like Amos. We are called to speak words of life in communities so that the words spoken "can go to work on us, through us, until the sound of them becomes like a heartbeat in our ears."[60]

In this meditation on the brokenness of language itself, notice how Brown Taylor keeps her orientation in the language world of the prophet rather than re-filtering the message of hope through the New Testament. The focus statement of this sermon may have been, "If God's defense against idolatry is to create a famine of the word in a land of plenty, then the best way to combat the famine is to let divine words be spoken among us as if they are nitroglycerine in our mouths." Analogically, the

---

[60] Brown Taylor's first lecture of the 1997 Lyman Beecher Lectures on Preaching, entitled "Famine," uses this same text as a focus for her words. Barbara Brown Taylor, *When God is Silent* (Cambridge: Cowley, 1999).

preacher affirms that the real world is the one in which Yahweh's concerns for "uncompromising love, perfect obedience, endless forgiveness, and justice for all" define what really matters. By revisiting—and thereby re-envisioning our language in Amos's language—we can recover language with which to speak the divine word that gives life in our context.

Sermons in a Testifying voice tend to be controlled by the persuasive intention of helping listeners be formed and reformed by an engagement with their corporate community's tradition of faith released to do a work of spiritual formation in their lives together. Sermons in this voice use language to re-form memory and set congregational consciousness free from a kind of culturally imposed amnesia. It allows them to rediscover who they are in Christ.[61]

### Negotiating a New Expression of Voice

Of these options in preached identity, the least familiar—the one for which we are still learning the language of its expression—is sermon as *Testimony*. In his essay "Shaped by Story," David Fleer recently argued for a post-liberal theory of preaching autobiography rather than the typical autobiographical sermon that always risks trumping the biblical story with our story.[62] Because he is concerned about "authenticity" in proposing a theory, his essay offers a final site to explore my proposal for determining congruence of identity in a preaching voice.[63]

His model of autobiographical preaching is both indeterminate, one that seeks to affirm corporate truths, and one that has the preacher adopt a *Testifying* voice that seeks to create a space for engagement with the biblical story. He does

---

[61] Campbell. *The Word Before the Powers*, 110-11.

[62] David Fleer. "Shaped by Story: Finding God's Limits and Outlets for our Passion," in *Preaching Autobiography*, Ed. Fleer and Bland (Abilene: ACU, 2001). 23-45.

[63] Fleer. "Shaped." 43

not invite listeners to find either his story or their story in the text's story; rather, he presents autobiography as making the story of the Bible his story, of understanding his own identity through the biblical story. As testimony, it seeks to engage listeners in a dialogue that invites them into the narrative world that is the "real world" of their own identity.

His proposal begins with the assumption that "Scripture confronts listeners, asking that its world and hope becomes theirs."[64] By naming the way his life participates eschatologically in the *unfinished* nature of Scripture's story while still being interpreted by it, he provides a frame of reference that permits his "identity to be shaped through the narrative of scripture."[65] This is one of the primary goals of post-liberal preaching. And rather than adopting the New Homiletic voice of a *sage*, who leads the congregation to the deep well of insight, Fleer argues that autobiography in the pulpit "needs community to reduce the threat of self-deception." This is preaching directed to a community and its self-understanding: "As my story needs the community, so the community needs my story crafted by Scripture."[66]

Fleer appears to have proposed an approach to preaching autobiography that is faithful to Brueggemann's culminating theses describing the post-liberal approach to preaching:

> The biblical text, in all its odd disjunctions, is an offer of an alternative script, and preaching this text is to explore how the world is, if it is imagined through this alternative script....[67] The invitation of preaching (not unlike therapy) is to abandon the script in which one has had confidence and to enter a different script that imaginatively tells one's life differently.... The offer of an alternative script (to which we testify and

---

[64] Fleer, "Shaped," 42.

[65] Fleer, "Shaped," 43.

[66] Fleer, "Shaped," 43.

[67] Brueggemann, *Cadences of Home*, 30.

bear witness as true) invites the listener out of his or
her assumed context into many alternative contexts
where different scripts have a ring of authenticity
and credibility.[68]

If Fleer were to shift his assumed ground of truth from the
corporate to the personal, or his purpose from indeterminate
to more determinate, or yet again, were he to structure the
sermon's strategy by one of the arrangement theories native to
a different approach, he might find that his sermon voice would
lack this "ring of authenticity and credibility."

## Faithful Intentions

My argument that preachers should consciously negotiate
voice as rhetorical resource in preaching is not a proposal for
a cookbook of personas one can don for different occasions.
Such a view subverts authenticity. Basic assumptions about the
differing natures of language and authority mark the choices
of a Rubicon many preachers would not cross. And those who
would should wonder why others see such a disparity in the
choice. In *Deep Memory, Exuberant Hope: Contested Truth
in a Post-Christian World*, Walter Brueggemann states, "My
thesis is that preaching is *sub-version*. You will recognize the
play I intend. Preaching is never dominant version; never has
been. It is always a sub-version, always a version, a rendering
of reality that lives under the dominant version, or an alternative
strategy of showing our 'under-version' to be in deep tension
with the dominant version."[69] It is unlikely that the author of
such a statement could find the voice to preach in determinate
language. *He would find it inauthentic testimony in his mouth.*

Constantly adapting one's voice across a ministry of
preaching is likely to create more confusion than help in
the way in which listeners learn to make sense of faith from

[68] Brueggemann. *Cadences of Home*. 34-35.

[69] Walter Brueggemann, *Deep Memory, Exuberant Hope: Contested Truth in
a Post-Christian World*, Patrick Miller, Ed. (Minneapolis: Fortress, 2000), 5.

hearing.[70] Of course there is some room for maneuvering, for no preacher has a single identity. Yet homiletics as taught in specific schools of thought has often dictated the identity its preachers should adopt by canonizing its preferred voice to the disparagement of all others. Perhaps, just perhaps, the task of teaching homiletics should be to help preachers find their own identity and, in the process, find their own authentic voice in the preaching of the *unfinished* story of the biblical text.

Miz Lil told her minister, "When you teach, I learn something for the day. I can take it home and, God willing, I can do it." Concerning his other voice she said, "But when you preach—God is here. And sometimes he's smiling and sometimes he's frowning surely." Miz Lil knew at least two of his voices, and she knew them by their preaching intentions. Invariably, when I have the privilege to listen to student sermons, one of my first questions in follow-up is to ask, "What did you want to have happen as a result of people hearing that sermon?" Without clarity of intention, it is rare that a sermon will be experienced as authentic. When the preacher is able to match his or her preaching intention and homiletic theology with a strategy of preaching that is consistent with the presuppositions of both, then the voice the preacher takes up has the potential to be experienced as authentic by listeners. Obviously other factors effect the experience of authenticity, but I have suggested that preaching identity is embodied in the way sermons reveal the intentionality of voice, in the way that this voice calls listeners into its confidence, and the way that this identity can, at times, be experienced as so authentic that it becomes the embodiment of voice as Word of God. That's what Miz Lil craved. And so do we.

---

[70] See Robert Stephen Reid. "Faithful Preaching: Faith Stages, Preaching Strategies, and Rhetorical Practice." *The Journal of Communication and Religion* 21.2 (1998): 164-99.

# II | *Sermons on The Eighth Century Prophets*

# 7

# *What Makes God Most Angry*

## *Amos 1-2*

Dave Bland

## Introduction

In chapter 2 on prophetic doom oracles, Rick Marrs touches on the nerve center of Amos' theology when he says, "Where the wealthy saw unlimited growth and prosperity, Amos saw social injustice;...Amos lamented a community devoid of righteousness, a society lacking a true moral compass." The oracles against the nations in Amos chapters 1-2 strike a deadly blow against the immoral and unjust lifestyle of the wealthy.

Rick highlights the reversal motif that Amos is so fond of. For example, "the day of the Lord" is not going to be a day of salvation for Israel but a day of doom (5:18-20). Instead of God's roar being an indication of protection for his people, it is an indication of God's stalking (1:2). Further, God invites the nations around Israel to come and surround Samaria and instead of witnessing the righteousness of God's people there, they will witness the "chaos of a society devoid of God's... righteous presence."

The most elaborate and rhetorically powerful reversal, however, is contained in the first oracle in Amos 1-2. This oracle is a good example of William Willimon's description of the prophets' speech: they "specialize in imaginative *disruption* in order to provoke social *transformation*."

Using Bob Reid's scheme, the dominant voice in this sermon is the Teaching voice. The purpose of this sermon is to affirm truths corporately for a community of faith in a persuasively determinate fashion. Reid assesses my sermon in the following way, "From the opening illustrative move in which the preacher [Bland] adopts the persona of the professor explaining the theory of literary expectation implied by texts to the final claim, the preacher's intention is to invite listeners to affirm that his assessment of the meaning and application of this text is correct."

My intention, though, was more than just to explain and invite the listener to affirm. I intended to do in this sermon what Tim Sensing calls on preachers to do in his chapter, to enact: "... the prophetic sermon will disorient the status quo by addressing the present issues with a Word of God so that a new orientation (reality) can be created in the lives of people. The new and future Word will faithfully represent the old Word in the turbulent present."

This and all subsequent sermons were preached at the Church of Christ at White Station in Memphis, Tennessee, where I have served as a pulpit preacher for the past seven years and worshipped for the past eleven years. This church is an urban-predominantly-white-middle-class congregation with a membership of about 900 and an average Sunday morning attendance of 600.

## *What Makes God Most Angry*

We can get a good idea of what to expect from a story, speech, or sermon when we hear the first few lines. We hear "Once upon a time..." and we know the final line is going to be, "And they lived happily ever after." The preacher says, "Dearly beloved we are gathered here today..." and we know the ending is going to be a couple saying to one another "I do." Certain forms generate certain expectations from us. There is satisfaction when the form is completed.

I'm going to clap my hands right now to a certain rhythm that you will immediately recognize. I'll start the pattern and you complete it. Are you ready?...(clap to the rhythm of "Shave and a Haircut...Six Bits"). Now wasn't that satisfying to complete the rhythm? If I had not told you to complete the pattern, some of you would have gone ahead and clapped out loud. Others may have been subtler about it and tapped your foot or patted your hand on your knee. If I had completed that pattern with a different beat, some of you would have been irritated and maybe even walked out of the service! At any rate, you would have experienced some dissonance. It would be like an itch that you couldn't scratch. Similarly, when a speech or sermon or literary pattern is left undone or is changed, it can leave the listener disoriented. Certain forms generate certain expectations and when appropriately completed, there is satisfaction.

Israel had a good idea of what to expect when Amos began his sermon in 1:3-5. All he needed to say was "Thus says the Lord" and they knew. His sermon is a series of oracles against seven different nations who are Israel's closest neighbors (chapters 1-2). The "oracles against the nations" is a common speech form found throughout the prophets. They were popular sermons. Whenever Israel heard this kind of sermon, they knew what to expect: judgment from God. On this occasion, Israel knows what's coming for these seven nations. At one time or another in her history, Israel had been at odds with all of them. These nations had oppressed Israel. But now a day of judgment was coming for them and a day of celebration for Israel. Israel would expect Amos to include seven nations, because seven indicated completeness. It meant that Amos' condemnation is comprehensive and inclusive.

God's judgment was about to rain down on these nations for their atrocities. And these nations are guilty of some pretty heinous crimes. With each nation, usually one crime is mentioned that represents their sin. For example, against Damascus, Amos says they used threshing sledges to run over prisoners of war. In other words, they tortured people. Gaza carried whole people into exile. That is, they engaged in slave trading and ethnic cleansing. The leaders of Ammon ripped open pregnant women, another form of ethnic cleansing. And on Amos goes, through the list. The nations are guilty of some horrendous acts of violence: torture, slavery, broken treaties, ethnic cleansing. All are war crimes, the worst possible acts of violence you can think of committing against another human being. And it makes God angry. Whenever God sees nations using their power against other weaker people to get what they want, he grieves. God deplores these heinous atrocities. These nations stand under God's judgment.

Last August (2002), *Newsweek* ran a special issue on the war crimes that had been committed against Afghanistan after 9/11. *Newsweek* discovered that U. S. allies loaded up hundreds of prisoners in unventilated cargo trucks to ship them off to prison camps. They packed them in like sardines, without food or water. By the time the trucks arrived at their destination, all the prisoners had suffocated. Witnesses said as the doors were opened, dead bodies spilled out like fish onto the deck of a ship. The trucks were intentionally used as extermination machines.

But atrocities do not occur only in times of war. They occur at other times and in other arenas as well. In the summer of 2001, CBS aired a special about the tobacco giant Philip Morris who lobbied the Czech government against initiating stricter health regulations on cigarette smoking. They argued that smoking has great benefits for the government. Smokers usually die prematurely, and these deaths save the government thirty million dollars a year in pensions, housing, and health care costs for the elderly. Basically, dead smokers save the government money. For them to die prematurely benefits the Gross National Product. God is angry when governments, nations, and corporations use and abuse people. We stand under God's judgment.

These are the kinds of atrocities Amos denounces. Amos condemns these nations for the carnage they commit against others. Israel had heard this sermon before. They knew where Amos was headed with it and they praised him for his boldness in speaking out against the violence. But Amos surprises them. He doesn't stop when he's supposed to. He adds an eighth oracle! It's like listening to a sermon and realizing it's about to conclude because the preacher starts offering the invitation. That's what you expect to hear, so you start reaching for your songbooks. Except on this occasion as Israel is reaching for the hymnal, Amos does the unexpected. He completely turns the tables and addresses Israel in an oracle that is three times as long as the other oracles.

Shockingly, Amos addresses them the same way as the other nations were addressed! Israel has lost her identity. Israel is no different from the surrounding pagan nations: "Thus says the Lord, for three transgressions of Israel and for four I will not revoke the punishment." No, this is not the way the sermon is supposed to end! Israel, like the church today, likes a religion that offers primarily comfort and affirmation, not accountability or judgment.

But on this occasion, Amos afflicts the comfortable. He starts naming Israel's sins (2:6-8). Not just one as in the other oracles, but seven! The verbs Amos uses depict wanton acts of violence: sell, trample, push, take, profane, drink, impose. But surely Israel's sins are no worse than the surrounding nations. There's nothing worse than war crimes, or acts of terror that take the lives of thousands of innocent civilians, or corporate crimes that destroy the lives of hundreds of employees, or random acts of violence that routinely occur in our cities!

Actually, yes there is. Amos announces to Israel, "your crimes are doubly tragic. For one, you are God's people. Look at the special love that God has bestowed on you. He's given you the law. He's given you land. He's given you leaders" (2: 9-11). "Look how God has cared especially for you over the centuries; he's always been faithful to you. You should know how to treat others because of the way God has treated you."

There is something else at stake here as well. Whereas the war crimes these nations committed were against other nations and people, "you, Israel, commit atrocities against your own people! The nations commit international violence, but you, Israel, engage in domestic violence. You mistreat the poor among you. You sell your own people into slavery. You sexually abuse the women who serve you right in your own household" (2:6-8)!

The God Amos describes is a God who is concerned with international affairs. But he also cares for the individual, "the least of these my brethren." The God we worship is a sovereign Lord. He orders the paths of nations and governments (9:7). But he also cares for each human being. When you and I, as God's people, show disrespect for one another, that is the worst crime in God's eyes. What grieves God most, even more than atrocities of war, is when you and I mistreat each other. We, of all people, should know better.

A church can be guilty of disregarding its own people; a church can become apathetic, calloused. When a church adopts the attitude of being more concerned with numbers and meeting budgets than with helping people, then we only see people as objects to meet our goal. The poor, uneducated, and handicapped aren't going to help us very far in that goal, that's for sure. And so we expend little energy on them. They are not the best use of our time and resources.

When we as ministers look at our role primarily as a profession rather than a calling from God, then people take a back seat. When we as preachers are more concerned with making you go away from here feeling good, than with disclosing to you both God's judgment and grace, we dishonor you.

Church members can grow indifferent toward fellow Christians. When you become so busy with your own lives that you have no time for hospitality, you disregard the body of Christ. When you spend time on the Internet perusing porn sites, you dishonor the women sitting around you this morning. When you find yourself in intimate conversations with others online, you dishonor the men sitting around you today.

Families can dishonor one another. When parents are so consumed by their own careers that they only spend "quality time" with their children, they treat them with disdain. When youth withdraw from their parents, when they speak disrespectfully to them, they treat their parents as objects.

In God's eyes, these sins are worse than the atrocities of war. What angers God most is when his people show disregard for one another. What we would like to hear this morning are condemnations of the state lottery, or of abortion, or corporate greed. God hates these sins, to be sure. But God has a *special* stake in the way his own people treat each other because it reflects on him. God's judgment is on us today. Our response is to accept his judgment for how we have mistreated one another. When we accept his judgment, then we are open to receiving his grace.

That's what we do as we now gather around the Lord's Table. As we eat the bread and drink the cup, we "discern the body." We assess the ways in which we have treated one another, we grieve over the way we have hurt or neglected a brother or sister, we accept God's judgment, and we plead for forgiveness. And as we eat the body and blood of Christ, we receive God's grace.

# 8

# Prophetic Imagination

## Amos 9:11-15

Dave Bland

## Introduction

This sermon flows out of struggling with the provocative material presented in chapter 3 by John Fortner. John's cutting-edge work on radical disjunction and conjunction uses an analogy from Deuteronomy and Exodus 32-34 to persuasively argue that prophetic doom and hope oracles are integral to God's covenant with Israel. Contrary to the majority of scholars who date the final oracle in Amos as exilic and not from Amos, John argues from a covenant theology that it is a vital part of Amos' prophetic word from God.

In the spring of 2002, John and I team-taught a Doctor of Ministry seminar at Harding University Graduate School of Religion on "Preaching from the Eighth Century Prophets." It was in that seminar that we interacted with each other and engaged students in discussions about the historical background, theology, and the relationship between doom and hope oracles. At the conclusion of the seminar, we as a class formed a panel in a local church in Memphis and, in an open forum, discussed the continued relevance of the prophetic message. All of this served as a rich background to the writing of this sermon.

In chapter 3, John observes that the prophets link the chaos and infertility of creation with the ethical demise of Israel (e.g., Amos 4:6-11). Therefore when the prophets imagine a future in which creation flourishes, an ethical connection is implied. John comments, "Thus, whatever grandiose form the oracles of weal may take, their realization may not be severed from an ethical walk." The sermon that follows operates under this theological assumption and, while highlighting the eschatological vision of Amos 9:11-15, attempts to keep the two aspects of God's covenant, judgment and hope, in dynamic tension with each other.

## Prophetic Imagination

We enjoy imagining the future. We love to envision what the perfect world would look like. Often these visions for a brighter tomorrow possess some common denominators: unity, freedom, peace, security, equality. The centerpiece of America's dream is, "We hold these truths to be self-evident, that all men are created equal, that they are endowed by their Creator with certain unalienable rights, that among these are life, liberty, and the pursuit of happiness."

We sing about this perfect world in our songs. The contemporary rock group, Creed, sings about such a world in a song called "Higher." The first stanza describes the singer striving to escape from the life he lives and staying in the ideal dream world he has created in his sleep. Creed sings:

When dreaming I'm guided to another world
Time and time again...

Can you take me higher?
To a place where blind men see
Can you take me higher?
To a place with golden streets

Although I would like our world to change
It helps me to appreciate
Those nights and those dreams
But, my friend, I'd sacrifice all those nights
If I could make the Earth and my dreams the same

God sets a vision in the minds of his people, Israel. It is not, however, a vision of personal success or wishful thinking; it is not a fantasy or a "day dream." It is more significant. It is a dream in which God creates a world for Israel where all people live in harmony and all serve the living God.

God's vision is not a wild and crazy vision that Israel could have never before fathomed. No, God's vision is grounded in Israel's past experiences with him. God envisions the transformation of human society. He will reunite the divided kingdom; Israel will be one. God envisions the transformation of the nations around Israel. Israel will no longer live in fear of other nations. All will live together in peace. People in Israel will live secure on their own land and in their own homes. The vision is also about God transforming creation. The land will be fertile. It will produce a bumper crop, the likes of which no one has ever before seen. Before a farmer even finishes harvesting the crops from one year, he will have to start planting the crops for the next year. No one will ever go hungry again. What a future to look forward to! What a vision!

But what kind of circumstance generates such a vision? Are there particular situations or contexts in which this kind of vision is most vivid? Does it come in the context of restful sleep, as dreams often do? In the quiet of the night do we envision, as Creed does, the perfect tomorrow engulfing our lives? Or is this kind of vision generated on warm sunny afternoons as we lie on our backs gazing into a blue sky while lazy puffs of clouds drift along on a gentle breeze? For Israel it was neither of these occasions. For Israel the vision came during her darkest hour. Amos announces God's impending judgment: The time for repentance is past. "Prepare to meet your God." All of Amos's words are oracles of doom, except for the final one.

From a human perspective, the moments that least likely generate vision and hope are those in which we find ourselves in the pit of despair, when we experience setback and loss, when we suffer. In those contexts humans do not have the resources to create within themselves a hope that can overcome. Oh, we can generate wishful thinking. We can manufacture positive thinking or possibility thinking. We can produce fantasies. But we can't create genuine hope. Out of our own resources, despair only begets more despair.

In the movie *As Good as It Gets*, Melvin Udall (Jack Nicholson) is an eccentric middle-aged recluse. He's obnoxious, bigoted, rude, obscene... and that's only the beginning. He makes a casualty out of every person he encounters. He's so obsessive-compulsive that he seldom ventures out of his apartment except to eat breakfast at a local restaurant. His life is a mess. On one occasion, he becomes so desperate for help that he risks leaving his apartment to visit his psychiatrist. The psychiatrist is not happy with Melvin's unscheduled visit and insists that Melvin leave. As he does, Melvin looks around at the other patients in the waiting room and says with disgust, "Have any of you ever considered the possibility that this is as good as it gets?" He sees no future in his life; he has nothing for which to hope. His life is pathetic. In moments of despair humans cannot, within themselves, produce life-sustaining hope.

But it is precisely in those moments that Israel is given hope. When Israel is in her bleakest hour, she has the opportunity to see most clearly a bright future. Israel has hope not because of who she is but because of who God is. It is a hope that is initiated, created, and sustained exclusively by God. It is a hope in God's future. Of all places, this hope arises in the midst of God's divine judgment on his people, when God is about to destroy them.

In Memphis in 1968, on the eve of his assassination, Martin Luther King delivered his famous speech "I See the Promised Land." Some of you may have actually heard that speech. In that speech he imagined God asking him this question, "Martin, if I allowed you to live in any time period of history that you would like, what period would you choose?" King answered, "I would want live in this present time." But why this time? The world is all messed up. The nation is sick. King's response was, "Only when it is dark enough, can you see the stars." King believed that it was in this period of darkness that people would be able to most clearly see God doing his mighty work.

In the eighth century, Israel as a nation was in her darkest hour, near the end of her existence. She had only a couple of decades left before God would destroy her. Yet out of death, God promised to produce a new and even better life. In the face of death, God gave Israel hope.

Hope is spawned in an environment of despair. It is fostered in situations that appear dismal. In 1962 my parents bought a run down piece of property in Northern Colorado. Over the next twenty-five years they tore down and built and planted and irrigated and transformed that piece of land into a beautiful little farm. Dad, who has been totally blind all his adult life, had a vision of what that piece of property could become. I recall many evenings around the supper table listening to Dad talking about the next phase of building the farm that he had already created in his mind. That vision sustained them through the toils and difficulties until it became a reality. Dad has never seen the farm that he and Mom built. But I guarantee you he has a better picture of it than the rest of us who have seen it. Only when it is dark enough, can you really see.

I think of a church that may be going through difficult times. But they maintain faithfulness through it all because they see a vision of what that church can become by God's grace. As long as they cling to God's vision for them, they can persevere through the most difficult circumstances.

The future that God sets before Israel through the prophet Amos springs out of the present destruction. It is a future that God brings about. The basis of hope does not lie in our human ability to pull it off but in God's power to bring it about. The hope that Amos envisions assumes that God is actively working to bring about that future. But we do not wait passively for its arrival. We respond. We respond in a way that fits the actions of God. Our actions strive for consistency with God's actions. Our actions and efforts, regardless of how inept they might be, serve as a witness to others that God is at work. In other words, we operate in the present as though the future has already come.

God gives the church a vision of what it means to be in God's kingdom. Those who chose to be a part of it, commit to a lifestyle that, however small and imperfect, reflects at least a glimmer of that vision. Every little effort to make things right between races or genders or generations or neighbors is a witness to the grand vision God is bringing about.

Robert J. Morgan tells of an occasion during Vacation Bible School when one day a little boy named Josh visited the 4-and-5-year-old class.[1] Josh was handicapped; he had only one arm. Since he had only come that day, the teacher did not have the opportunity to learn the details of his situation. All through the class she was afraid that one of the other children might say something insensitive to him, so she proceeded cautiously with the lesson. As the class time came to a close, she asked

---

[1] Morgan, Robert J., *Nelson's Complete Book of Stories, Illustrations & Quotes* (Nashville : Thomas Nelson Publishers), 2000, 123.

the children to join her in their usual closing exercise. "Let's make our churches," she said, clasping her hands together to form the church.

"Here's the church, here's the steeple, open the doors and..." Suddenly the awful truth struck her. The very thing she had feared that the children would do, she had done. As she stood there speechless, the little girl sitting next to Josh reached over with her left hand and placed it up to his right hand and said, "Josh, let's make the church together." This little girl participated in a rehearsal of God's vision. God's vision is seen most clearly in the midst of human frailty, suffering, and failure. Wherever someone extends a hand to another who is bruised or troubled or hurting, there you catch a little glimpse of the world that God is already at work bringing about.

# 9

# *The Knowledge of God*

*Hosea 4:1-10*

Dave Bland

## Introduction

The preparation of this sermon went through several phases of change. I began by developing a sermon on a smaller unit of material in Hosea 4, verses 11-14, which is probably the most complete description of Baal worship in the Old Testament. James Limburg's thoughts in his commentary in the Interpretation series piqued my interest in preaching from this text.[1] (The reader may want to refer to Limberg's commentary for good suggestions for preaching this text.) But after working with it for a while, I felt verses 11-14 did not get to the heart of the oracles in chapter 4. So I moved to look at a larger block of material, verses 1-14. There I discovered that the source of the problem in Israelite society was with the clergy. So I lived and worked with that idea for a while and decided to narrow the text to a more manageable unit, verses 1-10. But the audience to whom I am preaching is made up of laypeople, not clergy. I decided to place the emphasis on the responsibility of all of God's people to come to know him. With that in mind I developed the following focus and function statements to help

---

[1] James Limburg, *Hosea-Micah* (Atlanta: John Knox Press, 1988).

guide me in the process of writing the sermon. Sermon focus: A genuine knowledge of God leads to a desire to share life with God and with others. Sermon function: To create within listeners a stronger commitment to know God.

## *The Knowledge of God*

There are a few occasions in which I prefer to remain anonymous. When I've done something wrong. When I don't know the answer to the question the teacher asks. And when I've just made a fool of myself. In these situations, I relish anonymity.

But for the majority of my time, I like to be known. I like acknowledgement. I was disappointed that the *Commercial Appeal* did not publish my name in the paper when I contracted West Nile Virus last summer. I was just a statistic, "The Third Case of West Nile Virus in Shelby County." I wanted to be known, even if it was only because I contracted a virus. When my son B. J. and I went backpacking in Alaska a few months ago, we got our picture on the front page of the local paper because we happened to be in a visitor's center looking at a map of backpacking trails at the same time the newspaper photographer was there. I laminated that front page. I'm proud of it. We like to see our names in lights and on plaques and jerseys and dormitory rooms and buildings.

It's one thing to receive recognition and publicity. It's quite another, however, to be known in the sense of someone else understanding you, your joys and sorrows, your pleasures and pains. We often complain, "If others really understood me, they wouldn't be so quick to criticize." As Ray Stevens used to sing, "Before you abuse, criticize and accuse, walk a mile in my shoes." One of our deepest desires is for someone to really understand us, to get past the façade and to empathize with our feelings.

Children often accuse parents of being "out of touch." In moments of conflict a teenager sometimes complains, "My parents really don't understand me." A whole genre of literature and movies is devoted to the attempt of individuals to trade places or spaces or bodies in order to really understand the other. The latest in the genre is a remake of an old movie, *Freaky Friday*. A mother and daughter are at each other's throats. The mother nags the daughter about her dress and her music and her lifestyle. The daughter despises her mother's work and values and fiancé. She thinks her mom is totally out of touch with the times. Neither shows respect for the other. One day while in a restaurant an elderly woman with mystical powers sees the two fighting over whether the daughter can go to an important band tryout that just happens to fall on the night of the mother's wedding rehearsal dinner. The elderly woman decides to cast a spell on them. The result is that the two switch bodies. They go through the next day in each other's bodies, despising the experience.

According to the rules of the spell, the only way the two can rid themselves of the other's body is to do something totally selfless for the other. Such an opportunity finally presents itself. On the night of the wedding rehearsal, the mother must play in the daughter's rock band and the daughter must offer a toast at the rehearsal dinner and say something kind about her mother's fiancé. At that point they break the spell and reenter their own bodies, having come to a deeper appreciation of each other. It's an enjoyable movie. Unfortunately we don't have any magical spell that can force others to understand us. And so we lament.

It is not uncommon to accuse even God of not understanding us. That was Job's accusation. He felt that God was too big and too powerful to understand humans and in so many words railed to his friends, "Look at the mess God has created because God doesn't understand; God's out of touch" (Job 9). Many today would agree but conclude, "This is why God sent Jesus, to find out what it was really like to be human." Before God sent his son, some think, he did not know what it was like to live in a physical body and to experience the joys and sorrows, the successes and failures. And now the son is seated at the right hand of God, continually explaining to God what it is like to be human. But that is a dangerous position to hold. Theologically, just the opposite is true. Because God *already knew* what it was like to be human, he sent his son Jesus. God has always known what it was like to be human. Long before Jesus came, the psalmist declares:

> O LORD, you have searched me and known me. You know when I sit down and when I rise up; you discern my thoughts from far away... For it was you who formed my inward parts; you knit me together in my mother's womb. (Ps. 139:1-2, 13)

The reason God sent his son was not in order to know us better but in order that we might come to know him better. So the problem is not God knowing us; it is us knowing God. We have not responded to God's steadfast love. This was Israel's fundamental sin. In today's reading, Hosea announces, "There is no knowledge of God in the land" (4:1).

A couple of factors clearly indicate that Israel does not know God. According to Hosea, one indication is that the people are ignorant *about* God and his will. Knowledge of God involves a concrete understanding of God's word and commandments. That's why the phrase "knowledge of God" is so closely aligned in this oracle with the quoting of the last half of the Ten Commandments (swearing, lying, murder, and steeling, v. 2). Knowledge of God is also synonymous with "law" in verse 6. It involves knowledge of his instructions and commandments. Israel did not know God's instructions.

Another indication of their lack of knowledge, however, is that the people do not have a relationship with God. Knowledge of God is connected to an intimate covenant with him. It is not knowledge of God's *instructions* by themselves; that's cold and legalistic. But it is knowledge of God that is connected to a *personal relationship* with him. So there is not only an instructional dimension to knowledge of God, there is also a relational dimension. Knowledge of God is tied closely with "steadfast love" here in verse 1 and elsewhere in 6:6 where Hosea proclaims: "For I desire *steadfast love* and not sacrifice, the *knowledge of God* rather than burnt offerings." It is not a casual acquaintance; it involves one's whole being. Knowing God personalizes morality and makes obedience to God more than just fulfilling a set of rules. It becomes an expression of gratitude for what God has done.

Yet Israel lacks this knowledge and the results are disastrous. It is catastrophic for creation. According to Hosea, the created world becomes infertile (v. 3). Hosea explicitly links the fruitfulness of the soil with the practice of justice and righteousness (2:16-20). Thus, prosperity in the land is proportional to its inhabitants' moral walk.[2] But the lack of a relationship with God results in grave environmental consequences.

---

[2] See John Fortner in chapter three of this volume.

Preaching the Eighth Century Prophets

Besides being catastrophic for creation, the lack of knowledge of God results in the total breakdown of society. Hosea begins this oracle with a thumbnail sketch of the sin and corruption that prevail. These consist of sins of omission (v. 1) as well as sins of commission (v. 2). The sins of omission include no faithfulness or steadfast love. That is, there is a noticeable absence of intense loyalty in interpersonal relationships. The sins of commission consist of a series of one-word clauses taken directly from the Decalogue. There is cursing, lying, murder, stealing, and committing adultery. These people were in one another's wallets, at one another's throats, and in one another's beds: clearly an absence of steadfast love and faithfulness. There is no understanding of God's basic commands and there is no intimate relationship with him.

What the people desperately need is to know God. The starting point of knowledge begins not with trying to get others to understand us but with us trying to understand God. The leaders in Israel's day failed miserably in their responsibility to instruct the people about God. "My people are destroyed for lack of knowledge because you, O priests, have rejected knowledge. …[Y]ou have forgotten the law of your God…" (v. 6). The religious leaders of the day feed the people what they want to hear rather than what they need to hear.[3] However, the people themselves are accomplices with the leaders; they agree to be led in the wrong direction. So it's going to be "like people, like priests" (v. 9). That is, God will judge both for their unwillingness to learn and appropriate his instruction.

Knowledge of God is the fundamental quality of being God's people. This knowledge grows over time; it involves instruction, discipline, experience, humility, prayer, and commitment. Hosea describes it as a marriage relationship. God uses Hosea's own marriage to Gomer to describe his relationship to Israel. God reached out to Israel; he loved and accepted her. But Israel did not respond. In Hosea's case, Gomer displayed no faithfulness or steadfast love. She refused to develop an intimate knowledge of her husband. Israel refuses to come to a knowledge of God and it grieves God. What God

---

[3] See Rick Marrs in chapter two of this volume.

longs for is to enter into a relationship with his people in which they commit to a lifetime of growing in knowledge of him. That's what's supposed to happen in a marriage relationship. A couple seeks to grow in their love and understanding of one other. They desire to learn everything they can about the other: their likes and dislikes, their strengths and weaknesses, their dreams and goals. As they do, they bring out the best in each other and enable the other to grow.

In my own marriage, in order have a relationship with my wife, Nancy, I must know some basic facts about her. I must know her background and her family of origin. I must also know the little things that she likes or dislikes. For example, I know that she likes Dr. Pepper. I know that her feet easily get cold. She has repeatedly told me, "If I'm sick and unable to talk, be sure my feet are covered." I know she likes watching Andy Griffith reruns.

Though we have many common interests, I also know that we are different. For example, because of her servant heart she stops to help stranded motorists; I do not. She works better under pressure; I plan far in advance. Being around a lot of people energizes her. Being around a lot of people drains me.

In addition, we've also learned what buttons to push whenever we want to irritate the other. I know that she despises me *chewing* hard candy. So if I want to irritate her, I'll just pop a couple of Life Savers in my mouth and start chomping down. I like to have things in their proper place. For Nancy wherever an item is last used, that's where it belongs. That irritates me!

We've been married for twenty-seven years and we're still learning more about each other. After all these years, I finally figured out why the inside of her van is often so full of a variety of material like paper and pens and folders and other school supplies. It's because she sees the van as an extension of her purse. What we've also learned is that compatibility is not something that a couple either has or does not have. It is something that develops through commitment and by spending time with one another. That's what it means to know one another.

For us to know God means we spend time in listening to his word and talking to him in prayer. We learn about his character.

We know his likes and dislikes. We know what grieves him and what brings him joy. We reach out to those he reaches out to. We open our hands to the poor, the oppressed, to those who are suffering. We look for opportunities to serve those whom God serves. We spend time with people who love and worship him. In so doing we come to know God.

For those who come to know God, the results are not unlike a couple who has spent a lifetime together. Because they have committed themselves to one another for better or for worse, in sickness and in health, their relationship deepens. They reach a point where they experience love beyond what words can describe. They know what the other is thinking. They can complete each other's sentences. They even begin to look alike. They truly know each other.

Helmut Thielicke tells of such a couple he knew who radiated joy. The wife's body was riddled with arthritis. Yet she exuded gratitude for life. Why, he asked, was she so radiant in spite of her physical infirmities? He answered his own question when he saw how they interacted with each other. This couple loved each other deeply. She was like a stone that had been lying in the sun for years and years, absorbing all its radiant warmth, and now was reflecting back cheerfulness and warmth and serenity.[4]

Christians spend a lifetime basking in the knowledge of God. We learn his will, we know his heart, we experience his love, we associate with his people, and we begin to reflect his character. In the end we come to radiate a joy for life that no experience can quench, no pain can destroy, and no threat can defeat.

---

[4] Helmut Thielicke, *How The World Began*, (Philadelphia: Fortress Press, 1961), 99.

# 10

# *The Loving Father*
## *Hosea 11:1-9*

Dave Bland

## *Introduction*

In chapter 2 of this volume Rick Marrs speaks of three primary metaphors Hosea uses to communicate the shattering of the covenant relationship: the husband and wife, the vineyard owner and vineyard, and the parent and child. This text and sermon develops the parent and child metaphor. Rick discovers that with all three images, Hosea's theology remains consistent: Yahweh remains faithful to his people despite their rebellion. In Hosea 11, God loves in spite of the ingratitude of his children. God's love is fiercely personal and intimate. As Rick concludes, "He refuses to take the easy route and simply sever the relationship with his rebellious people."

In this text, the reader gets a glimpse of the heart of the prophet. Will Willimon points out, contrary to popular belief, that there is not a sharp distinction between prophetic and pastoral ministry. The prophets did not stand over against the community of faith and hurl oracles from God against them. Rather they stood within the community and took the anguish and suffering of the people and of God upon themselves. They spoke to the people through identifying with them. The prophets were not "lone rangers." They were loyal members of the faith community.

After reading the original manuscript of this sermon, Bob Reid classified this sermon in the Teaching voice. One of the keys that qualified it for this voice was my conclusion, of which Bob wrote, "The sermon concludes with a specific application of the sermon's implications for Christian living." Since I wanted the Sage voice to dominate in this sermon, I eliminated the final paragraph and allowed the contemporary story of the adopted son to stand on its own. Through the use of a personal story woven within the sermon, I invite listeners to explore the meaning of this text for their own lives. My intention is to permit listeners to evaluate their own feelings and thoughts on how God's grace manifests itself in their personal experiences. Readers can decide for themselves what voice dominates this sermon or whether my voice is "not authentic" but divided between Teaching and Sage.

This text is the Old Testament counterpart to Luke 15 and the parable of the prodigal son and the loving father. It encapsulates the heart of Old Testament theology.

## *The Loving Father*

It appears to me that next to the soaps, one of the most popular daytime TV programs is the courtroom judge. In the 80s it was *People's Court* with Judge Wapner. Judge Wapner was not afraid to come down hard on folks, giving them what they deserved. But these days there are a whole new breed of judges: Judge Marylyn is now on *People's Court* and her competitors are Judge Joe Brown and Judge Judy. These are judges on steroids! Joe Brown, who appears quite irresponsible with his own judicial duties in Memphis, doesn't let that stop him from doling out biting justice to those in his TV court in Hollywood.

Then there's Judge Judy, "justice with an attitude." Judge Judy rants and raves. She's not afraid to call someone a "jerk" or "stupid" or a "low life." She intimidates and humiliates. These judges are popular because they leave the impression that wrongs are righted, the lazy are rebuked, and the abusive spouse is punished. Whatever your impression is of these TV judges, they are a big hit with American audiences.

These TV judges are sometimes the image we have when we think of the prophets. Some may see the eighth century prophets like Hosea as counterparts to Judge Judy. These prophets stood before the people, railing at them, "Prepare to meet your God!"

It is true that the prophets called people to accountability and demanded justice. They were outspoken critics of oppression. They identified the sin that inhabited people's lives. But there is one major difference between the biblical prophets and the TV judges. The message of the prophets was rooted in the deep and long-lasting relationship that God had with his people. We can more easily disregard the anger of someone we perceive as an enemy than we can the anguished wrath that flows out of someone we love. The prophets' message flowed out of a posture of deep anguish and grief, more than anger, because they were servants of a God who was "slow to anger and abounding in steadfast love" and because they were intimately involved in the lives of God's people.

One cannot read the prophets without situating their message in its proper context: it is the context of grace and mercy. Yes, the heart of the prophetic message is not punishment and judgment but a message of grace. Hosea 11 represents this message.

We are quite familiar with the story of Hosea in the first three chapters of the book. He and his wife, Gomer, had three children, two boys and a girl. His wife, however, was unfaithful to him, an adulterer. She left him to follow after her other lovers. We're quite familiar with that part of the story. But what happened to the rest of the family while Gomer was sowing her wild oats?

What about the three children? We aren't told. But it might not be too farfetched to imagine that Hosea raised those children on his own. Hosea may have been a single parent. That's a pretty tough life. One can imagine that as the three children get older, they too, like their mother, become rebellious. They have no respect for their father. They begin to sow their wild oats. And it breaks Hosea's heart. Not only does Hosea have to deal with an unfaithful wife, but rebellious children as well.

This may be the personal background to the text in Hosea 11. Just as God used Hosea's marriage to Gomer in the first three chapters to describe his relationship with his wife, Israel, so in chapter 11, God uses Hosea's experience as a parent to describe his relationship to his children, Israel.

According to 11:1 Israel, described as a son, had been abandoned in Egypt. But God adopted him. God called him out of Egypt. God, as parent, cared deeply for his child. The verbs that describe his care dominate the first four verses: loved, cared, fed, taught, led, healed, took up in his arms. Here is a father who is daily involved in the life of his children, fulfilling not only paternal, but also maternal responsibilities. He is a nurturing parent.

But the son rebels. The more God calls him, the more distant the son becomes. Still, God does not withdraw. He is a patient and loving parent. He continues to care for his son in spite of the son's ingratitude. A point is reached, however, where the son's ingratitude and rebelliousness threatens the life of the whole family.

God is a loving father, but he is not an overindulgent parent who never disciplines. This father, like Hosea, grieves and becomes angry with his son whose actions are self-destructive. Coming through this passage, we hear all the anguish, the anger, and the disappointment of a parent whose son has ruined himself. The parent pours himself out to the child, but the child turns his back (v. 7).

I have a friend who is a Christian; she is the mother of two wonderful children. She is married to a dedicated Christian man. There was a time, however, when as a young adult in college, she was rebellious. She was a prodigal daughter. It grieved her parents deeply. They would probably tell you that that was the worst time in their lives. They begged and pleaded with her. They prayed earnestly for her but to no avail. They shed many tears.

Only a parent who has gone through such an experience can really understand such anger and remorse and grief, all mixed in together. Such parents cry out in anguish: "We thought we had taught him well, but he has rebelled." "How did this happen?" "Why won't she come to her senses and let us help her?" "Doesn't she know how much she's hurting us?" You see, even within the most nurturing environment, children can rebel. Hosea was a loving, nurturing parent. God was the perfect parent. But their children rebelled.

And God grieves. The legal background to Hosea 11 is Deuteronomy 21:18-21. When parents had a rebellious son who repeatedly disobeyed them, and would not listen to them, they brought him before the elders in the city gate for punishment. And there, before the elders, the son was put to death.

That is the legal background to Hosea 11. So what is to be done to this son on this occasion? What does the law say? In the father's anger, he says, "Punish him!" And the court agrees.

My friend, at one point, ended up in a jail in Dallas, Texas. Her parents found out where she was. And her Dad wrote a letter to the judge. He asked the judge, who was thinking of dismissing the charges, to not do so. He asked the judge to give her the sentence that she deserved. The parents made that request because they loved their daughter.

With deep remorse and with a broken heart, God pronounces his son guilty and calls for his punishment. But something happens, a change of attitude occurs. The father cannot, no he will not, abandon his son:

> How can I give you up, Ephraim?
>
> How can I hand you over, O Israel?
> How can I make you like Admah?
>
> How can I treat you like Zeboiim?
> My heart recoils within me;
>
> my compassion grows warm and tender.
> I will not execute my fierce anger;
>
> I will not again destroy Ephraim;
> for I am God and no mortal,
>
> the Holy One in your midst,
> and I will not come in wrath (vv. 8-9).

He will not stone his rebellious son as the law requires. Anger gives way to compassion as the father addresses his son. With tears streaming down his cheeks, his arms stretched out, he invites his prodigal son home.

What caused this about-face? The son certainly has not changed. Has God backed down? Gone soft? Not at all. The key is verse 9. "For I am God and no mortal...." God acts not according to what they deserve, but according to what love requires. Be assured, God's love did not cancel out the punishment. Israel will experience punishment. But punishment is not the final word. God does not give up. The final word is God's steadfast love.

What God has in mind is that some day his children, Israel, will remember the steadfast love and mercy their father poured out on them. He longs that they, like the prodigal son, will return home. But if they return, it is not because of who they are. It is because of the enduring love of their father. It is God's grace that initiates the return. When Israel finally recognizes what God has done, she will come running back to him.

My friend finally ended up in a little county jail in west Texas. She reached the end of her rope. She had nowhere to turn. She was utterly broken. But in her memory she could not forget the grace and mercy of two loving parents. And she came to herself. Her road back to recovery and wholeness was not easy; it was a long and difficult one. But she changed. That's what God's love does. It changes you.

Rubel Shelly tells about a student in his second year of college at a Christian University in the early 70s. He had to work his way through school. During his sophomore year he was working in the admissions office, doing some filing. One day, with a little time on his hands, he did something he shouldn't have done. He decided to go back into the files of students already admitted and look at his own application. He wanted to see what different references had said about him, his character, and his academic work. He opened up his file and as he was examining the sheet that his parents had filled out, this 19-year-old discovered for the first time that he was an adopted child. His parents had received him when he was four days old. For whatever reason, his parents had chosen to keep his adoption confidential.

When he discovered that, he literally dropped the folder, left the office, the school, got in his car and drove. A short time later, having come back into the office and seeing the folder lying open on the floor, different office workers pieced together what had happened. They called the parents who lived about three hours away and said, "Your son has apparently seen his files and discovered that he was adopted. He's headed your way. Be prepared!" Sure enough, three hours later, he wheeled into the drive, ran up the steps, threw the door open and tearfully confronted his parents and said, "If only I'd known how much you loved me. You adopted me. You chose me. You let me be yours." He hugged them and kissed them and thanked them in ways he had never been able to before because he didn't know. That's the way it is with God's love.

# 11 | *Worshipping God*
## *Isaiah 6:1-8; 1:10-15*

Dave Bland

## Introduction

In the following sermon, I call listeners to transformation of their understanding of worship in light of Isaiah's experience in the temple (Isa 6). I would locate this sermon in Bob Reid's Personal and Determinate quadrant, which puts the sermon in the mode of the Encouraging voice. My intention is to enable listeners to come to a new understanding (personal transformation) of what qualifies as acceptable worship before God. Bob Reid maintains that when a sermon's design is to lead listeners to a personal decision of transformation, that is an important use of the Encouraging voice. Bob adds, "Encouraging preachers shape sermons with the intention that listeners feel renewed hope, stronger faith, a desire to recommit, etc. They view preaching as an event in which listeners have the opportunity to meet the living God, have an encounter with grace, an encounter with the Holy, or renew their zeal to let the Spirit of God be released to affect some work of grace in their lives."

As both Bob and William Willimon point out, via Tom Long, one of the most significant turns in contemporary homiletics today is the turn to the listener. The New Homiletics is listener oriented. That also reflects the focus of contemporary worship; it is oriented toward the listener/worshipper. Isaiah's encounter with the Holy One in the temple challenges our contemporary focus. Will states it succinctly in chapter 1 in this volume:

> Much of current homiletic literature therefore tends to be mostly rhetoric, strategies for gaining a hearing, speculation upon the limits and capabilities of contemporary congregations. Prophetic preaching cares about none of this. Prophetic preaching worries more about listening to and speaking for God and less about listener approval, visible results, church growth, seeker sensitivity, user friendliness, and other ways that we pay more attention to what the congregation is able to hear than to what the Trinity is able to say.

Fred Craddock, in a recent lecture, concludes that the audience of our preaching is not the congregation but God because preaching is an act of worship. To help us remember that, he suggests that once a month before a particular Sunday comes, we go to the sanctuary, sit in a pew, and pray our sermon to God.

Isaiah 1:10-15 is the cleansing of the temple in reverse. Rather than God throwing out all of Israel's temple furniture and peace offerings, he simply shakes the dust off his feet and washes his hands of having anything to do with their public worship. God refuses to enter the temple. Following the preaching of this sermon, we moved directly into partaking of the Lord's Supper. Immediately following that, the congregation was led in a public confession of faith, "The Lord is gracious, merciful, slow to anger, abounding in steadfast love and faithfulness" (Exod 34:6). Following this confession, the congregation watched a video entitled "That's My King" in which the African-American preacher, Samuel Lockridge, describes God with one adjectival superlative after another.[1]

---

[1] Samuel Lockridge, "That's My King," Menlo Park Presbyterian Church, 1996.

## *Worshipping God*

Christian churches across this land are currently in the midst of what's been referred to as "worship wars." Protestant churches of all stripes are wrestling over issues of what goes on in worship. We in Churches of Christ have our own worship struggles. Representative of these wars is the issue of the type of music we sing. Do we go with a contemporary musical taste that emphasizes praise songs? Or do we settle for more traditional or classical hymns?

On the one hand, the "contemporary" music appeals more to the unchurched and speaks more to our own young people. It is important for such worship to be kept upbeat and moving at a pace where people can get involved and express their feelings (through hands and voices and visuals). But the criticism is that we fall into a kind of *Sister Act* syndrome. This syndrome believes that the way to revive a lethargic and dying church is to beef up the music. Upbeat music will transform a church into a vibrant and dynamic community. All that a church really needs in order to turn around is to give the music department a shot in the arm.

On the other hand, "traditional" music often appeals to the older members in the congregation. It carries a rich history that often expresses the central beliefs of our faith. But the criticism is that these hymns no longer speak to the younger generation. It's like the shopping mall that had difficulty with young people using its stores as a place to hang out and therefore attracting trouble. So mall authorities got the creative idea of piping in "easy listening" music over the intercom and in a short while the youth scattered to the four winds. Some would say that the church is playing easy listening music and driving the younger generation away.

For both groups, the starting point for what goes on in worship is "What am I comfortable with?" "How can I best express myself in worship?" In beginning at this point, we find ourselves bogged down in worship wars.

What is the beginning point of worship in Scripture? What does Isaiah have to say about it? An underlying question woven through Isaiah chapters 1-12 is "What's supposed to happen in worship? Why do you come into the presence of God?"

There was a worship war going on between Israel and God. In Isaiah's day people were quite concerned with the public assembly. In chapter one, Israel faces a crisis. Jerusalem is being invaded. Isaiah gives a description of their worship in 1:10-15. Notice the abundance of activities: a multitude of sacrifices, incense, new moon and Sabbath assemblies, appointed feasts, and prayers. Israel's strategy was to beef up their worship activity with the intention of putting God in a covenantal half nelson in order to force him to respond favorably to them.

But surprisingly God is not pleased with their worship activity at all. God is irritated! He's had enough of their burnt offerings, he hates their feasts, he's going to cover his eyes and close his ears to their worship. The irony is that while the sanctuaries are full of worshippers, God refuses to show up. He was fed up, angry!

So what's God's problem? Isaiah states it succinctly later in the book: "The people draw near with their mouth and honor me with their lips. But their hearts are far from me" (Isa 29:13). The problem was Israel's attitude toward worship. Israel was arrogant. Worship was an avenue for negotiating with God; it was a way of obligating God to them.

That was not what God desired. A contrast exists in Isaiah 1 between what the people do (vv. 10-15) and what God really wants (vv. 16-20). The worshippers come with an attitude of pride: "Lord, look what we have to offer." What God wants is worshippers who come into his presence in humility and as penitent sinners (vv. 18-19). What God wants is the sacrifice of a broken and contrite heart.

This is where Isaiah 6 enters the picture. Chapter 6 stands as the watershed point of the first twelve chapters. It serves as the interpretive key to chapters 1-5 that precede and chapters 7-12 that follow.

Isaiah goes to the temple to worship. There God manifests himself to Isaiah; Isaiah sees a vision of the Almighty. God's presence fills the temple. Isaiah sees the fierce-looking seraphim with their six wings encircling the throne. Normally in ancient near eastern literature, the seraphim are described as hovering over the gods to protect them. But here they cower (covering their feet and eyes) in the presence of the living

God. The seraphim must protect themselves from God! God is overwhelmingly powerful; it's a terrifying experience for those who come into his presence to worship. One of the seraphs cries out, "Holy, Holy, Holy is the Lord of hosts; the whole earth is full of his glory."

Worship in contemporary contexts is typically oriented toward the worshippers. We understand worship to fulfill one of several purposes. Sometimes it is designed to please worshippers so that they can escape the problems of the world for an hour and lose themselves in an aesthetically satisfying experience. Or sometimes worship serves as a therapy, intended to provide spiritual healing and enable the worshippers to feel better. Or sometimes its purpose is to educate the worshippers about the Christian life, which basically means preaching longer sermons. All of these purposes orient worship horizontally toward the worshipper.

The worship Isaiah describes is initially directed away from the worshipper and toward the living God who sits on the throne. The worship going on here expresses awe to a transcendent and sovereign God, a God who is shrouded in mystery and power. Annie Dillard is correct when she says that we don't come before the living God as "cheerful, brainless tourists on a packaged tour of the Absolute." Rather as we enter the assembly we should all be wearing crash helmets![2] I think we need to have, not flight attendants, but worship attendants who welcome us to worship and as we enter, issue life preservers and signal flares and announce, "Be sure that you are securely fastened into your body harness before take-off. If we reach too high an altitude during this worship, oxygen masks will automatically drop from the ceiling." We are in the presence of the Holy God, creator of the universe!

In describing worship in the holy of holies in the temple, Lawrence Kushner offers a spicy detail.[3] The holy of holies was so sacred that only the high priest could go in once a year on

<hr />

[2] Annie Dillard, *Teaching a Stone to Talk* (New York: Harper & Row, 1982), 40.

[3] Lawrence Kushner, *God Was In This Place and I Did Not Know* (Woodstock, VT: Jewish Lights, 1991), 96-97.

the Day of Atonement. If the High Priest dropped dead of a heart attack while standing before God, his body could not be retrieved. So before the high priest went into this most sacred place, they tied a rope around his leg, in order to have a way to drag him out without risk to themselves.

As Isaiah witnesses the sight of the fierce creatures cowering in the presence of the Almighty God and the thresholds of the temple trembling and smoke filling the house, he was overwhelmed, and shuddered with fear. His only response is to cry out to the Lord, "Woe is me, for I am lost, for I am a man of unclean lips amidst a people of unclean lips."

That's the starting point for acceptable worship before God. It is not our comfort level. Actually it's just the opposite. It's our discomfort with our sinfulness in the presence of a holy God. In his hallowed presence we feel more keenly our humanness and the burden of our own transgressions.

In the short run, worship does not seem to make Isaiah feel better about himself or his neighbors. In fact, he felt deep remorse for who he was in God's presence. It did not serve an aesthetic purpose in order to relieve Isaiah of his worldly problems. I wonder what Isaiah would have said about worship that day if you interviewed him afterward? My theology of worship has been that we leave with a word of hope. We leave encouraged and edified and often that should happen. But in light of Isaiah, I wonder if there are some occasions where we leave the presence of this holy, completely other God feeling overwhelmed about being there. And in coming into his presence we acquire a greater realization of our human frailty and sinful nature.

In past generations there was more of a persona of fear and trepidation generated when one came into the public assembly. Today the dominant posture is a casual one. God is my friend, my buddy; God and I are tight. We walk through gardens and fields together. "We walk and talk as good friends should and do." According to Isaiah, coming into the presence of the living God is an overwhelming experience. For God, Sunday is his day to "Shock and Awe" his people. The preacher of Hebrews reminds his audience of what it is like to come before the God of the universe. Though we do not experience the earth shaking or the blazing fire and smoke that Israel saw and felt at Sinai in God's presence, we still offer "God acceptable worship with reverence and awe, for indeed our God is a consuming fire" (Heb 12:18-29).

But as difficult as it is to imagine, there is something even more terrifying than coming into the presence of the living God. Isaiah says that what is more horrifying that being in God's presence is God's absence in our assemblies. As someone has said, "maybe we're spending far too much time trying to figure out how to comfortably express ourselves. Perhaps we should spend more time trying to attract an increasingly irritated God" who may, as in the days of Isaiah, be covering his ears and closing his eyes to our worship.

Coming before the living God begins with a broken and contrite heart. The posture in which I come into the presence of the Lord God Almighty, creator of the universe, is a posture that humbly acknowledges my sins, my transgression. The call to worship causes me to cry out in anguish, "Woe is me."

Last fall while I was in our chapel worship at the seminary, a student gave a testimony. He started off in this fashion: "I want to tell you my story. I was a cross dresser, a homosexual, and an alcoholic. I was into pornography and drugs. I was an adulterer." All the time he was listing these sins, he was using his fingers to count. He was only about twenty-five years old! He got up to nine fingers and then paused and said, "Let's see did I miss any?" I thought to myself, "Wow, I sure hope not!" He was not flaunting his sins at all. He was confessing out of deep humility. Then he added, "The reason it took me so long to face up to my sins and confess them is because I knew what you Christians really thought of people like me."

When we come into the presence of the sovereign, transcendent God, all bases for boasting are destroyed. All have sinned and fallen short of God's holiness. Maybe we should begin worship the way Alcoholics Anonymous teaches its members to introduce themselves, "Hi, I'm Jane, and I'm an alcoholic, but by the help of a higher power, a recovering one." This is the only posture in which I can stand before God and you today: "I'm Dave, and I'm a sinner. But by the amazing grace of God, I'm a recovering one." Only then can worship begin.

# 12

# *The Peaceable Kingdom*

## *Isaiah 11:6-9*

Dave Bland

## *Introduction*

William Willimon makes the astute observation that even though prophetic speech displays much variety, the oracles typically fall into three moves or categories: *"Judgment that indicts Israel for disobedience to God's Covenant and punishment that fits the crime. Grief. Call to repentance and return to covenantal obedience. Change. Promise of the gift of new life and open future that comes from a gracious and merciful God. Hope"* (italics Willimon). The sermon that follows falls into the third category: hope.

Will continues his comments regarding oracles of promise and hope:

> The prophets preach against a backdrop of faith in Yahweh's ability ultimately to make a new heaven and a new earth, to transform, convert, rebirth. Though our situation is grim, the prophets' fundamental faith in Yahweh's ability to get the family he deserves enables them to be not only brutally honest but also extravagantly hopeful. Any preacher who believes that things are unchangeably fixed, unalterably frozen by sociological, psychological, genetic, economic determinisms is not being true to the God of the

prophets who creates, plucks up, plants, brings a new heaven and a new earth. Prophets can sound so very pessimistic about human prospects for renewal because they are so unabashedly optimistic about God's ability to transform.

The oracle in Isaiah 11:1-9 is one of the most familiar eschatological visions in the Old Testament. The oracle envisions a new order in creation. Creation is transformed into a kingdom in which all of God's creatures live in peace with one another. Scripture closely ties peace in the natural world with peace in the human world; the two worlds are interrelated. Creation reflects the character and quality of the human community. The natural world is value-laden. John Fortner puts it this way: "A linkage between the well-being of the physical world and the ethical behavior of its inhabitants is as old as Eden." Later John observes "…Israel's sins are not only anti-Torah, they…are also anti-creational." This sermon attempts to establish that link.

This sermon also tries to perform the "homiletical model" that Tim Sensing engages from Zechariah chapters 7-8, except from the perspective of Isaiah. Both Isaiah and Zechariah believe that God has inaugurated the coming of his future kingdom in the present. Both also envision the coming of God's kingdom with children at the center. In Zechariah's case it is children peacefully playing in a public square. In Isaiah's case it is children peacefully playing over the den of poisonous snakes.

The description of animals living together in peace and harmony (11:6-9) has frequently been interpreted symbolically or allegorically. John T. Willis in his commentary on Isaiah interprets the text not as describing peace among animals, "but peace between men who would normally be hostile toward each other."[1] Similarly, Christopher Seitz speaks of the animals as symbolizing different nations at war with one another and a vision of world peace.[2] However, there is no other place

---

[1] John T. Willis, *Isaiah* (Austin, TX: Sweet Publishing, 1980), 203-205.

[2] Christopher Seitz, *Isaiah 1-39* (Atlanta: John Knox Press, 1993), 106-107.

in Isaiah 1-39 where this kind of allegory is used, except in the case of the vineyard in Isaiah 5:1-7 in which the prophet explicitly states that the vineyard symbolizes Israel. It is out of character for the prophet to use symbolism or allegory without explanation. Therefore I interpret the text literally to refer to the animal kingdom.

The sermon focus is the following: The vision of God transforming creation into a peaceable kingdom gives Christians hope for living faithfully in the present. The preacher might want to seek out the paintings of the American Quaker and artist Edward Hicks (1780-1849). Hicks painted over sixty versions of "The Peaceable Kingdom" based on Isaiah 11:6-9.[3] The preacher might also want to read Matthew Schully's recent work on the suffering of animals and human's responsibility to the natural world.[4]

---

[3] See *Christianity Today*, October 25, 1999, 98-99; see also Alice Ford, *Edward Hicks: His Life and Art* (New York: Abbeville Press), 1985.

[4] Matthew Scully, *Dominion: The Power of Man, the Suffering of Animals, and the Call to Mercy* (New York: St. Martin's Griffin), 2002.

## *The Peaceable Kingdom*

In a famous incident that occurred back in the 1960s, the World Health Organization tried to help residents of Borneo exterminate houseflies, which were suspected of spreading disease among humans. Officials sprayed the insides of houses with large quantities of DDT, an action that triggered a disastrous chain of events. As the flies died, lizards devoured the fly corpses and became sick from the DDT in them. Then house cats ate the poisoned lizards and likewise died. The loss of the cats resulted in an over infestation of rats. The rats then threatened the population with bubonic plague. Finally the government arranged for large numbers of foreign cats to be parachuted into the area in order to rid the country of rat-infested homes.[5] A delicate balance exists between humans and nature. When one suffers they all suffer.

The world in which we live is fearfully and wonderfully related. The prophets paint a picture of the interdependence of all creation. A bond exists between people and land because of a common bond both have with God. God is creator of all. But when that bond with God is broken, nature also suffers.

The best-known prophetic reference to this relationship and to a vision of the ideal world is Isaiah 11, the picture of the peaceable kingdom. No fewer than thirteen animals are listed in this text. The vision pairs predators with prey: wolf with lamb; leopard with kid; lion with calf. They will live together in peace. Domestic animals will no longer live in fear of wild animals. No more Discovery Channel programs that show scenes of animals attacking, killing, and shredding one another. This is a vision of an ideal world without violence of any kind.

The only humans pictured in the scene are children (vv. 6, 8). A small child has charge of the first group: wolf, leopard, and lion. And infants can play at will over the den of a poisonous snake. There will come a time when the world will be made safe for wild and domestic animals and children.

This is an amazing vision, an idyllic vision. Some church historians would say that we catch a glimpse of this peaceable

---

[5] Paul R Ehrlich and Anne H Ehrlich, *Extinction: The Causes and Consequences of the Disappearance of Species* (New York : Random House),1981), 79.

kingdom during the Middle Ages in the life and legend of Francis of Assisi. The next time you go by St. Francis hospital [in Memphis, Tennessee], notice the statue out front. It depicts St. Francis with a dove in his hand, one on his shoulder, and one at his feet. Francis of Assisi was known for his love for nature and for animals. The animals sensed his love and care for them and responded to him with no fear. Legends swirl around him about how he talked to birds: on one occasion as he was preaching, a legend goes, the swallows around him began chirping so loudly it was hard to for the audience to hear. St. Francis called them to silence and they obeyed. On one occasion he supposedly preached a sermon to birds. Such legends about him are reminiscent of the vision of the peaceable kingdom.

As Christians, what are we to do to enable this vision to come to reality? How do we take responsibility for initiating efforts to bring about this kingdom? A few months ago the *Commercial Appeal* ran an article about feedlots and slaughterhouses taking steps to treat animals more humanely.[6] Restaurant chains like McDonalds now have guidelines for animal welfare and will not buy from companies that do not uphold these standards. Here is an effort to treat animals with more respect and dignity. We applaud these efforts, but it still is a far cry from the vision portrayed in these verses.

Just ask Roy Horn how far removed we are from this vision. Horn, who lived with and trained tigers all his life, was mauled just a few weeks ago by one of his own "pet" tigers. Our human efforts to bring about peace and harmony seem to fail, more often than not. We are a long way from Isaiah's vision of the peaceable kingdom.

A key to understanding this text is to understand that it is closely related to what precedes. The vision of the peaceable kingdom contains a prerequisite that is described in vv. 1-5. These verses depict the character of the ideal king, the messiah that some day will reign. This messiah rules by the spirit of the knowledge of the Lord and the spirit of wisdom, counsel, and understanding. This king does not judge by what he sees (a bribe) or by what he hears (propaganda) but in righteousness. Righteousness and faithfulness will clothe his body. The result

---

[6] *The Commercial Appeal* (Memphis, May 11, 2003).

of his rule is that humans will live at peace with one another. Families will live in harmonious relationship with one another. Communities will look out for one another and care for one another and show compassion. No one will be left in want.

When humans treat one another with respect and care, the results are that all of creation is affected. The rule of justice in a new society (vv. 1-5) is followed by a transformation in the relationship among animals and between animals and human beings (vv. 6-11). Corruption within human society leads to destruction of the environment and all its creatures. When people are faithful in their responsibility to God and to one another, they will also demonstrate faithful stewardship toward creation, and the land will flourish. No more "dog eat dog" lifestyle. Human justice leads to a transformed relationship between human beings and the rest of creation.

Edward Hicks, a Quaker and preacher in the early 1800s, was a self-taught painter. He was not well known during his lifetime. It was only after his death that his work became popular. His favorite scene to paint was Isaiah 11:6-11. He typically painted it with William Penn in the background making a treaty with the Native American Indians. In the foreground are the domestic and wild animals and children living in peace with one another. It is significant that he connected the two worlds of humans and animals. Harmony in the human world influenced harmony in the natural world.

Isaiah says that nature is defiled because of ignorance of God. The languishing of creation is a sign that people do not know God. Creation suffering from pollution is a call for humanity to repent. But when humans come to know God, creation thrives. Isaiah says the peaceable kingdom will arrive when the whole earth is as full of the knowledge of God as the sea is full of water. When all of humanity enters into relationship with God, creation will be transformed.

In one sense this vision is a wake-up call for us to act responsibly toward other, to practice righteousness and faithfulness. But regardless of how responsibly we act toward others we will never usher in a peaceable kingdom on our own. That is ultimately God's work. So our first response to this vision is to praise God for what he is now working to bring about. When we allow this vision to fill our hearts and minds, we cannot help but break forth in praise to God that he in his own good time will bring this vision to reality. This passage does not command or admonish. We've come to expect sermons, especially from the prophets to chastise or rebuke. We expect sermons to challenge us to a call to action. And there are times when that's what Scripture calls preachers to do. But there are also times when Scripture simply calls us to rejoice in the hope we have in God. This text does not contain a persuasive appeal to go and do something. It does not even offer a criticism of injustices. These lines simply present unqualified good news. We rejoice in what God is doing right now to bring about that peaceable kingdom. It may seem far off but we believe God and his messiah are bringing it into reality. We praise God. The basis for hope in the Old Testament is not faith in human progress, but the assurance of a coming divine intervention that will introduce a new order of life that people have failed and will continue to fail to achieve. Our hope is in God and not in humans.

This vision gives us hope. It gives hope to people who are tired and weary, to those who are suffering, who find their world in chaos and who are discouraged. So we revel in this vision. We allow it to frame our life, to inform our thoughts to shape our decisions. The Quaker preacher, Edward Hicks, allowed this vision to captivate his life and passion. He spent his life painting pictures of the peaceable kingdom of Isaiah 11. Some historians estimate that Hicks painted nearly a hundred different versions. His life was absorbed in and infatuated with this vision. It was the inspiration for his life as a Quaker.

This vision provided inspiration for someone else as well. In 1939, as the Great Depression continued to wear on and wear the country down, Thomas A. Dorsey, an African-American composer, published a hymn for Mahalia Jackson. Later, Tennessee Ernie Ford sang it. And, finally, Elvis Presley popularized it. But in 1939 when this country and land was still in the grips of despair, Dorsey composed the hymn, "Peace in the Valley" based on the vision of Isaiah 11 that offered hope to the prophet's oppressed people.

Speaking through this text, God continues to provide his people with hope and inspiration. This text leaves us not with something to do but with something to rejoice in and to hope for. As you listen to this hymn by Thomas Dorsey, allow his version of Isaiah's vision to inspire, encourage, and give you hope in God.

Well, I'm tired and so weary,
But I must go along,
Till the Lord comes and calls me away,
O yes;
Well, the morning is bright,
And the Lamb is the Light,
And the night, night is as fair as the day,
O yes.

Chorus:
There will be peace in the valley for me some day,
There will be peace in the valley for me, O Lord, I pray,
There'll be no sadness, no sorrow, no trouble I'll see,
There will be peace in the valley for me.

There the flow'rs will be blooming
and the grass will be green,
And the skies will be clear and serene,
O yes;
Well, the sun ever beams,
In this valley of dreams,
And no clouds there will ever be seen,
O yes.

(Chorus)

Well the bear will be gentle,
And the wolf will be tame,
And the lion will lie down by the lamb,
O yes;
Well, the beast from the wild
Will be led by a child,
And I'll be changed, changed from this creature that I am,
O yes.
Chorus:[7]

---

[7] I want to express my thanks to Bill Roberts and the Everyday Singers of Portland, Oregon who recorded this song. While the song was sung, images corresponding to the lyrics were displayed on a screen. Examples of Edward Hicks' paintings of "The Peaceable Kingdom" were interspersed at the appropriate places.

# 13

# *The Snake in the Pew*

## *Amos 5:18-27*

Mark Frost
Trenton Church of Christ,
Trenton Michigan

## Introduction

In this sermon, I have attempted to pay attention to Robert Reid's concept of voices in preaching. Specifically, my intent was to employ what Reid calls the Testifying Voice, which seeks to "engage listeners in a dialogue with the language of their theological tradition." He characterizes this voice as "preaching to exiles."

Exiles, of course, are people cut off from their cultural roots who must reinterpret their traditions in a way that makes sense of their new reality. I have long seen my ministry in this light. For the past twenty-five years, I have worked with a Church of Christ in metropolitan Detroit. Most of the founding members of the congregation were exiles: Southerners who came to the area for jobs in the auto industry. For them, the church was their connection to the culture they left behind. In the local Church of Christ, people spoke with familiar accents, and the potluck dinners featured dishes that reminded them of home. The problem arose with the next generation. The founders' children were more midwestern than southern and often had difficulty separating biblical truth from the cultural trappings with which it was surrounded. In my ministry, I have sought to express the core beliefs of the founders in terms that connect with their children (and with our surrounding midwestern community).

A further dimension of preaching to exiles arises from the need to reach postmodern people in our secularized society. I believe the restoration plea of the Churches of Christ has the ability to resonate deeply with the postmodern mindset. The difficulty is that our restoration movement has roots deeply entrenched in the Enlightenment and modernity. In more recent times, I have attempted to champion the principle of biblical restoration while challenging our members to examine and reinterpret the framework of modernity in which that principle has been packaged.

A pattern of preaching that has been effective in addressing my congregation of exiles has been: (1) presentation of "what we've always believed," (2) disturbing the hearers' equilibrium by presenting a disorienting word from God, and (3) challenging the hearers to adjust their beliefs and behaviors in light of that word. This sermon follows that pattern, but with the added dimension that the reorientation is envisioned as a communal enterprise, not just a matter for individual reflection.

This sermon begins by bringing to mind some of the religious nomenclature that once made Churches of Christ unique. Next, listeners are invited to recall and value another distinctive element of our tradition: the weekly observance of the Lord's Supper. At this point, Amos 5 is inserted as a destabilizing message. Amos suggests that God is not honored when we seclude ourselves in the cocoon of our subculture and perpetuate our traditions; rather, he longs for us to engage the broader culture by championing justice and righteousness.

At its end, the sermon comes full-circle back to the Lord's Supper. But this time, the invitation is to come to the table not as a means of fulfilling some required element, but as a time of reorientation following a week of striving to act justly and live righteously. I intentionally left indeterminate the new meaning the Supper might take on in so doing. Rather, I suggest that by taking this challenge seriously, God's people will be able to join in rich and meaningful dialogue about the significance of the Supper for us as a community of exiles.

# The Snake in the Pew

*Woe to you who long for the day of the LORD! Why*
*do you long for the day of the LORD? That day will*
*be darkness, not light. It will be as though a man fled*
*from a lion only to meet a bear, as though he entered*
*his house and rested his hand on the wall only to*
*have a snake bite him. Will not the day of the LORD*
*be darkness, not light—pitch-dark, without a ray of*
*brightness?* (Amos 5:18-20)

Country songwriter Butch Hancock talks about his
upbringing in west Texas: "Life in Lubbock, Texas, taught me
two things: One is that God loves you and you're going to burn
in hell. The other is that sex is the most awful, filthy thing on
earth and you should save it for someone you love." This got me
thinking about the things I learned growing up. Though I spent
some of my formative years in Lubbock, my primary culture
wasn't west Texas as much as it was the Church of Christ. Deep
involvement in the local Church of Christ was the one constant
in my life as our military family moved from Texas and New
Mexico to Hawaii, California, and Arkansas.

So, what did I learn growing up in the Church of Christ?
I learned that pastors are elders, ministers are evangelists,
sanctuaries are auditoriums, and revivals are gospel meetings.
I learned to pray for God to "guide, guard, and direct" us, and
to grant the preacher a "ready recollection" of those things he
had studied. I learned that tithing, an Old Testament ordinance,
is no longer binding, but instead Christians must give the first
10% of their income to the church. But the main thing I learned
growing up in the Church of Christ was this: God's number one
requirement of his people is that we go to church faithfully.
I remember sermons on courageous discipleship featuring
stories of faithful Christians who gave up career advancement
opportunities, enticing vacation adventures, starring roles in
school plays, and even participation in state football playoff
games so that they would not miss even a single Wednesday
evening Bible study. Nothing was more important than one's
commitment to be in church!

Attending three times a week was the gold standard of faithfulness, the path of safety through which one could be as certain of salvation as humanly possible. But there was in practice a somewhat looser standard, though the preachers railed against it. The service on Lord's Day morning ("Sunday" isn't a biblical word, so we used "Lord's Day" instead, a designation occurring once in Scripture) was the supremely important obligatory meeting. And, while one's presence for the full hour of worship was certainly desirable, there was a strong feeling among the rank and file that one could miss parts—even large parts—of the service without seriously jeopardizing one's standing with the Almighty, so long as one was present to partake the Lord's Supper. And so it was that I concluded that being present in the church building for the fifteen minutes it took to pass the crackers and grape juice was God's strictest requirement, the *sine qua non* of a life pleasing to Him.

So every week, we came to church and took the Lord's Supper. And it felt good. It was a safe and comforting refuge from an often-hostile world. A family where you were accepted on a basis other than your good looks, your athletic ability, your money, or your brains. A place to be with friends who lived— more or less—by the same strict moral code as you, a moral code that was sometimes difficult to explain to the worldly kids at school. A place to show off to the cute girls (who largely ignored us) and to be told how handsome we were by blue-haired ladies with cataracts.

And church is still that place of safety and comfort for us, isn't it? Our lives are becoming increasingly complex, our schedules are hopelessly crammed, and the people around us are day-by-day more crassly irreverent. It's a rat race out there, and clearly the rats are winning. With a constant feeling that something ferocious is in hot pursuit, we almost literally come fleeing into church services shouting, "Lions and tigers and bears, oh my!" What a relief to come here, settle into the safety of our pew and sing "Sweet Hour of Prayer" in resonant four-part harmony! How comforting to lift voices in thanks to God that we are free to assemble "without fear of molestation."

Unfortunately, we can never be free from the fear of molestation if God is in the house! We may have escaped a mauling from the lions and tigers and bears outside, but the ancient prophet Amos slithers into the pew beside us and sinks his fangs into our flesh, all the better to inject God's venom into our veins and send it coursing toward our heart.

> I hate, I despise your religious feasts; I cannot stand your assemblies. Even though you bring me burnt offerings and grain offerings, I will not accept them. Though you bring choice fellowship offerings, I will have no regard for them. Away with the noise of your songs! I will not listen to the music of your harps (Amos 5:21-23).

Amos abrasively asserts that our church services are *not* the peak of God's week! In fact, if He comes to them at all He closes his eyes, stops up his ears, and holds his nose. And church attendance is nowhere near the top of God's list of requirements for us. In fact, through another of his prophets he demands, "who has asked this of you, this trampling of my courts?" (Isa 1:12). Obviously, it's not God who ruled that church attendance is the greatest commandment. In fact Amos, in verse 25, recalls the time of Israel's wilderness wanderings when God's people didn't go to church or do the Lord's Supper for forty years, and yet God was clearly guiding, guarding, and directing them the whole time. If they could skip church for forty years and still enjoy God's presence, where did we get the reverse concept that going to church is the sole requirement for receiving God's blessings?

Nor is God all that interested in making us comfortable when we come to church. Rather than guaranteeing our freedom from disturbance, he shows up for the purpose of disturbing us. More often than we think, he intends the Lord's Day to be the most unsettling day of the week. And today, God is in this place to upset your equilibrium, disturb your complacency, and leave you agitated. And he couldn't care less that you think he has no right to do so. Do we really think we can waltz into the presence of a Holy God without running that risk?

As it turns out, what God requires of us is something that happens primarily outside of church services: "Let justice roll on like a river, righteousness like a never-failing stream" (Amos 5:24). God is not one whit interested in what we do on the Lord's Day if we're not seeking justice and righteousness Monday, Tuesday, Wednesday, Thursday, Friday, and Saturday. We may be able to live one way during the week and pretend we're something different on the Lord's Day, but God knows what we're up to.

A wealthy entrepreneur retired and turned his business over to his four sons. Immediately, they began to fight for control of the company. Eventually, there was an acrimonious parting of the ways. The corporate assets were split up and each brother started his own company. The competition between them was fierce and dirty. Unlike their father, none of them had any qualms about cutting ethical corners or mistreating employees, as long as it helped the bottom line. Once a year, though, the brothers got together to throw a lavish birthday party for their father. Finally, he told them, "All I want for my birthday is for you to treat each other as brothers and to run your businesses honestly. Until that happens, have a party if you must, but I won't be there; it just hurts too much to be part of the charade." And our Father pleads with us: "Do right. Seek justice. Until then, spare me the party."

"Seek justice: encourage the oppressed, defend the cause of the fatherless, plead the case of the widow" (Isaiah 1:17). We look at the hour we spend in church and feel good about our devotion; God scrutinizes our day planner, discerning our true priorities. He sees us running from work to restaurant to recreation to Home Depot, with frantic stops along the way to drop our kids off at culturally mandated activities. How much time did you set aside to go with your kids to work at a homeless shelter this week? Last week? *Any* week? How much time did you leave uncluttered so you could seize opportunities to minister to those around you who are struggling? God looks at our day planner and sees a week so jam-packed that there is no time for Him. In truth, it's all about us and our comfort and our mad dash to live the American dream.

We look at the check we put in the collection basket in church and pat ourselves on the back. God looks at our

checkbook and sees our selfishness. He intended that we do
honorable work so that we could have something to share with
those in need. What does our checkbook reveal about our view
of our paycheck? It's ours, all ours, to spend paying back the
credit card debt we incurred buying stuff we just knew we *had*
to have. And how much slack is there to allow us to be randomly
generous to people we encounter? How much of what we have
spent is true *necessity* and how much is sheer self-indulgence:
toys, movies, CDs, electronic gear, sports equipment. Does it
disturb you that we can announce a yard sale for the Finland
campaign trip and in just a few days, we can fill our front yard
with thousands of dollars of fancy stuff (all no longer used
or wanted by the original buyers) from the bulging attics and
closets of Christian people, but we can't seem to keep our
benevolence budget funded because weekly contributions are
too low? And then there's the money you spent at the casino:
does it bother you that Christians have been so silent about an
industry that has moved into town that makes a disproportionate
share of its money off of poor folks by selling them false hope?
While we're at it, pull out the investment statements. Before
the market fell, you made significant donations of your wildly
appreciated stock to some caring ministry, didn't you? Oh, you
didn't? God saw that, too, and realized that like everything else,
your investments were all about you.

"Stop doing wrong; learn to do right!" (Isa 1:16c-17a).
What sites did you visit on the Internet last week? What TV
shows did you watch? What movies did you attend? Where
were you last night, and with whom? How did you conduct
yourself at work last week? What was your language like? How
did you treat your co-workers? Your boss? Those who work
for you? How many of your actions last week were in response
to the prompting of a holy God and how many were simply
going with the flow? How is it with you and your family? Your
neighbors? Your brothers and sisters in Christ? God consistently
tells us that we cannot have a right relationship with him if we
will not strive for a right relationship with human beings. Have
you sought reconciliation with those who've offended you?
Oh, *they* are responsible for initiating the process? Are you

sure? What about the people you've offended? Surely you took time this week to initiate the reconciliation process with them? Slipped your mind, did it? It didn't slip God's.

Are these questions disturbing to you? Well, they're disturbing to me! And these are just a few of the questions that could be used to focus our attention on the issues of doing right and seeking justice. I don't have tidy answers to all of them. I wrestle with them constantly. The snake in the pew has clamped his jaw down on me and he won't let go until I come to terms with them. I think he's trying to get me to realize that even though I sing, "Lord, I Lift Your Name On High," I still spend way too much time, money, and effort lifting up the idols of middle-class, self-centered, American values: "you have lifted up the shrine of your king, the pedestal of your idols, the star of your god—which you made for yourselves" (Amos 5:26). And the only outcome of idol worship is exile from God's presence.

Before we get completely depressed, let's reflect on a few other questions. What would happen if we left here and determined to make WWJD—what would Jesus do—a reality for just one week, Monday through Saturday? How would we be different, individually and as a church, if we rearranged our schedules and made time for things that are truly important? How would our faith, hope, and love grow if we tried really hard to be irrationally generous this week? What would we look like if we came together next week after several among us had started working toward the reconciliation of long-standing differences? And if we did these things, what would our worship next Lord's Day be like? Would we notice a difference? Would God? Would it be a celebration he would gladly attend?

Maybe after a week of trying—and ultimately failing—to achieve true justice and righteousness, we'd realize that we're desperately dependent on God for the very things he requires of us. Maybe instead of seeing church as a zone of safety and comfort, we'd see it as an opportunity to fall on our faces and beg God to be merciful to us sinners. And maybe God would soothe the desperation in our hearts and apply the antidote to our snake-bitten hearts. Maybe he would reassure us that the only sacrifice that pleases him has already been made, made himself when he turned his back on his crucified son. Maybe, just maybe, we would come to the Lord's Supper and see in it something more than the minimum weekly requirement for good standing in the club. What wonderful depth of meaning would we see in there? What motivation and strength would we draw from it? What healing would we find? I don't know. Why don't we spend a week seeking justice and doing right and find out? I'll see you back here next week!

# 14

# *Heartbroken for the Heartless*

## *Hosea 1-3*

Royce Dickinson, Jr.
Plymouth Church of Christ,
Plymouth Michigan

## *Introduction*

Although preached by Royce Dickinson, this sermon is the product of a collaborative endeavor by Royce and Craig Bowman. In particular, the convergence of three factors played a formative role for this sermon: (1) the insightfully provocative work of Abraham Heschel, (2) the intensely personal work of Craig, and (3) Royce's investigative pursuit of "heart" imagery in Hosea.

Through the sharing of insights and ideas, two striking aspects of the eighth-century-B.C. Hosea emerged. First, we recognized the challenge of making the scandalous story of the prophet shocking in today's culture, where R-rated movies rarely offend even Christians. Second, we realized that the significant metaphor of heart in Hosea had been obscured by English translations in which the apparent literalness of the Hebrew was characteristically changed to more eloquent contemporary phrasing. We have sought to address these difficulties in the preaching of this text.

The lengthy quotation from Calvin Miller that concludes the sermon functions to make explicit in the behavior of "the seller of friendship" what is (hopefully) implicit in the story of Gomer. Gomer's response is untold and, therefore, the story is open-ended. "The seller of friendship" suggests the appropriate response to the love of God.

According to Robert Reid, sermons that employ "[the sage voice] invite listeners to journey with the preacher and co-discover new possibilities of understanding and personal applications of faith." Such is the intent of this sermon as it seeks to wed the voice of the prophet and the voice of the sage. We believe this combined voice to be fitting and faithful to the prophet Hosea who himself finishes his oracle in the voice of a sage: "Let those who are wise understand these things; let those who are discerning know them. For the ways of Yahweh are right, and the righteous walk in them, but transgressors stumble in them" (Hos 14:9).

# *Heartbroken for the Heartless*

The first time God spoke to Hosea he said:
"Find a whore and marry her.
Make this whore the mother of your children.
And here's why: This whole country
    has become a whorehouse, unfaithful to me,
    God"
            (Hos 1:2, *The Message*).

With this startling and shocking statement, the word of Yahweh is spoken to the eighth-century-B.C. prophet Hosea. "Whore." The sound of the word is as ugly as the sense of its meaning. "Whore." Of all the English words to describe promiscuity or prostitution, perhaps none is as abrasive as the term "whore."[1]

The 1990 movie *Pretty Woman*, based loosely on George Bernard Shaw's *Pygmalion*, is the story of a transformation from whore to woman, from prostitute to lady. But a story depicting a whore who becomes a wife and mother, and yet remains a whore, is by no means a "pretty" story. Whereas Julia Roberts played the part of the "the pretty woman," Hosea's Gomer portrayed the plight of "the pretty whore." "Whore." There's that word again. "Pretty woman" sounds appealing. "Pretty whore" sounds appalling—which brings me to this unsettling and uncomfortable conclusion: *To read the story of Hosea and not be appalled is to be as apathetic as the audience to whom the tale was first told.*

But the salacious story of Gomer's indiscrete infidelity is not the most scandalous part of Hosea's prophetic preaching. The shocking scandal of Hosea's message is "the incomprehensible and incomparable nature of a God who loves

---

[1] See Craig Bowman's article in this volume where he maintains that attempts to soften the offensiveness of the Hebrew *zanah* and its synonyms "are probably unfaithful to the original meaning of the word given its wide use by Israel's prophets, especially when their intent was clearly in some cases to arrest the attention of an apathetic wayward people who apparently could not have cared less (e.g., Ezek 16 and 23)" (fn. 4).

the unlovable with an illogical loyalty."² The most scandalous character in the Hosea story is Yahweh!

Yahweh's demand that Hosea covenant himself to a whoring woman pales in comparison with Yahweh's decision to covenant himself to an adulterous nation. *The real scandal of Hosea is that of a heartbroken God who absolutely refuses to stop loving a heartless people.* Such love is as mysterious as it is marvelous.

This sermon is a struggle for me. Why? Is it because I must find a tasteful way to tell you the tantalizing tidbits about Gomer's sexual exploits? No, that part is easy. There are no such details. Is it because I must find words to express the anguish and anger of betrayed Hosea? No, that too is not difficult. We know very little about Hosea himself. Is it because I don't want to preach doom and gloom by portraying the sinfulness of Israel? No, most of you watch the news and so you've heard it all and seen it all before. This sermon is a struggle for me because the story itself compels me to speak to you about a God who chooses to reveal himself in ways that to us seem so completely out of character. *How dare God disclose himself to us in the disgusting imagery of steadfast love for a heartless whore!* What kind of God rips out his heart and places it before us that we may see both the awesomeness and awfulness of his emotional agony? This morning it doesn't matter how I feel. It doesn't matter how you feel. It doesn't even matter how Hosea felt. What matters is, how does God feel?³ And so I struggle as I strive to speak to your heart about the heart of Yahweh.⁴

I have chosen three texts to read. What I want all of us to see is that Yahweh cannot be apathetic. It is impossible for our God to be indifferent towards us. This is both soothing and it is scary. I want you to see the extreme range and incredible

---

²See Bowman's article in this volume.

³"Thus the prophet is guided, not by what he feels, but rather by what God feels" (Abraham J. Heschel, *The Prophets*, vol. 2 (New York: Harper/ Colophon, 1962), 94).

⁴Heart imagery is an important structural and connective thread throughout the Book of Hosea. See 2:14; 4:11; 7:6, 11. 14; 10:2; 11:8; 13:6, 8.

intensity of Yahweh's emotional steadfast love. I want all of us to see that no matter how unmoved we may be by God's feelings for us, he cannot be unmoved by our lack of feelings for him. Let's read from chapter 2, verses 14-20. (The translation is my own.) Listen to what Yahweh says to unfaithful Israel.

> *"And so, in light of all that has happened, I shall woo her [Israel] myself and shall lead her into the wilderness and shall speak to her heart. I will return her vineyards to her, transforming the Valley of Trouble into a Gateway of Hope. And she will respond to me as in the days of her youth, as in the days when I freed her from the land of Egypt.*

> *In that coming day," says Yahweh, "you will call me 'my husband' and will no longer refer to me as 'my master.' For I will cause you to forget your images of Baal; even their names will no longer be spoken. At that time, I will make for your sake a covenant with the wild animals, with the birds of the air, and with the critters that scurry on the ground. Bow, sword, and war I will banish from the land so that you can lie down in safety. And I will take you for my wife forever, pledging to you righteousness, justice, loyal-love, and mercy. I will be faithful to you and make you mine, and you will finally know me as Yahweh.*[5]

"I will woo her"..."speak to her heart"..."take her to be my wife and make her mine forever"...Yahweh speaks to Israel the romantic language of courtship and marriage—passionate words spoken to a promiscuous whore. Hollywood has never written a script that can match this!

But there is a problem: Israel is not "woo-able." Her heart is hard and so her ears are deaf. What is Yahweh to do? We turn now to chapter 13, verses 4-8. (Again, the translation is my own). Yahweh is the speaker.

> *Only I, Yahweh, have been your God ever since the land of Egypt. You have never known a [true] God*

---

[5] Hebrew—2:16-22. The translations here and throughout the sermon are my own

*but me, and you have never had a savior other than
me. I took care of you in the wilderness, in that land
of baking heat. When you were cared for you became
satisfied, and when you were satisfied you became
haughty, and so you forgot about me. Now then, here
is what I am going to do. I will attack you like a lion,
or like a leopard that lurks along the road. I will attack
you like a mother-bear robbed of her cubs, and will rip
to pieces the enclosure of your heart [the breast or rib-
cage]. I will devour you like a lion, and will tear you
apart like a wild animal.*

Oh my! Can this be the same God of chapter 2? We
have gone from the beauty to the beast. We have gone from
romancing the heart to ripping out the heart. *How can it be that
Yahweh is both Casanova and Hannibal Lecter?!*

What kind of god is Yahweh? He is a god with a heart.
And because he has a heart, this creates for him an emotional
dilemma when the people he so desperately loves are so
despicably unloving and unlovely. As I said earlier, *the real
scandal of Hosea is that of a heartbroken God who absolutely
refuses to stop loving a heartless people.* Look now, with me, to
chapter 11, verses 8 and 9. (My translation.) Listen not only to
the agony of God's heart, listen to God's assessment of himself
and to the actions he will undertake because of who he declares
himself to be.

*O Ephraim, how can I give you up? O Israel, how can
I hand you over? How can I treat you like Admah or
surrender you to the fate of Zeboiim? My heart is torn
within me; my compassion is aroused. No, I refuse to
act in angry wrath and I will not change my mind and
destroy Ephraim. For I am God and not a mere mortal.
I am the Holy One living among you, and I will not
come in fury.*

I am speechless. What can I say? God has already said
it all.

Perhaps some of you are thinking, I wish Royce had spent

more time telling us about Hosea and Gomer's marriage. After all, who names their children "You're Going to Get It!"[6]—"I Don't Care What Happens to You!"[7]—"You're Not My Kid!"?[8] Exactly what type of woman was Gomer? Was she really a whore or is the language only metaphorical? If the language is literal, was her prostitution secular or cultic? Or does it only refer to the loss of virginity in a fertility initiation rite? Was she promiscuous before her marriage or after her marriage or both? What happened after Hosea and Gomer were reunited? And what about the language of spousal abuse in chapter 2? The list of questions goes on and on, and they are good questions.[9] But none of them is the question that matters most. The question that matters most is: *How does God feel about us when we no longer feel for him?* The answer: he still loves us. And what makes that love so scandalous is the fact that we are such scoundrels. To borrow from the seventeenth-century French mathematician and Christian philosopher Blaise Pascal, "The heart has its reasons of which reason knows nothing."[10]

Our contemporary culture has at least one thing in common with eighth-century-B.C. Israel: *It is difficult for us to hear the message of Hosea because we believe ourselves to be spiritual.* However incomprehensible may be Hosea's picture of Yahweh, it is inconceivable to us that we would be portrayed as Gomer.

---

[6] Jezreel (Hos 1:4-5, 11; 2:21-23a).

[7] Lo-ruhamah (Hos 1:6-7; 2:23b).

[8] Lo-ammi (Hos 1:8-9, 10; 2:23c).

[9] See Bowman's article in this volume and Craig D. Bowman, "Prophetic Grief, Divine Grace: The Marriage of Hosea," *Restoration Quarterly* 43:4 (2001): 229-42.

[10] Blaise Pascal, *Pensées*, trans. A. J. Krailsheimer (New York: Penguin Books, 1966), 154, no. 423. Interestingly, this oft-quoted statement of Pascal occurs in the context of how God is known by humans. Pascal goes on to maintain, "It is the heart which perceives God and not the reason. That is what faith is: God perceived by the heart, not by the reason" (154, no. 424). Although Hosea may not have a similar negative assessment of reason, he does proclaim that "the knowledge of God" is a matter of the heart and not merely of matter of the head. See Abraham J. Heschel, *The Prophets*, vol. 1 (New York: Harper/Colophon, 1962), 57-60.

Modern-day-self-serving spirituality is far more palatable and pleasing than the thought of serving a sovereign, saving, scandalous God. But that doesn't change who God is, nor does it change what that makes us to be.

Calvin Miller has written a trilogy of books in which he retells the story of the New Testament in a poetic and metaphorical way. The first book, *The Singer*, is the story of the Gospels. Jesus is the Singer and his song is the good news of God's redeeming love. Of course, Jesus has competition. Satan, called the World Hater, also sings his song. His song is seductive and deceptive—it appears to be a love song but it is really a song of hate. The excerpt I am going to read to you concerns Jesus meeting a woman who is engaged in the business of selling herself. Like Gomer, she is a whore. Listen as I read.

He met a woman in the street. She leaned against an open door and sang through her half-parted lips a song that he could barely hear. He knew her friendship was for hire. She was without a doubt a study in desire. Her hair fell free around her shoulders. And intrigue played upon her lips.

"Are you betrothed?" she asked.

"No, only loved," he answered.

"And do you pay for love?"

"No, but I owe it everything."

"You are alone. Could I sell you but an hour of friendship?"

Deaf to her surface proposition, he said, "Tell me of the song that you were singing as I came upon you. Where did you learn it?"

His question troubled her. At length she said, "The first night that I ever sold myself, I learned it from a tall impressive man."

"And did he play a silver pipe?" the Singer asked.

She seemed surprised. "Do you know the man who bought me first?"

"Yes. Not long ago, in fact, he did his best to teach that song to me."

"I cannot understand. I sell friendship and you your melody. Why would he teach us both the self-same song?"

The Singer pitied her. He knew the World Hater had a way of making every victim feel as though he were the only person who could sing his song.

"He only has one song; he therefore teaches it to everyone. It is a song of hate."

"No, it is a love song. The first night that he held me close, he sang it tenderly and so in every way he owned me while he sang to me of love."

"And have you seen him since?"

"No, not him, but a never ending queue of men with his desires."

"So it was no song of love. Tell me, did he also say that some day in the merchandising of your soul, you would find someone who would not simply leave his fee upon the stand but rather take you home to care for you and cherish you?"

Again she seemed surprised. "Those were indeed his very words—how can you know them?"

"And have you found the one that he has promised?"

"Not yet."

"And how long have you peddled friendship?"

"Some twenty years are gone since first I learned the song that you inquired about."

The Singer felt a burst of pity. "We sometimes give ourselves to hate in masquerade and only think it love. And all our lives we sing the song we thought was right. The Canyon of the Damned is filled with singers who thought they knew a love song...Listen while I sing for you a song of love."

He began the melody so vital to the dying men around him. "In the beginning was the song of love..."

She listened and knew for the first time she

was hearing all of love there was. Her eyes swam when he was finished. She sobbed and sobbed in shame. "Forgive me, Father-Spirit, for I am sinful and undone...for singing weary years of all the wrong words..."

The Singer touched her shoulder and told her of the joy that lay ahead if she could learn the music he had sung.

He left her in the street and walked away, and as he left he heard her singing his new song. And when he turned to wave the final time he saw her shaking her head to a friendship buyer. She would not take his money.

And from his little distance, the Singer heard her use his very word

"Are you betrothed?" the buyer asked her.

"No, only loved," she answered.

"And do you pay for love?"

"No, but I owe it everything."[11]

In just a few minutes from now, we will all leave this place of worship. As we each walk out the door, we will either walk away from God's love or walk in God's love. We will depart to live as if God's love means nothing to us or to live as if we owe everything to God's love. *And no matter how you leave, God will still love you—although there is a word, that I will not repeat, that he may use to describe you.*

How do you feel about God? More importantly, How does God feel about you?

---

[11] Calvin Miller, *The Singer* (Downers Grove: InterVarsity, 1975), 62-66.

# 15

# *In Micah's Courtroom*

## *Micah 6:1-8*

David Fleer
Rochester Church of Christ,
Rochester Michigan

## *Introduction*

Bob Reid's Matrix of Preaching Voices proposes different ways contemporary preachers make choices about the nature of language and the nature of authority that control the way reality is structured for listeners. His essay demonstrates the utility of the Matrix in four sample sermons from Amos, one in each voice. In the following sermon I adopt the *Testifying* voice in an attempt to *engage* listeners in a formative dialogue, inviting them to join me in reaffirming our identity as a people called to "Do Justice." I asked Bob to introduce the sermon through a sharpened focus of his essay. He graciously responded with the following observations.

Fleer's sermon invites listeners to enter the world of the biblical text by way of an extended story—a story that we soon discover is our story. Fleer engages the text by cautiously permitting us to adopt the role of one who overhears—for who among us would readily embrace the role of the one judged? Yet before the sermon's end we discover that this is an identity we willingly assume: for only as a people so judged are we capable of living out the claims of being a people of God who "Do Justice" in the world today.

Fleer's sermon is devoid of fuzzy correspondences between religion and meaningful experience.[1] He creates a world in which dreams, visions, and oracles, so characteristic of prophetic speech, become the very means by which we, as listeners, must decide in the end which world is real and which world is dream. Rather than preaching as *argument*, as *advocacy*, or even as *analysis*, this is preaching as an *articulation* of the world of the biblical text, a dramatic reenactment of the text that invites listeners to find their role in the story, to rediscover and reaffirm their identity as the people of God.[2]

Walter Brueggemann argues that this kind of preaching "is analogous to preaching to exiles. More broadly, biblical preaching is addressed to a particular community of believers committed through baptism to the claims of biblical faith addressed to the community of the baptized in order to articulate, sustain, and empower a distinctive identity in the world."[3]

Fleer's sermon would have listeners willingly suspend their belief in the difference between the dream-world of oracle and the supposed world of reality in order to see how their own story can continue to finish the drama of the biblical story in which God, in the name of Jesus, says "I want you to do the same." In choosing to respond to this script listeners can join one another in living out the drama of life in a whole new way.[4]

---

[1] See Richard Lischer, "Preaching as the Church's Language," in *Listening to the Word: Studies in Honor of Fred Craddock*, Ed. Gail R. O'Day and Thomas G. Long (Nashville: Abingdon, 1993), 126.

[2] See Walter Brueggemann, *Texts Under Negotiation: The Bible and Postmodern Imagination* (Minneapolis: Fortress Press, 1993), 68-69.

[3] Walter Brueggemann, *Cadences of Home: Preaching Among Exiles* (Louisville: Westminster/John Knox, 1997), 78.

[4] Brueggemann, *Texts*, 68.

## In Micah's Courtroom

It has been a while since I was last with you. A lot has happened since then. In the last week we've had a "fracus over the College's historic barn" to the west of us. And, in the last year the showcase facility for Lifetime Fitness is up and shining to the east of us. Since we last met we have had a war and our nation's economy has struggled. We were told this week that the jobless rate is the highest its been in nine years. But, interest rates have never been lower and many of us have been busy refinancing our home mortgages, money in the pocket for home repairs or vacations as a result. Since we last met a sister congregation in Flint shut its doors, but the Rochester Church of Christ looks to be busting at the seams, construction an obvious sign of numerical growth.

A lot has happened since we last met which makes the hearing of today's text all the more difficult. The reading will be from Micah 6:1-8. In different places different congregations try different ways of creating a hearing. Some have the congregation stand, a sign of reverence. Others employ different people to read, especially helpful with narratives, women and men reading different characters. This morning, however, the burden will be on your ears. Listen carefully.

Not much to say to introduce the reading, except that the setting is a court room, and that God's people are on trial, and that you'll hear several voices. You will hear the voice of God. You will hear your own voice. [read Mic 6:1-8].

Now that we have heard the passage, how shall we talk about it? I require freshmen at Rochester College to memorize the punch line of this passage, "He has told you, O man, what is good and what does the Lord require of you, but to do justice, to love kindness and to walk humbly with your God?" First thing every semester, they commit this verse to memory. I don't know how effective this is, like knowing the answer before figuring out the question. But today, let's listen to this text and the terrible question that it raises.

Since none of us is eager to enter the court room, especially if we're the ones on trial, the best way to move into the world created by this text is to watch someone else enter and maybe, in so watching, we might see for ourselves.

So, I will tell you the story of Richard, a white-42-year-old man, married with two grade-school-aged daughters. Their home is just east of town. They have two new cars, paid for.

Richard has settled nicely into business. But maneuvering for a promotion, he took on some travel this spring that has wearied him, even while earning him his position enhancement. His last travel installment sent him out of town last week to make a couple of presentations at a conference in Dallas.

And so, on Monday morning Richard drove to Detroit Metro's Park-N-Fly and as he stood outside his car, waiting for the airport shuttle, he thought, "The promotion will eliminate the travel and bring an end to these inconveniences." The shuttle van arrived and Richard found himself riding with three others, all black men. Snugged next to one, Richard clutched his Eddie Bauer satchel close to his chest and he couldn't help but notice the contrast of the color of his hands with those of his traveling companion. At the first stop, two passengers got out and the driver went to the back of the van to help with luggage. As Richard repositioned himself to take the available space, he glanced back and saw both passengers' hands peel bills out of their wallets to tip the driver.

"Oh brother," Richard thought, "I forgot again. Easily solved. At my stop I'll just grab my own bag and turn quickly toward the terminal and save a dollar in the process." Which is exactly what he did.

The flight to Dallas went well as did the first two days of the conference. On Tuesday evening, however, as he was heading back to the motel, he once again found himself in a shuttle with others, all black. Having the conference and the motel in common, Richard struck up a conversation and asked his companions about their motel's service. "Just fine," one said, "You having some problems?"

"Why, yes," Richard explained, "Trouble with the towels and the sheets weren't changed Monday."

"Leave a tip?" one asked.

Leave a tip? The notion hadn't occurred to Richard.

"You leave a tip, and she'll put a little chocolate mint on your pillow," his companion said, and all the travelers laughed.

At the conference there was an abundance of fine cuisine and Richard had to discipline himself, as he always does at these events, to avoid eating too much. The conference site was quite nice, new carpet, chandeliers in the meeting rooms and portable comfy chairs, what Richard likes. Starbucks in the morning and iced water in the afternoon.

The space outside the conference, however, troubled Richard. Panhandlers were visible. Homeless people, with their grocery carts and black plastic bags. And the only alternative for lunch out looked to be the Denny's across the street, with what Richard called, "Greasy food for greasy people."

On Friday Richard flew back to Detroit and took the shuttle to Park-N-Fly. The luggage had arrived safely, and Richard tucked it into his trunk. He walked around his car, unscratched. A successful trip.

The weekend home meant catch-up. Solving problems and seizing opportunities. The problem, his wife reported, was another poor job by the cleaning service. "What's with labor? Where's gumption and pride in a job well done?" The question was how to deal with it. Should they talk to the lead cleaning lady? Doubtful. Speak with their boss? Unlikely. Should they just upgrade companies?

The opportunity, however, made Richard happy. The real estate lady had called saying that she'd found a house in their price range, in that new subdivision off Adams.

Sunday, of course, was church. New outfits for the girls. Very cute. Matching dress and shoes. And, a sermon from this passage, Micah 6:1-8. What it meant then and what it means now, images of a courtroom, an exhortation to help the poor. Richard tried to listen but his mind wandered. He was busy solving problems and plotting to seize opportunities and planning next weekend's getaway to their cabin up north.

After church he shook hands with the preacher. "How was the trip?" the minister asked.

"Travel is wearing me out," Richard replied. "I'm happy to be done, looking forward to staying close to home," which, for Richard, is 23 Mile Road and north.

I have told you all of this as a context so that you might better hear what took place that night. Richard's Sunday night sleep was restless and fitful and filled with uneasy dreams, the most troublesome was more of a nightmare. Here is what happened.

In his dream Richard was standing, anklecuffed and handcuffed, wearing an orange jumpsuit and tennis shoes without shoe strings. Huddled with other villains wearing the same jail clothing, he looked to be in a courtroom, an ancient courtroom. The sky was blue above him, the air was dry and tall gray stone walls surrounded him. To his right was a huge wooden gate, wide enough to accommodate chariots, with double doors, metal plated. A large wooden post, positioned horizontally, braced the doors, which were shut and locked. Richard was standing with others on a stone foundation, alongside the entrance to this walled city. They were in an alcove area, adjacent to the gate, with three long stone benches lining this bay.[5]

As Richard listened, he could hear that he was in a courtroom. Phrases like, "All rise...your honor...I object... Overruled....We find the defendant..." were audible. He was standing in a courtroom, all right.

Richard looked straight ahead and he realized he saw familiar faces looking back at him. He saw the driver of the shuttle, the waitress from the conference, and the bus boy. He saw the woman who cleaned his motel room and the four Molly Maids who scrubbed his house's floors. He recognized some by their faces and others by their uniforms. And, at that very instant, Richard realized that the people looking at him weren't wearing the jailhouse orange. They weren't anklecuffed or handcuffed. They weren't on trial. He was on trial. Why was he on trial? What were the charges against him?

Among the stone benches was a throne. King David's throne. Only, David wasn't on the throne in the courtroom, God

[5] See Philip J. King and Lawrence E. Stager, *Life in Biblical Israel* (Louisville: Westminster/John Knox Press, 2001), 234-239 and Philip J. King, *Amos, Hosea, Micah – An Archeological Commentary* (Philadelphia: Westminster, 1988), 72-78 for descriptions of ancient city gates which have been conflated in the sermon's dream scene.

was on the throne. Still cuffed, Richard was now standing before God, and God was describing all of his actions in history. He created the world and he rescued Israel from terrible bondage and delivered them into the Promised Land and about Jesus' life and death and the beginning of the church and throughout time and specific kindnesses to Richard and to his family. And God was going on and on; as Richard was listening he was crying. Tears welled up in his eyes and fell down his face because at this moment he could see the purity of God's motive for every act God had ever done. Like a bright light shining behind all of God's work, sharply defined, Richard could clearly see that every thing God had ever done God had done because of his steadfast love. Richard was crying, too, because he was feeling an overwhelming sense of responsibility. And, like thunder rolling in from the distance, a roar growing louder and louder, he could hear the question, "How do you plead? How do you plead?"

And then, with a start, Richard awoke. He had been dreaming and now he was awake. But, the dream had been so real, that, although the air conditioner was working nicely, his body was damp with perspiration. His face was wet from tears; he had really been crying. It was still the middle of the night but Richard arose from his bed and walked down the staircase and into his den. He stood before the bookcase and pulled a Bible off the shelf. He sank into his overstuffed chair and clicked on the reading light, opened his Bible, thumbed to Micah, and turned to chapter six. He looked carefully at the passage and he was thinking very clearly now, as clearly as ever before in his life. He realized he had been dreaming Micah 6. He said to himself, "I was in God's court room. I was hearing these words. It was so real."

As Richard examined the text, some images stood out. Balak and Balaam, for one. He remembered from Sunday School days, mostly the donkey, but he also remembered the story line, how Balak tried to bribe Balaam to curse Israel and although Balaam would have loved the money that came with the request he could not curse Israel because God intervened. God's righteous act on behalf of his people.

He recognized Moses and Aaron and Miriam, of course, and that God had used them to lead his people out of the oppression of hard labor, impossible work. The Egyptians had murdered innocents; little Hebrew babies were killed with the torture and cruelty of slavery, because of their bondage. God used Moses and Aaron and Miriam to bring all of that to an end. God's righteous act on behalf of his people.

Then, Richard's eyes fell on one word. It stood out as if it were written in 3D and highlighted: "Remember." And his mind began to connect the dots. He remembered that God said, "When you get to the land flowing with milk and honey, when you live in the land of milk and honey, remember that you were once a slave in Egypt and the Lord redeemed you from there and therefore you had better not pervert the justice due an alien, an orphan, or a widow." God had said, "When you get to the land of milk and honey, when you're living in the land of milk and honey and you harvest your crops, harvest your olives and grapes and whatever else you produce, always leave plenty for the helpless in society. Remember that you were a slave in Egypt."[6]

And then Richard recalled the black hands peeling out a tip at the airport and he thought, "they remembered." And then he recalled the conversation on the way to the motel, "You leave a tip, and she'll put a mint on your pillow," and he thought, "evidently they remembered."

In his dream Richard had wondered, "What are the charges?" The charges he now saw were scattered throughout his world: "wicked scales, deceptive weights, rich men, leaders judging for a bribe, coveting fields and seizing them, coveting houses and taking them, evicting tenants." The rich getting richer and the poor getting poorer.

I'd like to tell you more about Richard, but I cannot. I'd like to tell you more, because you'd like to know. You'd like to know, "What happens next? Does Richard stay in this world where he sees with such clarity? Does he dream again? What

---

[6] The quote is paraphrased and adapted from Deut 24:17-22. I've framed the paraphrase with the word "remember" and added "the land of milk and honey" to preserve the context of the covenantal promise.